Skye Stories

Volume 3 Not the Skye Years

By Raymond Moore

First published in 2021 by Redshank Books

Redshank Books is an imprint of Libri Publishing.

ISBN 978-1-912969-27-2

Cover and book design by Carnegie Book Production

Libri Publishing
Brunel House
Volunteer Way
Faringdon
Oxfordshire
SN7 7YR

Tel: +44 (0)845 873 3837

www.libripublishing.co.uk

Contents

Dedication
For Janya, Isis, Isaac, and Noah.
My heart, my soul, my loves, my life.

Foreword

I first met Raymond on August 5th, 2009. I was freshly arrived to Saudi Arabia from New York and was getting the report from the Nursing Coordinator about the overall patient situation in the hospital. In walks a very sleepy, cranky Scotsman complaining about his mattress like he was in some version of *The Princess and the Pea*. He said he didn't think he could make it. My first thought was: 'He's no Jamie Fraser for sure.' I did replace his mattress, however.

Ever since that day Raymond has been enlightening me with stories of Skye, Glasgow and Edinburgh. To be fair he made me practise saying Edinburgh until I was so good at it I could have gotten a part in *Trainspotting*! He never fails to surprise me, and we are so proud he has written down his stories for us all to enjoy. I have travelled to Scotland now numerous times and I must say I am a huge fan of the country but more importantly the people. Raymond is truly a one of a kind. Every Nursing Director should have at least one Scottish Nurse to make sure she is entertained to say the least.

Dawn Parker

Director of Nursing, Imam Abdulrahman Bin Faisal Hospital

Introduction

If someone had told me two years ago that I would be a published author with two books under my belt I would have asked them for a wee taste of what they were drinking. Imagine my surprise then, when I now find myself having to write an introduction for Volume 3 of my Skye Stories series. WTF?

Originally my plan was for one book filled with wee stories of my time living in Linicro. That was it. As you, my beautifully formed reader, already know, that plan morphed into two books containing stories and poems about my life in Linicro and Uig. What an effin' achievement for someone like me who suffers from a serious case of being bone lazy.

My work was done... or so I thought! After completing *The Road to Uig*, I thought...is that it? Is that all I've got to say? Obviously not. In my mind it made sense that in order to complete the series another book was needed. A what-happened-next book, if you like. This what you are now holding in your gorgeous hands. For those of you lovelies who have stuck with me through Volume 1 and 2, I now present Volume 3 for your delectation.

In this rather hefty tome, you will find out a wee bit about my life in Glasgow before I moved to Skye and a whole lot about my life after I left the island in 1982. It makes sense, right? Go on... you know it does. There is a lot of years to get through in this book so this time there are no poems – only stories that I hope will entertain and bring a smile to that cute wee face of yours. To the best of my recollection everything is as true as true can be. Some of it is sad, a lot of it is happy and there is the occasional unbelievable tale told too.

In getting here there are many folk I have to thank. Too many to name individually but some that deserve a special mention. Firstly, to the members of Something Skye and Skye and Lochalsh Memories Facebook groups. Your encouraging words of support have kept me going especially when I felt at my laziest! Without you I would not have had the pick of wonderful photos that have been donated to me and featured in my first two books. A big Shokran Jazeelan as we say in the desert of Saudi Arabia.

To my editor Steve Lane I have to show some love. Working with him over the last year has been a steep learning curve for my old brain. I've learned so much and I'm truly in his debt. That goes for everyone at Libri Publishing whose support has been critical to me completing my mission.

My pal Les, whose video calls and advice throughout the writing process has been totally invaluable. Cheers mate. To my boss Dawn and my colleague Richard who have kept me afloat during some rough mental weather and to all my workmates at Imam Abdulrahman Bin Faisal Hospital. I couldn't have gotten through this past year without your friendship.

Last and most definitely not least is you my dear reader. You're the reason I put finger to keyboard. It's your lovely self that I endeavour to entertain and without you it would all be rather pointless. A big thanks and a virtual hug to each and every one of you.

Glasgow

Beginning

Like most Glasgow kids born in the 1960s, my mother delivered me at the Rottenrow Maternity hospital on the morning of March 22nd 1964. For the first four years we lived in a 'room and kitchen' on Ardgowan Street, Kinning Park. I don't have many memories from that period, but of those that I do have, the main one is the toilet. The toilet seat, to be precise. Being a 'room and kitchen', my mother informed me that we had the rare luxury of an indoor toilet. Most other 'room and kitchens' or 'single-end' accommodation had communal toilets. These were known affectionately (and sometimes literally) as 'bogs' or 'cludgies' and were situated in the corner of the stair landing. One corner bog would be shared by two floors. I have a vague recollection of standing holding on to this toilet seat and my memory tells me they covered the wooden seat in some yellow sticky plasticky stuff. Perhaps used in an effort to make the aesthetics of our small W.C. more attractive to the eye. I can't be 100% sure, but that's about all that I recall of that time.

The funny thing is, I remember more clearly two incidents that did not happen! I don't know why, but I had a powerful memory that I broke my leg. I believed that it got caught under a wooden play park roundabout and I broke one bone. It was not till recently I asked my Mum about this and she says it never happened! Weird. I even have a memory of my Dad telling me about this and that they were worried that one of my legs would be shorter than the other? Strange. To me, that story felt totally real. Perhaps it was a recollection of a past life? Who knows?

The other vivid memory that I possess was that I remember flying down the close stairs. A 'close' is the term used for the communal entrance and stairwell of a tenement building. I don't mean running fast and falling. I mean actually flying down the stairs. I was above the wooden bannisters and flew to the close entrance! Obviously, that did not happen!
Or maybe it did?

The only other vague glimpses into my past in Kinning Park are from faded black and white photos in a biscuit tin in my Mum's living room closet.

<figure>
◌
</figure>

52a 7 Galloway Street

It was 1968 and my folks got offered an apartment in Springburn in a brand new scheme known as the 'maisonettes'. These council flats were highly desirable back then. I read that they had received some design award too? Galloway Street's red-bricked apartments looked better than your average council flat, and in the early 1970s they were a decent place to live. We stayed on the end of 'new Galloway Street' which carried into 'old Galloway Street'. Old tenements stood to our side, and opposite us were post-war tenements.

There were two floors or 'decks'. We stayed on the ground floor 'A' deck and up the stairs was 'B' deck. The corridors ran all the way from our side until they reached Balgrayhill Road leading on to Springburn Road. At one time you could walk all the way through and not get soaked by the Glasgow rain. Opposite the flat doors in the corridor were 'drying areas'. People could hang their washing in these purpose-built spaces and lock the door. Also, as you climbed to 'B' deck, there were more 'drying areas' on each landing. At the top of the first flight of stairs was a 'chute' for rubbish. This emptied into big metal bins in the locked bin rooms, which hid behind the wall outside our front door. On either side of the apartment front doors in the corridor were 'cellars' which people could use as storage. In theory, all of this was nice but for these things to work nice relied on honest people being around as opposed to others who would want to rob you naked. The long corridors on both decks were covered with black ridged rubber tiles.

Ours was a three-bedroomed apartment (we called it our hoose) with a living room, kitchen and a 'veranda'. Our hoose was roomy, and I would be happy staying in a flat that size now! When you entered our front door, there were two flights of stairs separated by a landing. This landing was the parking area for my Dad's bike. You then came to the bedrooms. My sister in one room. Me and my brother Gary sharing a double bed in the other and my parents were in the master bedroom on the end of the landing. Two more flights of stairs to climb and you would find the toilet and the living room door there to greet you. Our bog contained a bath and no windows. The living room was a spacious square shape with windows looking onto Springburn Road. The kitchen had a sliding door and had room for all the usual kitchen stuff, plus a dining table with four chairs. We accessed the veranda via the kitchen. These flats were definitely much bigger than most tenement flats. I have only happy memories of living there and my Mum and my sister continued to live there until the late 1980s when they eventually moved to the West End.

Local amenities at the time were Jackie Wilson's shop on Galloway Street below tenements on the corner of Huntershill Street. He also had a shop on Huntershill Street. The tenements on our side of the street stretched all the way on Springburn Road, in front of our building. These also had shops beneath them. I have fond memories of the 'paper shop' on Springburn Road near the turnoff to Huntershill Street. There was also an Asian grocery shop in front of us, which we accessed by going down the 'back' (which was our front) and cutting through the close. We went there to buy McCowans Dainties and chocolate-covered toffee bars on our way to school. Chocolate-covered toffee was my favourite. Over time, all these old tenements got demolished. It was in the Asian grocery shop I got caught shoplifting. Chocolate-covered toffee, of course!

It was Glasgow so there had to be a 'local' pub. The Spring Inn sat in front of our apartment building on Springburn Road. This flat-roofed building still stands today but is no longer a pub. Back then it had a Lounge, Public Bar and an Off Sales. The Public Bar is where my Dad drank. There was another pub, The Talisman, known locally as 'The Tally'. This was up near Viewpoint on the Balgrayhill and the building there also contained a supermarket, Galbraith's and a paper shop called 'Billy's'.

It was hardly a concrete jungle where we lived. There was a reasonable amount of greenery. In front of our building there was a long strip of grass the length of 7 Galloway which stretched out toward Springburn Road and carried on all the way to Balgrayhill. Opposite us and in front of the Viewpoint maisonettes there was a green grass expanse dotted with trees. We played a lot of football there during the summer months. For some real greenery there was Springburn Public Park, which was situated just opposite 'The Tally'.

My Mum

Most of my pals on our street called their mothers Ma or Maw. We always had to call her Mum. Rena (or Rene to her friends) looked after the three of us kids extremely well. She always made sure that our clothes were clean and ironed. She also made sure that we washed and that every Sunday we had our weekly bath and hair wash. We had a cooked dinner every night of the week, and she made us a 'play piece' for primary school 'play time'. Our hoose was always spotless and our rooms were always tidy. As a kid you take these things for granted, especially the fact that your mess miraculously gets cleaned up. I would go into some of my pals' houses and wondered why they were not as clean as ours. Some kids in my class always looked dirty, and some of them smelled as if they had pooped their pants. My Mum made sure we were all presentable.

She took a part-time job as a 'maid' in one of the psychiatric wards in Stobhill Hospital, which was our local healthcare facility. She still made sure our hoose (and us) were shiny and clean. My Mum was strict and would not let us stay out late like other kids on the street. It was usually down to her to discipline us, and by that, I mean the occasional slap! She made sure that before we went to bed, we had to give her and my Dad a kiss and say 'night night'. She was the boss of our place and everyone knew it. Including my Dad. He gave her all his wages plus the money he earned playing bass in various Glasgow Country and Western bands. She would give him pocket money. She took care of all the shopping and paid all the bills. She was rarely sick. The only time I remember her being ill was soon after she first started wearing contact lenses and she had left them on too long after a night out. It floored her for a day or two in eyeball agony. If she was ill any other time we did not notice it.

She treated me like I was the responsible one of her three kids as one time I had to go into Springburn to pay the rent. This was an enormous responsibility, and it was a lot of money. Good thing for me was she kept me off school that day. I might have been around ten years old. She told me where to go and gave me money for the bus. The rent money was in a brown envelope hidden inside my trousers and as I made my way there, I was always checking around me for potential muggers. The rent place was full of adults, and I eventually found a desk and felt relieved when I handed over the rent book and the money. They stamped the book, and I made my way out with a smile of achievement on my face. I walked back home and used the bus money to buy sweeties.

My Mum was and still is very house-proud and decorated our apartment nicely, making it look modern and fresh, unlike some of my friends in old Galloway whose apartments looked unchanged since they had built the buildings.

When I asked if I could stay in Linicro and go to school in Portree on the Isle of Skye, she agreed and supported my decision. That meant that I left home at 13 years old, never to return apart from brief vacations. As I got older and started going to pubs, many a time I went out drinking with her and her friends. In the 1980s, the first time I went to a gay pub was with her and Ali Aitken. We went to the Vintners by the Clyde as it had a late licence. She had been there many times with the nurses she worked with at Stobhill. I must admit because I was young and immature, I was a wee bit scared being a straight guy in a gay pub but as the drink took effect, I realised there was nothing to be scared about!

The first time I got up to sing in a pub it was on a night out with her; my vocal debut took place in Chamber's lounge on George Square. I remember being very nervous and it showed, but I wanted to do it for the longest time but never had the guts! I got up and sang the Everly Brothers 'Bye Bye Love'. It was not the best ever version of that song (I was reading from a lyric sheet) but it got me over my fear and a few months later, in the same pub I got up to sing a half decent version of the James Taylor 'You've Got a Friend'.

Scottish parents are good at hiding their emotion and although she might not have shown it, I know my Mum was proud when I qualified as a Registered Nurse and always supported me when I was managing the bands. She even came to watch one of my bands D.C. DeSouza play at Shadows in Bath Street.

I consider myself very lucky to have two loving parents who are still with us today. I'm also happy that after an endless wait both of them became grandparents to Isis, Isaac and Noah. I wish that they could see them more often, but as I have lived abroad for so long and their mother is Thai, it's not so easy. Thank God Mum's mastered the art of video calling and we can keep in touch regularly and she can see my kids growing. Facebook also helps as every day there is usually a kid's photo posted by my wife.

What else can I say about my old dear? Thanks for loving us and taking real good care of us when we were children, Mum. Love ya always.

St Aloysius Juniors

Being born a Roman Catholic to non-practising parents meant that if you lived in Galloway Street, you would attend St Aloysius primary school. Actually, there were two St Aloysius

– one you attended from primary one to three and the other you went from primary four till primary seven. Both these schools were close to each other and the junior primary building remains in use to this day but not as a school. It's used by some local government body. The bigger school stood until around 10 years ago when it was demolished. In between both these schools was the Protestant Elmvale Primary, and this building remains standing too.

I started school around 1970(ish); my memory of this time is not the greatest, but I remember the first few days. I was taken to the class by my Mum and I remember seeing a kid who lived in the same scheme as us but in the Viewpoint road maison-ettes cry for his 'Mammy' when she left. I did not cry so that obviously made me tough! I recently messaged him on Facebook and he still lives in Viewpoint!

It's strange, I have absolutely no memories of the teachers and, as I probably paid little attention in the classroom, I have little information on how we were taught! I remember they gave us each a small 'slate' blackboard type thing with chalk, and I surmise that was the beginning of our reading and writing. I also remember being given a set of small wooden blocks which I think were multi coloured with different shapes and sizes and these we used to start our number counting career!

I have a clear memory of the Jannie's (Janitor's) face and that he lived in the cottage attached to the school. For the life of me I don't remember his name, but as I sit here in my office in Saudi Arabia typing this, I can see his smiling face as if it was yesterday!

They heated the school via a coal-fired boiler that the Jannie spent his day stoking whilst keeping us young folk away from the boiler room. I have a memory that it was down in a basement and from the top of the stairs you could feel the heat and see the coal piled below!

My strongest memory of the junior school was being part of a play about Noah's Ark! I remember a song that went something like 'the animals go in by two-by-two hurrah'. My part in this production was ... wait for it ... the rear end of a hippo! My pal

John was the front end of said hippo. What is clear in my mind was how badly behaved we were and that we were always being pulled up by the teachers for carrying on! The other thing I remember was that John's two arms had a cardboard mouth which he would clap together as I – covered with something grey – bent down at his back with my face squashed up against his behind! I don't remember too much about the actual show, so obviously we must have behaved!

One other clear memory of that school was about the school dinners. I don't think I partook of them, but I remember our fascination with the leftovers which were all slopped into big shiny metal containers! We were told that these would be fed to the pigs. Where they kept these beasts I don't know.

That's about all that I have from my time there although I have memories of us 'fighting' the pupils from Elmvale on the spare ground where they erected the Fernbank scheme, all concrete and bare. And the chant we made was 'Proddy dogs eat the frogs' to which they replied, 'Catholic cats eat the rats' and I remember thinking at least eating rats was a good thing!

As I type this I'm struck with another memory of that time when we would be given a lift home perhaps by somebody's father and as we made our way to the Balgray Hill flats where we were deposited, we would sing Glasgow Celtic songs! In particular, the one that starts with 'oh it's a grand old team to play for' and ended with 'because we only know that there is going to be a show, and the Glasgow Celtic will be there!' This song sticks in my mind because at the end of it I used to sing (to the annoyance of the others), and I write this in the vernacular, 'Yogi Bear peed the fler licked it up and asked for mer.' It was funny at the time!

Big Gerry

What can I say about the man who helped create me? Easy? Love ya, Big Man! My old Dad has always been known as Big Gerry for obvious reasons. He was a rather tall guy! He was born in Kinning Park and from the late 1960s till the late 1970s he worked at Slater and Rodger's Whiskey Bond. It does not exist anymore as far as I'm aware. Back in his day there was very little 'Health and Safety' at work, and it was commonplace for the workers to 'sample' the products! This meant that he returned home many a night slightly 'tipsy'! The Big Man was tough as he cycled to work every day. As a teen he loved cycling, and this carried on into his working life. No doubt he was under the influence of the water of life on more than a few occasions! The last bike he owned was made by Peugeot, all purple and new! I remember that it was a ten-speed gear which he removed as he preferred a 'fixed' wheel. Through sun, rain, hail and snow he cycled every day. I never recall him having a sick day. To him though, this was just a job which was a necessity for a father of three. Come every Friday he would dutifully hand over the brown wage packet to my Mum, who would give him some 'beer money'!

Big Gerry's passion was music and in particular American country music! He was a huge Hank Williams fan, and he was also a musician. The bass guitar was his instrument of choice although he always had a six-string acoustic propped up in the corner of our living room, which he would strum now and again. This beast would also be produced at house parties where he sang a song or two! For as long as I can remember, he played bass. Over the years he played with many bands and was a well-known 'character' in the Glasgow country music scene. Country was big in Glasgow and there were many clubs and pubs that catered solely for country fans.

The first band I have memories of was called The Long Horns. Glaswegian C&W bands of this era were frequently named after animals found in North America. The big man played with them for several years in the early 1970s. I can remember being taken to my first gig in a place called (and I'm not sure of the spelling) 'Delearn House'. This was a regular gig for him and the band. Throughout the years he was in and out of many bands and casual groups, and in any given week he could play up to three or four gigs a week. He would be out playing on a Thursday night, come home late very 'merry' and then would be up early for work the next day. The band I have the most memories of (and the fondest), was Carmel and Country Pride. He played with this band from the late 70s to middle 1980s. More about them later!

Now you have to remember this was the early 1970s, and he was dressing up with cowboy shirts and cowboy boots, walking proudly down Galloway Street. A sight for sore eyes indeed! As kids we used to have to help pull off these boots, which seemed to be super-glued to his big ponging feet! His boot would be between our legs and his other foot pushing against our back. More often than not we would go flying across the living room head first, boot in hand!

Now it's safe to say that my Dad likes a drink. Or two or three! He could fair put it away and luckily for us he was like me, a very decent drunk. He just liked to spread the love man! When I would go home to Glasgow (from Skye) on school holidays and if he was out playing with the band, he'd usually come home late (and steaming), come into me and my brother's room and wake me up to cuddle me and to tell me he loved me and missed me! I would get annoyed at his beer breath and scratchy beard, waking me up, but I suppose it was also nice.

He has always been very supportive of anything I have ever done and never been negative about any of my failed attempts to be a band manager (more of that later too). Big Gerry loved the Isle of Skye and he began taking us there from a very early age. I think I was just over a year old when we first went to Linicro. In 1977, when I had asked my Aunt Margaret if I could stay and go to school, he was thrilled and agreed immediately. He visited me a couple of times whilst I went to school and – being my Dad – he liked to head to Uig's Ferry Inn for a pint or two! He would walk there cutting down the Bealach shortcut and spend the evening getting 'merry' and talking to the locals.

He made it back up the Bealach hill (which is steep), without injuring himself... much!

We have been lucky with him, but we did nearly lose him to a stroke. In 2001, when he was sixty-one (the same age that his Dad was when he died), Big Gerry was in the pub on a Saturday afternoon when he keeled over onto the floor. Fortunately for me, I was doing Agency Nursing at the time in Glasgow. I was in my sister's flat that day when I received a call from my Agency, who had gotten a call from the Glasgow Royal saying that they had taken my Dad in with a stroke and he could not talk. How they found out about me and got the Agency to call I'm not sure, but at the time I did a fair amount of shifts there. Immediately after the call, I jumped in a taxi to the hospital. When I got there, he was awake and lucid, but he could not talk, and I realised he had had a dense stroke. He had a bleed, not a clot, probably because of undiagnosed high blood pressure. After speaking to the doctor and being a nurse, I was pessimistic about his chances for recovery. They had also seen what they thought was a 'growth' in his lungs. My sister was on holiday in America at the time and annoyingly, a friend of my Dad's had phoned her to tell her about his stroke. My sister loves her Dad and immediately made plans to fly back. I had hoped not to tell her until I saw how things went. He then went downhill and for a good while it was touch and go whether he would pull through. It was depressing as I had seen many stroke victims in my career and those with bad strokes almost never made a full recovery. Most were left with a one-sided weakness. My old man is tough though! He eventually recovered enough to be moved from the Royal to a rehab unit on the Southside. Eventually he got back his speech and was left only with a mild paralysis. My sister got him into a new Housing Association flat in Govanhill, very near all his local pubs. Result! He never played his bass again though, but at least we still had him with us. He still got out and about for several years and still enjoyed a pint or two... or three. Over the last decade or so his health has slowly deteriorated and mostly he has become house-bound, only venturing out for special occasions, the last big one being for my daughter's Christening. My sister Angela lives in Glasgow's West End (as does my mother, my folks divorced). She got him a nice wee apartment close to the Kelvinhall Underground Station. With the support of carers coming in to check on him, he is happy enough with his TV, fags and occasional half bottle of whisky! My brother Gary ended up moving to Partick, so it means that they are all close together in the same general area. Living and working abroad means I only see him about once a year, but I try to video call him regularly. I'm just glad he is still alive and almost kicking!

Grandparents

Unfortunately, all of my grandparents died relatively young, the last being my Granda Cusack (Mum's Dad) who died when I was around 17 years old. I had not seen him in a long time as I was at school on Skye. His wife, my Granny Cusack (née McKenzie) was originally from Linicro so she was our connection to the island that I would grow to love. She was only in her 60s when she passed in the mid-1970s. My Dad's Dad was only 61 when he died around 1970 and his wife probably passed around the mid-70s too. It's sad because as kids you don't really have the capabilities to appreciate your grandparents. To you they seem ancient and out of touch. It's only as you get older you can see them for who they are and for me I never had that opportunity. I just want to share some memories I have of them so that my kids will have an idea who they were.

Around about 1968-69 they hospitalised my Mum with tuberculosis. We were lucky not to have lost her and although the only memories I have of her at that time are from black and white photos of her in the hospital, she was lucky to survive. She would have been in hospital for months and as my Dad worked, he could not look after us kids. My brother Gary would have been a young baby. What I remember was that they sent me to live with my Granny and Granda Moore. They sent my sister Angela to Linicro to be looked after by my Great Granny and Great Auntie. I really have no clue who looked after my young brother.

This is probably the reason I felt closer to my Granny Moore. I only have very vague memories from that time. They lived in the white high flats on Caledonia Road. It was a two-bedroom apartment and an older relative who I knew as 'Uncle Mattie' lived with them. I think he was a cousin of my Granny's. Although I did not know it at the time, Mattie was handicapped. In the 1960s they would have called him 'slow' but to me he was just a friendly old guy and I shared a room with him. One thing I remember was that on his dresser he had toy cowboys and Indians, and I thought this very cool. My only memory of my Granda Moore, which is hazy, was of him teaching me to tell the time and to tie my laces. That's it. I wish I had more time with him because I think I would have really liked him. From what I was told, he was just an unassuming, decent guy. He let his wife be the boss. I know that this wee Glasgow guy shipped out to Burma during World War Two and did his bit for King and country. I have huge respect for him for being brave enough to do that.

I spent one Christmas there and I remember getting a shooting game that came with a rifle. You had to shoot at Dr Who's Daleks as they slipped down a metal ramp from their tin plate spaceship.

Once my Mum was out of hospital, they would take us to see their parents on a Sunday. This was when my Granny and Granda Cusack moved to a horrendous concrete scheme in Pine Place just across the river in the Gorbals, near to the Caledonia Road turn off. The flats were notorious for their poor construction, ugly looks and dampness. These were eventually demolished in the early 80s. By the mid-70s, my folks would let us kids go to visit them on our own. The three of us would be dressed in our Sunday best and we would walk up past Galbraith's supermarket and the Talisman Pub and get a 37 bus on Balgrayhill Road. This bus would take us right to the scheme where my Granny and Granda Cusack lived. They were on the ground floor.

My Granda Cusack was of Irish descent and had terrible eyesight. He wore these really thick glasses. He liked to play tricks on us and would buy stuff like chattering teeth from his trips to Blackpool and try to make us laugh. We considered the Cusacks old fashioned. My Granny always wore a pinnie and still kept her Highland accent. My memories of her are few, but she seemed always tired. We would do our best not to spend any time at all with them as we were in a rush to get to Granny Moore's. We would leave them and cut through the scheme to get to my Granny Moore's high flats. Granda was gone by then and Mattie moved into sheltered accommodation, so she was on her own. Her place was more modern, and she had a colour TV. Sunday's must view for kids was Glen Michael's 'Cartoon Cavalcade' which he hosted with his sausage dog and a talking oil lamp called Paladin. We loved that show.

Granny Moore had worked in Grey-Dunns the biscuit factory and would sometimes buy us a bag of 'broken biscuits'. If she did not have that she would always have some chocolate biscuit in her kitchen. She would also make us a bowl of her thick broth, which we scoffed with glee. She could be rather stern, I recall, and after we had eaten our food and watched the TV, it was time for us to return to Galloway Street. On our way back down Caledonia Road we had noticed that there was this area that had big white writing on the roof that said, 'Adventure Playground'. It looked very intriguing. We made a plan that on our next visit we would leave Granny Moore's early and see what this 'Adventure Playground' was all about. Sure enough, we left early the following week and went over the road towards the playground. We thought you might have to pay to get in, but it was free. We really had no idea what it was, as there was nothing like this in Springburn. Once inside we were amazed with the swings, slides, climbing areas and they even had a short zip line to slide down. We were a wee bit scared as we were unknown faces plus the fact we looked like we just came out of church! Nobody bothered us, and we did our best to play without getting dirt on our clothes. From then on, we would leave early every Sunday and play in that place. It was great. Afterwards we would board the 37 bus home and say nothing of our secret. Only our muddy shoes gave a hint that we had got up to some mischief.

As I have said, I really wish that I had known both sets of grandparents better. It was thanks to my Granny Cusack that I had the opportunity to be taken to Linicro – my first love. I miss the life that we could have shared with them as we kids got older and all that is left to say that I love each one of them and that a part of each of them lives on in the eyes of my kids. My Isaac when he was about one was the spitting image of my Granda Moore (to my eye, at least).

Tenements

Until the early 1970s there were old tenements right beside our block that stretched over Galloway Street, round the corner to Huntershill Street and round and along Springburn Road, ending right beside the local boozer, The Spring Inn. One of the earliest memories I have of Galloway Street was of an old woman always sitting outside of her ground-floor window in the first close by our opening. There was also a cat that would sit on her windowsill. Outside of the building was parked an old motorbike with a sidecar. I played with a young girl from that close and one day when it was pouring with rain, I imitated my mother pouring the water on our heads in the bath to rinse off the soap. For this poor wee lassie, it was water that was running down a drain on the road that I scooped up and poured over her head! She ran to tell her Mammy, and I got my bum spanked! I think by that time most of those flats were empty because we did our best to smash all the windows with stones.

Just before the corner was Jackie Wilson's shop, and this was where we would buy our lucky bags. I remember having a pal called Dougie who lived up the close near the shop. His family might have been the last in that building, and their door had a black-and-white marble effect design. At night these buildings along our street were really creepy, especially during the power cuts of the 1970s. Most of the flats either side of Huntershill Street were empty too and people used to tell us wee guys not to go there at night because Bible John will get ye! For those not

familiar with this name, Bible John was a guy who murdered a
number of women in Glasgow in the early 1970s. He supposedly
quoted passages from the bible, hence the name. He was never
caught for his crimes. We didn't go there alone. Just around the
corner on Springburn Road there were some shops, including a
paper shop that sold toys. There I would buy the Bassetts
sweetie cigarettes that had cards from the Gerry Anderson
show, UFO. These I collected madly. Along the way going
towards the Spring Inn there were at least two Asian grocery
shops. As more and more of these flats became empty, we
would try to break into them to see if we could find anything
worth taking. We also looked for lead to sell. There was one flat
that we got into that was full of old TVs. Every room from floor
to ceiling. We ended up smashing a lot of the screens (we were
young and stupid)! This flat was not inhabited by anyone and
the building was completely empty and stripped of all its lead
(not by us)! It was creepy though because most of the time we
went at night and there were no lights on the stairs. They still
had lamplighters then, going around lighting the gas lights in
all the closes.

The first of these old buildings to get knocked down were the
ones right beside us. I remember the sunny day we all sat up
outside the close opposite us and watched in awe as the roof
came down! We all cheered! Eventually the entire block was
demolished. Huntershill was next, and then eventually they got
round to the block on Springburn Road. Before that though, we
would enjoy going down the back and building wee fires. Most
of the time nobody would bother you as long as you didn't
make it too big. Stuart Wallace and I would take lead-covered
wiring and squash it into an old can and melt it. I loved seeing
it poured molten on the ground, just like silver or mercury. By
this time most of the closes were bricked up and with chalk we
would write on the grey cemented bricks Ray + Stu or Stu + Ray
– writing so big that I could look at it from my living room
window and get a feeling of pride!

Other than a Church, the ground on which these tenements
stood remains empty till this day. If only they had spent the
money on refurbishing them, they would still be standing and
would give the street some much-needed character.

Bus to Butlin's

In the early 1970s there was a genuine sense of pride and community within the residents of 7 Galloway Street. Along at the 'bridge' near the 'lift', they had a caretaker who would do his rounds making sure that us kids were not playing in areas with 'no ball games' signs. I remember him to be a bad-tempered old codger, who was intent on spoiling our fun!

Residents took turns in cleaning the floors in front of their front doors in the corridors and inside the shared 'drying areas'. The A and B decks were always looking clean and tidy, and people took pride in being a resident.

There was also a 'bus run' organised and we would head to Butlin's holiday resort in Ayr. We were all very excited about that. The night before we could hardly sleep because of the excitement. The day came along with two green double-decker buses parked up near the bridge. All I recall about the journey was singing 'the tap ae the bus they cannae sing for peanuts' sung by us on the bottom and the retort being 'the bottom of the bus they cannae sing for peanuts'! The journey for us kids was overly long and, on the bus, they fed us with sandwiches and sweet diluted orange drinks served from a Tupperware container.

Finally, we arrived, and we decided that we would go to the 'swimmin' first. There were two large pools, outside and inside. For us kids, we wanted to experience the luxury of an outside pool. The weather was pleasant, but the water was totally effin' freezing! I can't remember which pool had windows under-neath, but we were beyond excited to swim under the water and look through the windows and see people walking by!

After being fed a lunch of chips and 'ginger' (the generic Glasgow name for any soft drink), we went mad at 'the shows' or Butlin's amusement park, as most people called it. My chief memory of that is being on a (rather small) roller coaster. I want to say that we also went to the beach, but I might be getting that mixed up with a later family day outing to Saltcoats.

Eventually we had to pack up our stuff and travel back on the bus for a sad journey back to Springburn. That was the last bus run I was on.

Lost

As a parent of three kids out shopping, you constantly have to monitor them for fear that they get lost. Here in Saudi Arabia most of the time we go to shopping malls, so if we happen to misplace one of ours, it's usually easy to find them. Having said that, not too long ago I was in a computer shop with my boy Isaac asleep in his stroller. I was checking out some new gadgets when I walked out of the shop and left him there. It took me a couple of minutes to realise what I had done. My heart in my mouth, I ran back in to find him still sleeping where I left him.

I got lost only once, briefly, and it was scary as hell. I was probably around seven when I had been at my Granny Moore's with my Dad. On the way back there were the 'shows' on Glasgow Green. Big Gerry took me around them. With all the flashing lights, smell of toffee apples and candy floss, he gave me some money to go on a ride of my choice. I saw the dodgems, and I told him I was going on them. He said fine and let me go. The fare was too much, so when another kid about my age came up to me and asked if I wanted to share the ride. I said ok. He drove, and then I drove and it was fun, but when we stopped, it was on the other side from where we got on. I said cheerio to him and happily walked to where I thought my old man was. He was not there. Not thinking to walk round, I walked away from the dodgems. At first, I was not too worried, but after about ten minutes I panicked. My heart was pumping and my tears were flowing. I almost walked out of the amusement area completely when I double backed and did what I should have done in the first place. I found the dodgems and walked all the way round, but this time no sign of the big man. My wee heart sank. I was almost about to go into full crying mode when I heard a familiar voice shout my name. I breathed deeply and never felt so happy to see Big Gerry. I didn't tell him I got lost and typical parent he didn't ask. He thought I was still playing on the dodgems. For the rest of the afternoon, I stuck close to the big man's side.

Bools, Football Cards, Collecting and Homemade Toys

Collecting crazes came and went as a kid, as did playing with homemade toys. It appeared to be cyclical, like collecting football cards that came with a stick of gum. We would then avidly swap our 'doublers', trying to make up our favourite teams. Then came the phase of crossbows made from two pieces of wood nailed together, cross shaped. We hammered two nails either side of the cross and strung these with a thick rubber band. Wooden clothes pegs were our projectile, and the aim was to hit anyone hard. One summer someone made homemade darts from sewing needles and cut playing cards. These would then be thrown at any and everybody's arses. Dangerous, painful, and very good fun! It got even more dangerous one summer when air guns were a thing. Some big guys would go around with their GAT pistol shooting at us wee guys. In the summer of 1975, I came back from the Isle of Skye with a highly desirable Diane air gun. Everybody wanted to be my pal so they could get a shot. At night we would fire from Davie Cosgrove's close window, aiming at the Viewpoint maisonette windows. Sometimes we actually hit them!

I was mad for collecting birds' eggs, and I had a proud collection of local Glasgow birds' eggs in an old wooden drawer.

This wooden display had sawdust on the bottom with my precious collection laid out all nice for me and others to admire. The prize of my collection was a buzzard's egg that I had nabbed in Totescore the year before. Many a time I would go to Springburn Park on the hunt for eggs. Any type would do. The problem was the 'Parkies'. If they saw you, they would give chase. It was always a cat-and-mouse game. I was not good at climbing trees, nor was I very brave. One attempt saw me get very high only for my foot branch to break and I smacked every branch on my way down to the ground. It was a soft landing though, and I was unhurt. Some egg collectors would take all the eggs, but not me. If I was successful in finding a full nest, I would take only one or two. Some people also 'rooked' the nest after snatching the eggs. Destroying the bird's wee house. Again, not me.

Some birds nested in the drying areas of B Deck, and this day I was trying to get close to one directly above my house. It was almost impossible, but as I got near, I got my hand inside to find it empty of eggs. At that moment Davie Cosgrove was looking outside his bedroom window directly opposite me and he thought I was 'rooking' the nest. I wasn't, but this did not stop him waving his fist at me and mouth something like 'I'm gonnae batter you'. I had to hide from him for a couple of days until I could explain myself. He never did batter me! Newly collected eggs required you to 'blow' them. This entailed pin pricking top and bottom and then putting your mouth to one end and gently blowing. This was to remove the yolk and was difficult. Especially if the egg was small. Some guys on the street were expert 'blowers' and you would always seek their skills.

Stamp collecting became a big thing for me and a few of my school pals. You could buy big bundles of worthless stamps from across the world very cheaply in the town. To see all the different countries and the unique designs was very cool. You always hoped that you would find a stamp worth loads of money. I loved old pre- and post-war British Stamps and was very proud of my extensive collection. I found it amazing to think every one of them had at one time been sent by someone all those years ago.

One other craze that hit our street was finding detonators from the railway lines across the dump. This was a dangerous thing; not only could you put yourself in mortal danger of being hit by a train but also you might get caught by the Transport Police. These yellow metal discs created a very loud noise once hit correctly with a brick. They also shot off shrapnel and I think it was Jim Price who lost a piece of a front tooth to this very injury. I still don't know what these things were used for by British Rail.

I was also mad for anything to do with aeroplanes. Especially World War Two planes. Airfix and Matchbox models I made frequently. I collected cards and books and every Saturday I would buy a magazine from Billy's paper shop called Speed and Power. This magazine had loads of planes and boats. It also had the very first photos of the Space Shuttle and it was just crazy to think there would soon be the aeroplane for space flight!

Another game that came round in cycles was playing with 'bools' or, as they are known in England, marbles. We could buy these glass spheres with coloured insides from many shops, including Woolies in Springburn. There were also the big green ones called 'conkers' and one day a bunch of us went to a fibre glass factory somewhere over in Milton. The green balls were a by-product of whatever the factory produced. If you were lucky one worker would bring out loads of them for all of us to share. I took an old paint tin and used it to carry a full load home. We would play the games on the drain covers or 'stanks'. There were many of these along Galloway Street. These games we could play for hours, and if you were on a winning streak, you could win many of your pals' bools. I used to have a 'lucky bool', this would be one of those fancy multi-coloured marbles and before playing I would make an agreement that should I lose I would give them another from my bool collection but not my lucky one! Sometimes people didn't agree and I would lose my precious ball of glass. Then you needed to hunt for another colourful 'lucky bool'.

Peg Ya Bass!

Anyone who grew up in Glasgow in the 1960s and 70s would be familiar with their local area 'Gang'. Now I'm not suggesting that you were part of them but undoubtedly you would, at the very least, have seen their name spray painted on a wall somewhere!

Springburn and Galloway Street had the 'Springburn Peg' or 'Young Springburn Peg' (YSP). Sometimes you heard somebody shout, 'Young Galloway Street Peg'. In the surrounding areas we had 'Milton Tongs' and the 'Memel Toi'. We also feared 'The Bundy' and 'The Fleet' and there was a rumour that there was a gang called 'The Skinhead Mafia', scary!

Who were in these gangs? I don't know. For the Springburn/ Galloway Street Peg, we supposed that it was big guys from both old and new Galloway Street. There was one guy in Galloway Street who was artistic and poetic with his graffiti. I can remember this ditty spray painted on the floor of one of the 'drying areas' on our block. It went something like this.... 'In the land of rips and scars there are these names, and they are stars'. It listed nicknames of people from old Galloway. He would also paint big logos and army stuff, which was pretty good if a wee bit fascist!

The 'Pegs' mortal enemy when I was a kid were 'The Milton Tongs', from Milton obviously. This was not too far away and any time there was trouble it would be 'sorted out' on the 'dump', opposite my building across Springburn Road – usually on the unused railway bridge over the train tracks at the far end of the 'dump'. I was too scared to be involved in any of their shenanigans and watched the 'battle' from the safety of my veranda!

The norm would be a bunch of 'Tongs' at one side of the bridge and a bunch of the 'Peg' at the other. In the 70s, the 'Peg' had an alliance with the 'Toi', who would join the 'battle' on the bridge!

This would usually mean a bunch of guys running at the other with sticks waving and the occasional half brick being lobbed! Unlike the battle scenes in Braveheart, the two groups would never actually clash as at some point one group would turn and run! Very occasionally, a couple of guys may get into an actual fight, but I do not recall hearing of anyone receiving any serious injuries. Glasgow then was notorious for knife crime and in particular getting 'ripped', which meant getting cut down the side of the face with a razor. We were always in fear that this could happen to us if we wandered into unknown territory!

As sidebar to this there was one time my pal Stuart and I were hunting for newts that could be found in puddles of mud at the far end of the 'dump', close to the railway tracks. This day I remember well as both of us took our newly purchased penknives with us. Being unsuccessful with the newt hunt we headed for home on the path next to the Springburn 'Plots' (allotments) and as we came out of the gate going onto Springburn Road, a car braked in front of us, and two guys got out and grabbed us saying they were the police. Unbeknownst to me, Stuart had surreptitiously dropped his knife, but mine was still in my pocket! They took us in the back of the car and started asking us questions about fighting on the bridge. Stuart immediately cried, and I wanted to as well, but I kept thinking about the knife in my pocket and not wanting to get caught. This kept the tears from my eyes. We explained to them that we were just playing, looking for newts, and we were too small to be involved with gang fights. They asked us where we lived and then they took us to Galloway Street. Thinking back, I see how easy it could have been for adults to have snatched us, pretending to be the police, and we would have gone with them without question! They dumped us on our street and sped off to God knows where.

The Shows

Now and again during the 1970s 'the shows' (travelling amusement park) would come to Springburn and set up on the spare ground called 'the dump' or 'coup' as it was also known, across the road from our house. These amusements were located near where the old 'Perthshire Club' was. This generated a lot of excitement on Galloway Street.

I don't recall ever seeing any adverts telling of their arrival. The first sign would be when we were walking home across 'the dump' from St Aloysius. There you would see the gathering of the mobile homes and the trucks with the amusement rides on them! We would hang about and watch the guys set up the rides. We would be super excited to see which amusements they brought. In only a couple of days that part of 'the dump' was a full-blown amusement park with flashing lights and the smell of candy floss!

Most evenings, money or not, we would all cross the road to wander about and listen to the hits being played from the 'waltzers'. They had the 'chairoplane', the 'big wheel' and my personal favourite, the 'sticky wall'. There were also smaller amusements like the 'rib tickler' and of course the 'dodgems'. Another firm favourite with me was the amusement arcades.

The Rotor aka the 'sticky wall' was great fun where you all stood inside a rotating barrel that would turn so fast that when the floor moved down, the G forces would keep you stuck to the wall. Brilliant! I also liked the 'dive bombers' but they were scary and did not seem that safe. In fact, I saw the aftermath of an accident where the door had opened, and the two people had fallen out. One of them landed on the wooden ramp up to the ride. It was two girls, and they were crying but did not seem to be badly hurt.

We were only given enough money for one or two rides, so it limited our choice. I remember the 'dodgems' were too expensive, as was the 'big wheel', which I went up on one time and was pretty scared! People would try to win coconuts and goldfish, much like they do today. In the amusement arcades, we scanned the floor for coins and tried our best to win something with the penny shuffle machines. One year they brought this semi-video game called 'Destroyer'. The front of the machine looked like a submarine periscope with a red button on the right handle. You would insert a coin and peer through the scope and what appeared in the distance was a wee plastic destroyer ship moving from left to right and back again. You scored points if you could fire your submarine torpedo and hit the ship! You had to time the pressing of the red button just right. When you did, a red light flashed across the 'sea' towards the ship. If you hit, there would be flashing lights beside the plastic boat! If you got a direct hit right in the middle, you heard a rather tinny explosion sound. It was pretty basic, but I found it addictive.

The only downside to 'the shows' was that older teenagers from all over Springburn and beyond would gather – some looking to chat up the girls who would sit around the 'waltzers', most looking for a fight!

There were many skirmishes and a couple of full-on battles. Lucky for us we were too young to get involved, but sometimes you got caught up in the crowd. There was one year when a big fight kicked off near the entrance. I was standing beside the 'big wheel' when two groups of teenagers went at it! Scary. The police showed up, but it was only one car and two officers, and I remember them standing on the stairs of the portable toilets when the crowd pelted them with stones. They jumped inside to hide until back-up came, when the crowd of guys went to tip over the porta potties! That building was shaking as if it was in an earthquake. Thank God for the two cops that a couple of vans filled with their colleagues turned up, and they quickly dispersed the crowd. We heard of stabbing and slashings going on, but I saw nothing like that!

Halloween

For us 70s Springburn kids the build up to Christmas started at the end of October with Halloween. This we got really excited about and the thought of getting money, peanuts or sweeties kept us awake at night. My parents never gave me a budget for a costume, so you had to make your own. Mine were all pretty lame. My last Halloween in Glasgow was in 1975, as by 1976 I was in first year at school and had 'grown out' of such childish things!

I was struggling to come up with a fancy-dress idea when I found an old pair of spotted pyjamas. I asked to use some of my mother's makeup on my face and she helped to give me a creepy white face and some red lips and cheeks. I stuck a pillow up my shirt and became a fat clown from hell! Not very convincing, I know, but that was the best that I could do.

I had arranged to meet my pal from school, Stuart McKenna. He lived up old Galloway Street, and we had a plan that we thought would ensure a very successful evening. Rather than go around Galloway we made our way towards Colston and further on to the beginning of Bishopbriggs. There were plenty of detached and semi-detached villas around and we thought there would be less competition! We were right about the competition, there were few kids around, so we just started knocking on every door. This was before Halloween got 'Americanized', so we never said, 'Trick or Treat' we would say 'anything for Halloween'? Sometimes they would give us what we called 'monkey nuts' and some fruit. Other times it was small sweeties and said nuts which were peanuts in their shells. Sometimes we were asked to do a 'turn' before getting a reward. Stuart usually told a joke, and I would sing the chorus of 'Hey Jock Ma Cuddie'. More doors remained closed than open that night, but we had fun and it did not rain. We had a bag each for our treasure and as we ventured further into Bishopbriggs, they were both getting very full. Our only problem would be when we returned to Galloway Street with full bags, some older kids would try to 'knock' (steal) our stuff. As we walked back on to

Springburn Road, Stuart cut through one of the tenement closes and then went through their 'back' until he reached his own back and entered his close's back door, running up the stairs to safety. This left me alone, so I rushed along the road and I cut up Huntershill Street and got back to my door as quick as a flash! How proud I was of my haul. Funny thing is though that I didn't like the 'monkey nuts' (and at that time I did not know that these were just unroasted, unsalted peanuts), I enjoyed the sweeties, though!

Guy Fawkes

Next in our pre-Christmas calendar was 'remember, remember the 5th of November' – Guy Fawkes or bonfire night! In the weeks leading up to this night there would be indiscriminate firework usage on our street, usually 'bangers'. Nobody had much money for anything else! My mind tells me that 'bangers' or 'squibs' from earlier years, were bigger and more powerful than the weedy ones of the mid-1970s. Maybe something to do with health and safety? Astra was the company that sold most fireworks that I remember. How we would stare with wanting eyes at the big boxes in Woolworths. Us wee guys could not even buy a box of 'bangers' even if we had the money because we were too young. If we scraped together enough cash, then we would ask a big guy on the street to buy us a box. The box looked like a cigarette carton with ten anorexic 'squibs' inside. You would pull one out, light it with a match, hold for as long as possible and then throw it at someone! I don't know of anyone who got injured by a firework on my street, but I'm sure Glasgow's A&Es were full of victims on November 5th. Sometimes you could walk along the street when suddenly a lit firework landed at your feet! Some people even put fireworks through letterboxes in my corridor. Luckily, no house fires ensued.

A few days before the 5th we would make up a life size 'Guy' and take it around to the Public Bar door of the Spring Inn. It would sit at the side of the steps and we would shout 'Penny for the Guy' at any adult entering or exiting – the hope being that those pub punters under the influence would be more generous with their contributions. We never made loads of money, but whatever we made was given to the big guys to buy whatever they could in the way of firework entertainment.

Traditionally in Glasgow, you made your own bonfire. Organized events were few. This would become a competition to see who could build the biggest. Earlier years we would have a smallish fire at the back of the tenements opposite us where my pals Stuart Wallace and Davie Cosgrove lived. My last Guy Fawkes Night in Glasgow was in November 1976 and that year we would build a bonfire on the spare ground beside our building where the old tenements used to sit and where the Church is now. Guys from old Galloway were building there too, closer to their side of the street. We had been planning our fire for weeks and our wood collecting began in early October. The problem with collecting so early is where would you hide your wood stash? If it was outside, it was easily knockable (*stolen*)! I asked my folks if we could use our 'cellar' to store our wood, and they said yes. This room was in our building corridor, so behind our black painted door lay our stash.

For weeks we would wander everywhere looking for any wood. If we found old furniture, we would break it up. We would purloin wooden planks from building sites with scaffolding. All this booty would be safe in my locked room. By November 5th we stacked our cellar to the ceiling. It was lucky that we could close the door – there was that much burning material inside! That evening it was all hands on 'A' deck to remove the wood and take it to the spare ground.

Some big guys were in charge of bonfire construction, probably including Gerry McDade and Stephen Wallace. Once the cellar was empty, we all went to see our wood all stacked and ready to be lit, and although it was pretty impressive, it was not as big as the one made by the guys from old Galloway. Theirs was gargantuan. Unlucky for them though was when a police car stopped and told them it was too big, and they had to remove a lot of the wood. That night both fires blazed into the night and we saw a collection of fireworks being set off. Jumping Jacks were my favourite, if a little scary. Catherine Wheels would be nailed to a standing plank of wood to be lit and to spin, and the very occasional Roman Candle was set off from the ground. All over the city was the noise of fireworks and fire engines. Our eyes would scan the night sky for the selection of rockets that would have been stood in an empty milk bottle and set alight and to blast and explode above our heads. They were nothing like the fancy fireworks you see these days, but we still enjoyed it and got excited at every bang!

Christmas

As kids, we were very lucky to have parents who made an effort with our Christmases. That's not to say we got hundreds of presents or got everything we asked for but considering how tight money probably was for my folks, we were always very happy. For us, Christmas was the only time you got toys. We got nothing except a card for our birthdays, and any toy bought throughout the year would have been by us from our saved-up pocket money.

The Christmas excitement would begin in earnest by the end of November. It was around about then that you would see adverts for the latest and greatest toys on STV. Usually, these adverts were screened at the weekends and after school until teatime. My brother, sister and I would also look through the Autumn and Winter Great Universal catalogue and spend hours flipping through the toy section at the back. Great fun. In the early 70s, my mother would make Christmas decorations from crepe paper rolls on her sewing machine. Occasionally she would buy some extra ones. For years we had the same old 'fake' Christmas tree, not particularly big, but we liked it. It had a thick wooden 'log' base, and my Mum would wrap cotton wool round it to imitate snow. Cotton wool balls would be placed on the tree branches like 'snowflakes'. There would be tinsel wrapped around too and hanging decorative balls and the obligatory flashing lights. Usually a star at the top, although we might have had a fairy too.

The weeks before Christmas were so exciting for us. School would get into the Christmas spirit and the workload was less. In Mrs Carr's classroom at St Aloysius we would make our own paper decorations, colourful and fun. Usually on one wall we would have a 'frieze' (poster) typically depicting a Nativity scene. Every year the school would put on a play of the Nativity and perhaps another musical show on the dining hall's stage. I got to play a shepherd one year and my only line was 'oh look there at that beautiful star' or something like that!

In the town there would be Christmas lights slung along city streets and George Square would have a selection of festive decorations. It really was pretty cool, and it was also a treat to go into the town centre, not to buy anything but to look at the lights on Sauchiehall and Argyle Street. There Lewis's would have a Christmas tree outside, and I loved going up to their toy department, although I never bought a thing!

Another Christmas treat would be to go to the 'shows' in the Kelvinhall. To be inside out of the cold and have many amusement rides was totally brilliant. One year they also had a small 'petting zoo'; there are some photos of my sister, brother and me standing in front of a camel! Great fun.

One thing me and my brother Gary would do usually a few weeks before Christmas was to 'practise' at getting up early on Christmas morning. We would pretend to sleep and then wake each other up saying 'it's Christmas' then pretend to go to the living room and open our presents! Those last couple of days before Christmas would be sleepless as our excitement would build and build.

Before long it would be Christmas Eve and we would not have long to wait before we could get up super early and find our gifts. Our plan would always be to wait till we heard our folks go to bed. Wait another 10 minutes, then get up and go to the living room. Most of the time we were fast asleep by the time they went to bed, but we woke up very early. The excitement of the three of us climbing the stairs to the living room was obvious. Then we opened the living room door and over by the window would be three piles of presents. Like mad men we would be ripping open the packages to see what we got. It was great. We nearly always got what we wanted in the way of a 'big' toy and plenty of other stuff including sweetie 'selection' box. Depending on how early we got up we would go back to bed only to wake up again excited for a second time. Some of my toy highlights through the years was Action Man Sailor (with beard). Subbuteo European Cup Edition, TT stunt car and one of my absolute favourites was Major Matt Mason's UniTrac and Space Bubble. Depending on the weather and what was on TV we would go out to show off our new toys. I don't remember it ever being a white Christmas anytime when I was a child in Glasgow.

Another Christmas treat was the TV shows and movies. Back then a blockbuster movie being shown on TV was a big deal. Essential viewing for us was also the Christmas edition of Top of the Pops and finding out who had the Christmas number one! Back then we only had BBC1, STV and BBC2 so the choice was not great. Not like today. Usually either the *Daily Record* or *Sunday Mail* would have a Christmas TV 'pull out' so that you could check when and where a show or movie was on and plan your viewing day accordingly.

Our Christmas dinner was always chicken which was fine by us as we loved it roasted. All shops generally were closed so my Mum would usually buy enough provisions for three days. As kids we loved it and we have our folks to thank for giving us these precious memories.

We would also have to buy our Mum and Dad a wee gift which usually was very small as it would have had to have been purchased from our meagre pocket money!

One other thing that happened up until the early 1970s was that our extended family on my mother's side would get together, usually at my Grannie and Granda Cusack's (my

Mum's Mum) or my Auntie Annie's Maclellan Street tenement in Kinning Park. There my Mum's sister's Margaret and Annie would bring my cousins Flora, Bobby, Veronica and Andrew (I don't think wee Jason had been born then). My uncle Peter was always there too. We would all get wee gifts to open, and we would have a great time. This stopped though as we got older. Usually after Boxing Day we would go and see my Grannie Moore in her Caledonia Road apartment. There we could watch her colour TV and get a present from her. We used to leave her place and go down to the paper shop near her building and buy sweets and play in the nearby playground. This was a fun day out for us too.

By my last Christmas in Glasgow, I was getting too old for toys and in 1976 I received my 'big' Christmas gifts before Christmas as I had to try them on before they were bought. I got an Admiral Leeds United football strip which was the white strip with the blue and yellow Admiral logos down the side and a pair of Adidas Beckenbauer football boots with rubber studs. The boots were black and lime green Trefoil and 3 stripes! Very cool. I also remember that year that my brother Gary got a Hornby Rural Rambler train set which he was very happy with!

One more standout memory of that Christmas was at our last Boys' Brigade meeting before the Christmas break. Tariq Benison, Jim McClusky and I were walking back from Albert Secondary school late on a Friday night and as we passed the Talisman pub, we burst into a very loud rendition of Johnny Mathis's song 'When a child is born'. Great fun!

∽

St Aloysius School Trips

I suppose we were lucky during the early 1970s as we got to go on several school trips, which did not seem to cost that much. The first one for me was a trip to Blantyre and to the David

Livingstone Centre. All that sticks in my memory was that it was a pretty miserable rainy day and I remember walking across the Livingstone Bridge looking on to the weir which was in full flow because of the weather. That bridge was very high to us primary school kids. The only other memory I thought I had of visiting there was that a few of us went walking in the 'countryside' near a hill only to be told to stay away because they were blasting! This only made us more curious, but eventually we retreated. When I looked on Google to see the Centre and its surroundings, I did not see any hills nearby? Maybe I'm just making that memory up?

Our next trip was to Ayr and to the seaside! I was particularly excited about this, as a few of us had planned to go fishing! My Dad had a sea rod and over the months I had gathered weights and lures including 'spinners', all neatly packed into this wee white plastic container with a handle. The night before, Big Gerry had promised to hook up the rod with its reel all ready for me to attach my favourite spinner. The big man may have had a few drinks after work because he fell asleep on the sofa and took an age to wake up. I waited patiently with all my gear. Wake up, he did, and as promised he sorted everything for me. I remember the rod cover being blue and I recall one guy from along Galloway Street who had a fancy rod that we were all jealous of. It was a single decker Plaxton Panorama coach that took us to the seaside town on what was another rainy day. We had no clue where we would fish but I remember getting off the bus and being very excited by the sight of the sea. Rather than go to the end of the pier I tried to get closer to the water near to a green slimy embankment. The inevitable happened when I lost my footing on the greasy rocks and slipped to the water's edge! I narrowly avoided going into the sea. It was not an easy climb back up, and thankfully nobody saw me (to laugh at)! Eventually I made my way to the pier's end and cast my favourite spinner. Within five minutes I had lost it to thick seaweed. The rain pelted down. Disheartened, I made my way to the bus where I met my classmate Stuart McKenna. We had planned to go to Ayr baths and with the rain on it seemed like a good time to go. Luckily for me the coach driver was still in his seat and he let me in to dump my fishing gear and off we went to the 'swimmin'.

What stood out about Ayr baths was the diving pool, which housed springboards and diving dales (boards in English). We of course wanted to climb to the very top and as we made our move, we were told by the pool attendant that there was no jumping, only diving. It was high but did not seem too high. Well, not until we reached the top dale and looked over! My heart began pumping, fast and my bravery left my body very quickly. Stuart was not afraid of anything and immediately he dived off! It was by no means an Olympic quality dive, but he hit the water straight and surfaced with a smile! I looked over the edge again and said 'no effin' way'. I travelled all the way down to the ground with my tail between my legs and only attempted to use the springboard at the pool's edge!

The last trip I have a memory of was going to see the Cinderella Panto at the Glasgow King's. This was near Christmas time and I remember being in the balcony on the plush red seats. The Panto was good fun, but what I remember most was that during the performance one of the cast threw bags of sweets into the audience. He threw a few up to the balcony and I was lucky to grab a bag. I remember it was full of white chocolate candies, which I scoffed without sharing!

Doorstep

One of the annoying things about my mother having a part-time 'maid' job at Stobhill was that many times I would come back from school and nobody was in! This meant I would miss my kid's shows on TV. My Dad would not be back from his work till around 6 o'clock and there was nobody to play with because they were all inside watching TV! Davie Cosgrove's mother would take pity on me and she would tell him to bring me up to their place. At least I got to watch the box whilst waiting for my Mum's return. All this could have been solved by giving me or my big sister a key, but I don't think they trusted us! Then I had a brainstorm. Inside our front door there was two screws that held the letter box on. My small hand could squeeze inside side and reach the screw, but a burglar's hand could not. I then suggested that whenever my mother was going to be late, she hang the spare set of keys from the screw. When I came home, I would check the corridor, make sure nobody was looking, and reach in for the keys. Easy! I never had to wait for her again!

Staying In

With my Dad being a musician, he played in various bands and sometimes my mother would go with him for a night out. I have faint memories of being baby sat by a neighbour's daughter who lived upstairs on 'B' deck. As we got a bit older, we convinced my folks that the three of us could look after ourselves and anytime they both went out, which was rare, we had the house to ourselves! This was great for us because we could run amok without fear of skelp from my Mum!

We played many games inside the house and with no adults this meant that we could watch what we wanted on TV. Friday nights on STV had a horror movie showing known as 'Don't Watch Alone'. They would usually show old Frankenstein and Dracula movies, and we would do our best to stay awake to watch this and get ourselves scared! The problem was we had to go to our beds alone and after a horror flick our young imaginations would run riot and we would be convinced that a ghost or monster would be hiding in one of our closets!

Our old sofa was one of those that could be folded into a double bed and on that we could play 'King of the Castle' and throw each other on to the floor. One evening we were playing 'Camel', which was my brother at the front, my sister bent down behind and me sitting on my sister like I was on a camel! We would run around mad in the living room. This time my brother ran straight for our sofa which backed on to a wall and my sister helped speed him up. He then halted, and the momentum made me fly off onto the sofa with my arms straight in front of me so my noggin (head) would not hit the wall. Unfortunately, the forces of my arms hitting the wall caused a cracking sound to my right elbow! The pain soon followed! I was in agony and had obviously hurt myself. Later on we went to bed before my parents came back, but I awoke early because of the throbbing from my arm. I woke my Mum, who obviously had a hangover and told her what happened and that I was in agony. She eventually had to get up and take me to the A&E at Stobhill. An X-ray showed that I had fractured my elbow, but they would not put a cast on just a sling. As the nurse tied the sling around my neck and pulled my arm up, I suddenly felt very weird. As if everything in front of me was dimming. Almost the same as when you turned your TV off and you would see the wee white spot in the middle of the screen. I half fainted, and they got me on a stretcher and called the doctor again. This time he ordered a full arm cast and once applied I felt much better. My elbow was bent and my casted arm was in a sling. Having this made me feel great! I could show it off on our street and at school, and people could sign it! Even better, because it was my right hand I did not have to do any school work for a couple of weeks. I could only sit, listen, and read! Pretty good! Once they removed the cast, my arm was better and of course when my folks went out, we would again play 'camels'!

Millport

It was a summer that I did not go to Skye for the school holidays, probably 1974. I was offered a chance to go to Millport with my bestie Stuart Wallace and his family. I jumped at said chance. It was kind of his Mum and Dad, Sadie and Big George to take me along. I ended up having a cracking time!

George was a train driver for British Rail, so all the tickets to Largs to catch the ferry were free. The group comprised the two adults, Stuart, his brothers Steven and Scott (who was just a baby), their sister Susanne, their cousin Alan and me! What an adventure. We boarded the ferry sailing to the island of Millport, and the accommodation that they had booked was up a hill near to the pier.

Basically, it was a room with two double beds, and I think a cot. All the boys shared one bed, top and tail, and their sister was in with her parents. There was probably a small kitchen area and a table and chairs, but I remember little else!

Millport (unlike Skye) is a tiny island, and most of the action occurs along one road opposite the pier and beach. It also very safe for children. For Stuart and me, we were most excited about the ability to hire a bike. which we did almost immediately! We did not spend much time with the family as we were always out on our adventures and exploring. Beside the pier there were these steep steps leading down to a small sandy beach area. We played there a lot. We also liked to play at the well-known 'crocodile rock'. Also, near there just off the beach, moored in the water was a raft. The weather may have been fine, but that did not mean the sea was in any way, shape or form, warm. We did swim to the raft a few times, though!

I came a cropper on my bike one time and I'm lucky I did not give myself brain damage (maybe I did)? I was trying to mount the pavement but came in at too sharp an angle and tumbled off the bike, my head hitting the concrete. I definitely had a concussion as I was dazed and confused for more than a wee while. Most of the time, though, I was injury free. Millport is relatively easy to cycle around, and this we did several times before stopping at 'The Fintry Bay Café' for fluids.

It was a fairly family-orientated place and there were many kids' activities like Punch and Judy shows and trampolines. These I was too scared to try as a metal edge surrounded the trampolines and it did not look safe. I remember Stephen doing somersaults!

Big George and Sadie Wallace are no longer with us now, so I just wanted to share that memory in honour of them and to thank them for taking me on holiday because I really had such a good time!

Games

On the walls of our maisonettes there were signs placed strate-
gically all along Galloway Street saying: 'No Ball Games' and
'No Loitering'. I did not know what loitering meant but laughed
at the idea of 'No Ball Games'. This sign we totally ignored.

 Looking back, it's weird and funny to think that the small
stretch of road from our opening of the maisonettes to the
bridge which was the boundary of 7 Galloway Street was my
world for a good many years. It was nothing much to look at.
Our building on one side, the tenements and a stretch of grass
on the other. You can include the corridors and open areas in
our building too and occasionally the grass out in front of our
flats, but that was about it. Not huge at all. Yet every day that is
where we would all go out to play. Rain or shine.

Most of my pals lived opposite in the tenements and for as long
as I can remember we played football. We played it directly
under my bedroom window. We played in the next opening,
going towards the bridge. We played in the parking area two
openings up before the bridge and we played it on the grass
opposite to the side of said tenements and the front of
Viewpoint's maisonettes. When it rained, we would play in the
corridor outside my front door. I wasn't even that good, but I
liked to play. We would always play a mixture of big guys and
wee guys. In the next opening up one person would use that
opening as their goal mouth and we would all play 'wan and
aff'. Meaning we all played for ourselves and whoever scored a
goal went off and was through to the next round. We played on
till everyone got a goal but one. They were 'oot'. They watched
until the rounds ended and there was a final winner! I never
ever won, but I was rarely the first 'oot'.

Without fail very Saturday I would show up for our Boys'
Brigade football team which guaranteed me a game every
single week. I even scored a goal now and again! For a wee
while I even played for Springburn Boys' Club purely by
showing up to practise, I would get a game just so that they

could field a full team! We were hopeless and I remember getting beaten by some ridiculous score like 18-2!

We did not always play football. During the better weather we would vary what games we played. As previously mentioned, we did a lot of biking around. Racing to the bridge and back and the occasional long runs out of the city boundaries.

Kick the can was popular then. This entailed one person being in charge of the can and the others hiding. That person would then have to find those hiding. If they saw you, they would run back to the can and say your name 'Raymond Moore, bock tae bock bock'. This meant you were caught, and either had to wait until they found all the others hiding or if someone crept out and got to the can first and kicked it, then all of us who were caught could run and hide again!

Two-man hunt was played by two people 'hunting' the others and catching them. Once caught you had to join the hunt till everyone was found. Occasionally we would end up hiding as far as Viewpoint in an effort not to get caught!

At the back of the tenements opposite, there was a patch of green grass used as a clothing drying area and in the summer months we would gather there for 'British Bulldog' and 'May I Cross Your Golden River Mr Alligator'. Both games similar in that one person had to catch someone who would then join them and help catch the rest.

Now and again, we would go on the hunt for a 'lucky midgie bin' which saw us rake through back yard dustbins for thrown out treasure. Not too much treasure was ever thrown out in Springburn, though!

The long corridors of our building were ideal for 'chap door, run away' that is until the ground floor corridor had the prison-like iron gates installed so that nobody could walk, run, bicycle or sometimes motorbike in that corridor ever again!

During the power cuts of the early 1970s, we could run amok in the corridors. We drove the neighbours crazy and often got chased outside by torch-holding Dads.

No matter what day it was though, I was always called in at 9 o'clock by my mother. She usually came to my bedroom window and no matter how much I begged her; I was shown no mercy. Other kids were allowed out till 10 o'clock but my brother, sister and I had to be in our beds at that time. Weekends we had a little leeway, but Mum was pretty strict about getting us in before it got too late.

Toy Boy

As briefly mentioned before, my brother, sister and I only ever got toys at Christmas. Nothing for birthdays. This didn't stop us from wanting them. Sometimes you swapped. Sometimes you saved up your pocket money and other times if you were very lucky (and this was rare) you would be given some for nowt!

I bet that any adult of my age watching old 1970s toy adverts will get a warm fuzzy feeling in the bottom of their stomachs, even if they never owned the actual advertised toy. I sometimes watch these on YouTube, and over the years I have collected some highly desirable toys that I could not have as a kid. If any of my pals owned a fancy (expensive) toy, then at least I got a 'shot' of them. It was better than nothing!

Dinky Toys I loved. In particular, the Gerry Anderson related vehicles. First, the SHADO 2 Mobile from UFO. This green tank-like vehicle had a rocket launcher that hid inside the roof. By flicking a wee lever, the green roof flipped round revealing the yellow and red launcher. Sadly, I never owned one as a kid. Some school friends did and getting a wee shot of theirs was the closest I ever came to one. Now I'm an adult I own two. In mint working condition! With working rockets! Yaas! Again, from UFO was the green Interceptor with firing front missile. I was so desperate for it but never got one. Now I own two of those as well. Still working.

Another Dinky toy of desire was Ed Straker's golden car which I never saw in the flesh but knew of its existence. A few years ago, I bought a well-played one from the wee toy shop 'Pastimes' that used to sit at the bottom of Maryhill Road. I plan to buy a mint one before I leave Saudi. The 'Eagles' from Gerry Anderson's Space 1999 were always on my wish list. It's only as an adult that I own two models purchased from eBay, the green one with the white passenger pod and the blue one with the radioactive drums. Both mint! Captain Scarlet's red car and the Special Patrol Vehicle I found well used in the aforementioned 'Pastimes' (now closed due to retirement). From Joe 90 again from Mr Anderson I found a well-used Joe's car and hope to buy Sam's car one day. I always wanted Thunderbirds 2 but never got one until recently when I purchased a Dinky re-release.

Ker-plunk – I only ever got to play this toy with a pal, but it was a favourite during the Christmas season with several other Ideal Toys and was constantly being advertised on the telly.

Mousetrap – Who didn't play this game? Who actually got it to work? Stuart Wallace had it, and we never got it to work the way it did on the advert! It was good fun trying, though.

Striker – I had Subbuteo, but Davie Cosgrove had Striker. This five-a-side tabletop game was great fun. You pushed down the players' heads to get them to kick the ball.

Billy Blastoff – This fabled toy I saw once in an advert and made a Santa request for it. Never got it though, but I got Major Matt Mason toys, which were even better.

Hot Wheels Racetrack – I had plenty of cars, but never the track. Wee Jim McClusky had track which we would play with in his close. The track could be purchased in long length rolls and over in the stairwell of my pal's tenement close we'd stretch and contort it downstairs and around corners. We fashioned loops and if your car could build up enough speed it would reach the end of the track without falling off the side. This unfortunately was a rare thing.

TCR Racing Set – Was desperate for this slotless car racing set. Unlike other racing sets the cars didn't fit into 'slots', the track was smooth and underneath it ran wire with an electrical current. Beneath each car there was a piece of metal that ran across the track picking up the electric. In theory this meant that you could swerve and overtake your opponent on any stretch of track. From YouTube I've seen that in reality that doesn't happen. Anyway, they were expensive and nobody I knew had one, but some had Scalextric. I now have a complete working set in a box in my office. Not played it yet.

Colditz – This board game was from the BBC TV series. Stuart had this, but we never really knew how to play. Reading the rules might have helped! Basically, you played a prisoner of war who had to escape from Colditz Castle in Germany. You rolled a dice and advanced through the board occasionally picking up cards that allowed you to do things like bribe the guards. It was not particularly exciting.

Monopoly – Someone always had this, and it was great fun to play. Even as an adult. It felt good to have loads of money, even if it was just Monopoly money! Luckily the property game was easy to play so we didn't have to read the rules!

Meccano – I got one small set for Christmas and loved playing with it. These construction sets were great fun and allowed you to assemble cars, bridges and a myriad of other contraptions by connecting metal strips and plates together with nuts and bolts. Still a great toy for today's kids.

Hornby Trains – My wee brother Gary was right into train sets and I must admit I would love one today. Train sets were ubiquitous, and Hornby was the king. The problem was that the sets came with very few accessories, so these had to be self-made with anything that you found lying around. I made him a mountain tunnel with a box and paper mâché, two holes cut and the application of some green paint. It wasn't great but it was better than nothing!

Clackers – These injury-causing toys had their moment in the 70s. I had one pair that I threw up towards the light post opposite our door on Galloway Street. It wrapped round the wires where it stayed for years. The last time I saw it was the late 1980s before my Mum moved away. I checked one time when I worked an agency shift at Stobhill. By that time, it had gone!

Raving Bonkers – This robot fighting set was owned by one of my classmates, who occasionally would bring it to St Aloysius. This toy was of plastic construction and it had two robots in a ring. Either side were two hand-controlled levers that allowed you to move the robots' arms. Basically, you just punched the heck out of your opponent's robot and the first to connect with a head punch would send the neck flying upwards on a metal ratchet. Great fun.

Lego – Over the years I would play with Lego. It was a toy brick building set that you could always return to. Good fun to make forts for miniature toy soldiers and garages for your Matchbox cars.

The Six Million Dollar Man – The same classmate who had the Raving Bonkers also had this Action Man Rival. Steve Austen was a man barely alive. This doll had a number of unique 'bionic' features like a telescopic eye and plastic limb 'flesh' that could be rolled up to reveal his cyborg parts. I still want one and who knows one day I will get.

Airfix Super Flight Deck – For a while I was desperate for this toy because the advert made it look very cool and I loved aeroplanes. This contraption was meant to be the deck of an aircraft carrier ship. At one end there was a control stick and a line of wire that you stretched out and connected to something high like the top of your bedroom door. On the deck there was a catapult that launched a yellow jet along the wire. It turned round, and you then had to guide it back on to the deck successfully. I know it was not as good as the adverts made out, but I still want one now!

That is just a wee selection. There were loads of other toys that we all fancied but most of us never got our wee hands on. Check out YouTube and give yourself a wee fuzzy warm feeling tonight.

Comics

I was a bit of a comic collector when I was a kid. Even now when I see some Marvel or DC Comics covers it transports me back to the happy Saturdays when I would go up to Billy's Newspaper shop besides Galbraith's and buy my weekly Spiderman comic. I would occasionally buy other American comics mostly for their adverts. They used to sell things like X-Ray Spex and magic tricks. There was always a big advert for Sea Monkeys. Imagine my disappointment when as an adult I purchased some Sea Monkeys from Toys R Us to find out they were just wee sea larvae. Not nice.

Being Scottish, I loved to read Oor Wullie and The Broons in the Sunday Post. Someone always got an annual for Christmas so you could overdose on these great Scottish Characters. There was The Beezer, The Topper and Whizzer and Chips. I preferred The Sparky to the Beano or Dandy. I loved the character Peter Piper, who could make things come alive with his magic pipes.

Two of my most favourite comics of all time were Action and Bullet. Action in particular was brilliant because it had real blood and gore. The Hookjaw story was a Jaws rip-off, but it really had some fantastic bloody stories. There was Dredger and my other favourite story Death Game, which was a Rollerball-like game that would ultimately end up in death. The first run of Action was so violent that it caused a real furore in the press and on TV. Eventually they had to tone down the violence, and then I lost interest. We devised a 'Death Game' at St Aloysius. Stuart McKenna, John Mackintosh and I would run in one entrance door being chased by each other. To make it 'Death' we had to slam the swinging doors as hard as possible, to try and hurt each other. We ran along the inside corridor and slammed the fire doors on whoever was chasing behind. Great fun apart from one day I ran head first into a girl. I really hit her head hard with mine. I must have given myself a concussion because I don't remember what happened next. What I do remember was 'waking up' sat at my desk in Mrs Carr's class with no memory of how I got there and having one terrible headache. I don't even know what happened to the poor girl I ran into.

Bullet was another brilliant but less gory comic. It had all these free spy gifts, like a medallion and a codebook and club member stuff. I used to train Gary and his pal John Fyfe to be special Bullet agents and would make them do stupid stuff for 'exercise' like run up and down the stairs between A and B deck. They obeyed me like good wee spies.

Comics like The Victor and Commando I also liked, but I was always more drawn to Sci-Fi stuff like the brilliant artwork of 2000AD and the Gerry Anderson comic books. I wish my kids would read comics, but I doubt if they will. iPads have taken over. Even if they read soft comics downloaded. Any kind of reading is good for the young mind. Let's see what happens when my kids get a bit older.

Recently I purchased a couple of copies of the original Action comic from eBay. I'm hoping to frame them and stick them in my man cave if my wife ever lets me have one in our house in Thailand.

∽

Skye Summer 75

As the school holidays approached, I could barely contain myself. The last few days in Mrs Carr's St Aloysius class were long and drawn out. I had been preparing for my Linicro holiday for weeks. I had been swapping stuff like mad and gathering as many comics as I could find. I stacked them in the wee white wooden bedside cabinet in my room. It was almost full. I thought that I would need plenty of comics to read on the bus journey and over the summer. The plan was that my folks would take us on the Wallace Arnold bus, and they would spend some time in Linicro before leaving my sister Angela and I for the rest of the summer holidays. It was going to be great!

The long bus journey for us kids was a complete nightmare. I could not even read my comics because it was hot, and I felt sick. I just kept wishing and praying that it would soon be over, and we would land in Linicro.

Eventually we made it there, and it was great to be back on the island. After my folks left, Angela and I slept in one of the double beds in the wee hoose. My Granny and Aunt Margaret slept in the other. We thought it was great. The bed was lumpy and comfy. The blankets were scratchy. At night, it was creepy, and we absolutely loved it.

Every day was an adventure and being on the croft, following my Aunt Margaret around as if she cast three shadows, was a joy. I have to say that Margaret was great with us kids. She had a lot of patience and very rarely told us off. She and my Granny had a real soft spot for Angela as she had lived with them when my Mum was hospitalised with tuberculosis. She was their favourite.

We loved to help with Murdy the milking cow. It was a treat to take her to the byre and watch my aunt squeeze the warm cow juice out into a white metal pail, then look on as she transferred it to a plastic bucket using muslin as a filter.

At that time the hens were housed all over the place, the main hen house being my Great-Great Uncle Murdo' s bachelor pad across the burn, known as the 'Rookery'. Between the wee hoose and the big hoose there were also a couple of smaller houses for the bantam hens. We loved to feed them and happily shouted 'chook chook' at the top of our wee voices. Not having seen the Macinnes boys for over two years, it surprised us when one Sunday we met them walking on their way to church. We could not believe how tall Duncan had gotten. Man, he really stretched. We agreed to visit them in the weeks coming and my love of Totescore began.

On a hill walk with Norman, Duncan and Archie, way above their house on the Totescore hill I was amazed to find this wee lochan (a small highland lake) surrounded by a rickety fence. The location stayed in my mind and as the summer progressed, I planned a trip there.

A family from England, who regularly rented my Aunt's big hoose, arrived and their kids were around our age. The Taylor family were very nice and friendly. There were two boys and one girl. This would be my explorer group, and I asked them if they wanted to see something amazingly wonderful. They did, and one afternoon we set off up the hill. We made it to the top easily, it's not too steep. We then carried on walking in the direction of Uig. In reality not that far but when you're a kid it seems like hundreds of miles. As we neared the spot, I noticed a boggy hole and inside was a drowned sheep! I warned everyone to be careful and minutes later we found the peat black water of the lochan. None of us went close to it and soon after we decided we had better make for home. As we came over the hill way up behind the big hoose, we heard the long tooting of a car horn and could hear some disembodied voices. As we got closer, we saw the Taylor parents at their car, shouting and beeping their horn. They saw us and as we approached; we wondered what all the commotion was about? We were gone longer than I thought, and the adults were really worried that we had gotten lost in the heather!

One other incident stands out from that holiday and it was the time Angela and I got caught behind the byre throwing kittens in the air and letting them land on the soft dung heap! I know it sounds cruel, but we did not mean any harm and they were unhurt. We had only thrown them a couple of times when my Aunt Margaret caught us. She was furious and told us to go up to the wee hoose and take down our trousers as we were going to get a spanking! Scared, we did what she said. There we were pants down waiting when my Granny came in and asked us what we were doing? We told her through tears what had happened, and she laughed and made us pull up our breeks and that it was all right. We never got that spanking and we laughed about it later.

All too soon the summer vacation ended. My Dad picked us up, and we were full of tears as we said our cheerios. My Granny was crying too, saying that she might not be alive the next time we come for a holiday. She said that to everyone. Every year!

I remember we returned to Glasgow by train via Mallaig. It seemed a long journey to us, but it was better than being on the bus!

Two things I remember about being back home in Galloway Street. One was the song 'Barbados' by one-hit wonders, Typically Tropical. The other was that night we got back I was lying on our sofa and was crying. Mum asked me what was wrong, and I did not want to tell her I was crying because I was not on Skye. I just told her my stomach hurt after the long journey.

Efter Ye

It was not all sweetness and light on Galloway Street! Sometimes people, even your friends, could be 'efter ye' looking for a fight for some perceived grievance or other. Luckily it was a relatively rare occurrence for me, but it happened all the same. The one time that sticks in my memory happened at Colston Secondary where they had a Youth Club on weekday evenings. I was a regular there, and it was pretty good. You could swim at the pool and there was table tennis and other activities. I went for the swimming and table tennis. Usually, me and my pal from old Galloway Street, Stuart McKenna, would go together.

This evening did not differ from others until something happened to one of the younger guys and he was crying. His brother was a hard-of-hearing guy from old Galloway Street who had the unfortunate moniker of 'Dumb Dumb'. He would have been maybe a year older than me, and he was built like the proverbial brick bog (he was huge for his age)! His wee brother had gone outside to tell him about whoever had made him cry, so 'Dumb Dumb' came looking for the culprit! They would not let him in the Youth Club door. And it was at the door that somehow, I was identified as the one who had caused his wee brother's tears! WTF? I was playing TT and had nothing to do with it! As they shut the door on 'Dumb Dumb' he looked over at me and mouthed something like 'I'm gonnae get ye'. Nightmare! I was now worried about going home and getting 'battered'. I really did not want this Youth Club night to end. End it did and as we all walked outside. Who was still waiting there? Yep! 'Dumb Dumb'. The worst thing about this powerful guy was that because he was deaf, he could not hear your cries for mercy or your screams of pain! Many gathered round as he grabbed me by the neck and pushed me against a wall. He began to throttle me, and it was then my survival instinct kicked in. I tried to punch him a few times and escape his grasp. Luckily an adult from the Youth Club came out and dragged him away and I beat it, running all the way home. Phew! Now all I had to worry about was him catching me outside. When someone is 'efter ye' you live in constant fear of being caught. He was not at my school but people who knew him were, and they would taunt me with 'Dumb Dumb is gonnae bust ye'. Not nice! I was in an anxious state!

Weeks went by and our paths had not crossed. He was a collector of 'ginger bottles' (soft drink empties) which he would exchange for money. I had seen him a couple of times, but he had not seen me. One evening the doorbell rang and my brother told me it was Tabby from across the street. I went down and sure enough Tabby was there but so was 'Dumb Dumb'! My wee heart sank, then sprang into my mouth.

He was smiling though, and he put out his hand to shake mine as he had been told the full story by his younger brother. He now knew I had nothing to do with hurting him. Wow! 'Thank God,' I thought as I shook his hand!

Years later in 1978 when I was back in Glasgow for a two-week visit during Portree High School summer holidays who was I to meet but this guy 'Dumb Dumb' who was even bigger! He made some joke about the time he was gonnae batter me and he grabbed me in a bear hug and nearly popped out my eyes! That was the last I ever saw of him! Who knows, he might still live in Galloway Street?

The Pictures

Growing up in Glasgow in the early 1970s, inevitably you went to the pictures. Back then we had a fairly wide choice of cinemas that had genuine character, unlike the Multiplexes that exist today! My first cinema recall is from the Alexandra Parade in Dennistoun. I remember going on a Saturday morning to watch 'The Munsters' and 'Where Eagles Dare'. During the break they would play music and at that time they had this wee guy who had Down's Syndrome, who would dance. That boy could bust a move and kept us all entertained!

As we got a wee bit older and more adventurous, we would head into 'the toon' on the 45 bus. Mostly we would go to the Odeon or The Regent on Renfield Street. Occasionally the ABC on Sauchiehall Street and sometimes to the Classic (no, not for X-rated)! My favourite cinema and where I always felt safe was The Regent. I wish they had not knocked it down some years later.

The two movies that had the biggest impact on me in the 1970s were, firstly, 'Jaws' released late 1975, early 1976. I remember going to see it at the ABC and it was the only time that I ever saw queues all the way down the street and then up a side street! What a movie! Still is a magnificent film. And who did not jump when that head came out the hole in the sunken boat?

The other movie was 'Bugsy Malone' released in the summer of 1976. As I was not going to Skye for my holidays, we spent more time going to see movies. This movie was on at the Odeon and I absolutely loved it. Still do! I loved all the songs, and it really made me want to be some kind of stage performer! I can remember a few weeks after seeing it, I really wanted to watch it again, but most of my pals on Galloway Street thought it was a movie for 'poofs' (a term used indiscriminately in the 70s to describe anyone who, like me was a wee bit artistically inclined. We were young and stupid and didn't know any better)! A bunch of us went into town to see some other movie one Saturday but it was full, so we looked to see what the other choice was, and Bugsy was one of them, but I didn't want to suggest it in fear of being called a 'poof'! I lost my pals by design and went to watch the movie again on my own. Later, back on the street, I told them that I went to see another film! Funny thing was that one guy I was with said he saw me going into see another movie in the Odeon. Luckily, he did not see me go to Bugsy Malone as I would no doubt face a lot of 'slagging'. I would have gone to see a third time if I could!

∽

Retyred

It can be dangerous for a kid being brought up in the city. I reckon I have a guardian angel looking out for me as there were three times I could easily have been killed (or seriously hurt). The first time would have been in the early 1970s; it was a sunny day, and I was walking across the 'dump' to go home for lunch. At this point in my St Aloysius career, I would walk across the grass that led me to crossing Springburn Road to the stairs that took you out at the bridge on Galloway Street. The reason we did not take the dirt path was that 'big' guys from the nearby Colston Protestant secondary school would walk home that way, and us 'wee' guys feared them. By the time we were in primary 7 we used that path but still were wary of Colston pupils. This day I came out of the 'dump' on to the pavement, waiting to cross Springburn Road. I made it halfway when I was hit by a car. It was weird and in slow motion, the front of the car did not hit me. I had been waiting in the middle of the road and had run out as a car was passing. I glanced off its back wing which knocked me flying onto the road. The driver stopped immediately but before he was out of his door I was up on my feet and I made it to the other side. I was standing on the pavement in a bit of a daze but appeared to have been uninjured. I still remember the guy's face. He was white as a sheet. He asked me if I was ok, and I mumbled yes. He asked if I wanted him to take me home and I said no, I could manage by myself. That was it. A split second earlier, I would have been in front of that car. When I got home, I said nothing to my mother.

The next danger time was again crossing Springburn Road, but this time it was a dreary Glasgow morning, and I was crossing at the front of our building near to the Spring Inn. This was morning rush hour, and I was standing next to this wee fair-haired guy. I knew him by sight, but he was younger than me and came from old Galloway, so we were not pals. We stood at each other's sides waiting to dash across to the 'dumps' mud path to school. As I think about it now, I can still feel that urge I had to cross, but as I was about to make a move, I stopped. The wee guy didn't; he ran and was immediately hit by a car. Not from the front, but from the back wing (similar to what had happened to me before). The difference being that the force of the car knocked him straight to the kerb with a crunching blow to his forehead. He was unconscious in front of us, and a big lump formed on his wee forehead. He looked like he was sleeping and as a child I thought that he would just wake up. Just like on the TV when someone is knocked out by a punch. It would be a matter of seconds and they would be awake and on their feet. Not for this guy named Stephen Toll. He never woke up. Several of us who were crossing that day were asked questions by the police, and they took our names and addresses. The driver of the car was an old grey-haired guy who looked in shock and I just remember him saying something like, 'I didn't see him; he came out of nowhere'. Maybe he didn't say that, but that's what I remember.

Months later a few of us were called as witnesses and we had to go to court. We thought this something exciting. We went into the town somewhere and I remember sitting on a wooden bench in a corridor when the mother of the dead boy came to us and just told us to tell the truth, exactly what happened. Her eyes showed pain. Grief was obvious in her face. We did not get called to give our 'evidence' and I don't know what, if anything, happened to the driver. Recently, on Facebook I've been in contact with Stephen's brother Frank. I wanted to tell him my memories of that day and that his brother and mother's faces are forever imprinted on my memory. A truly tragic event for his family. Frank appreciated my memories and thanked me for telling him. We are now FB buddies.

One thing that stands out from that day was that our mothers took us out to lunch near the court. I think they gave my mother some lunch expenses. We went to an actual restaurant, not a café. I still remember its name 'The Salad Bowl', the worst type of restaurant to take Springburn kids to as it served mostly salad stuff which we hated. We got some chips, but no tomato sauce.

The third time I was in an accident, I really was lucky not to have been killed or injured for life. Around May 1976 it was a running joke on my street that Raymond had retyred (and no, it's not a typo)!

Our council apartment block on Galloway Street had two 'decks' top and bottom (we lived on the bottom). Across Springburn Road was the 'dump'. It was land belonging to British Rail and comprised black ash which over the years had accumulated topsoil and nature grew green grass and bushes. Sometimes at the weekend, if we were feeling brave, we would go play there. To be honest, it was not my favourite play place. It always scared me we would get jumped or chased by people from Milton who would yell 'Tongs Ya Bass'. I must have been feeling brave that day!

It was a Sunday because I was not worried about getting dirty amongst the black ash as this was bath night. My pal Stuart discovered an old car tyre, and we thought that we could have some rubber fun! It was quickly decided that we would haul our rubber booty across Springburn Road and up to our street so that we could play safe knowing that no 'Tongs' would disturb us!

After rolling this dirty, worn, rubber donut up and down our street for a while, I came up with the idea to take it up the stairs to the top deck of the building and throw it off (what a total genius)! It was high on B Deck about the equivalent of a four-floor tenement building. We enlisted Stuart's older brother Stephen to help carry the tyre up the stairs. As we neared the top, I decided I wanted to go back down onto the street to see the tyre fight gravity and land on the tarmac!

This is what happened next!

As I swiftly jumped the stairs, I reached the bottom deck and ran out into the street.

I have no memory of this so we will rely on an eyewitness report which stated that I came zooming out onto Galloway Street and just at that moment they threw the tyre from said top deck and it landed round my neck!

That is the honest truth!

What are the odds of that tyre landing round my skinny neck? It knocked me unconscious, and I hit the ground with a death-like thud, blood coming out of my nose and mouth! Everyone thought I was dead, and they were all too scared to come close to me. A passing adult rushed into their flat and dialled 999 and soon an ambulance arrived. As the drivers came towards me, I opened my eyes and had a strange ground-level view of blood and feet! I was unsure if it was New York or New Year, but the first comment the ambulance guy made struck a dagger of fear into my young mind. As he knelt beside me, he said to his colleague, 'His neck could be broken'! WTF?

By this time someone had gotten my mother and they bundled her into the back of the blue light machine and off we sped to Stobhill A&E. It was all a bit of a blur and goodness knows how long it took me to come round but the good news was my neck was still intact! Yaas! Eventually I was transferred to the general kids' ward for observation.

Here's the embarrassing part now.

Remember where we got the tyre?

Remember the black ash??

Remember that it was bath night?

I was totally manky!

I mean, I was bogging black with dirt and it was everywhere!

The first thing the ward nurse said was, 'You're no gettin intae that bed until you've hud a baff'! I was taken into the bathroom and steeped in soapy water! The nurses were great and made total fun of me as they removed my clarty claes! Once all clean and in my PJs I was secreted into the coolness of two highly starched hospital sheets. I had the mother of all headaches for three days and then I was discharged. Back on my street, I know my two friends felt an enormous relief as they welcomed me home because they honestly thought I was toast!

I have had no lasting side effects after this freak accident, and I remain unafraid of tyres unless they are flying through the air!

All Saints

Having spent all my school years so far at St Aloysius Primary, the August of 1976 saw me go to the 'big school' which was All Saints' Secondary School in Barmulloch. Over the years I have tended to bad mouth this experience but the reality of that first year as a first-year was not that bad.

The chief thing that I really hated was the distance of the new school from Galloway Street and the fact that I had to walk there and back every day! This journey took a good 30 minutes, and we had to traipse the length of Springburn Park before walking through a succession of streets and roads until we finally arrived at our destination.

My first day in first year I had to line up with the rest of the pupils in the morning under the direction of 'Harry O' the school's deputy Headmaster. I can remember the face of our form teacher but do not remember his name. What I do remember was getting the belt from him on my first day! The tables in the classroom could be folded horizontally by moving the lever underneath. This is what I did and this is why I got the belt. Ouch! I don't think anybody from my St Aloysius class was in my new class and, as kids do, I soon made friends with my new classmates.

I think the only subject that I liked was English, the rest I could do without. All Saints had 'one way' corridors, and if they caught you walking in the wrong direction, they gave you the belt! I particularly loathed French given by either a Mr or Mrs Scullion (they both worked there). Our Science teacher was a bit of an eccentric and mostly the class was OK if a little boring. The Music class was all right, but the teacher was a bit stuffy. Gym class was fine too except for 'cross country' which involved us running round all the red ash football pitches God knows how many times! The school had a swimming pool, which was good.

I was lucky because I never really got bullied at school and only had to have one fight with this guy in my class whose nickname was 'Stunty' (he was rather short), and I don't remember what the fight was about, but it did not last too long, and I was declared the winner!

For about half that year I used to walk home for lunch which was crazy as it gave me only a few minutes to eat my tomato soup with bread and then I had to rush off again to get back in time for afternoon classes. I think the reason I was walking was that Davie across the road would go home every lunch, so I just followed him! Eventually after some pleading with my Mum she would buy me a weekly 'dinner ticket', which would allow you a main course and a sweet in the 'dinner hall'. The food was not too bad, and I remember queuing up loads of times for extras, especially if there were any leftover desserts!

All Saints was the only school that I 'dogged' (played truant), occasionally, and I would get my sister to write me a note and sign it as my Mum.

Sometimes, instead of walking that long walk home, I would try and 'skip' on the bus that would take us down Petershill Road and onto Springburn Road. Then try to skip on a 37 to Balgrayhill. My 'skip' success rate on the Petershill Road was almost always 100% as there were loads of pupils trying to get on the bus! I was less successful on the 37 and more often than not I had to walk the length of Springburn Road to get back home! The rush home at four was only so I could get to watch children's programs on the TV before the Six o'clock News. I loved Land of the Giants, The Tomorrow People and John Craven's Newsround. We watched anything because it was the only time we controlled the TV channels as the rest of the night my mother was in control!

The BB

Around 1975, I joined the Boys' Brigade 202 Company. Previously I had been in the Cub Scouts, but after a while I got fed up with it and never went back. I think I joined initially because my pal Stuart was in it and so was his brother Stephen, along with some other 'big guys' from Galloway Street.

If I'm not mistaken my pal Tariq 'Tabby' Benison joined around the same time and so did Jim McClusky, all from the tenements opposite our block.

Every Friday at seven all of us would head up to Albert Secondary School where the Company met. It was predominantly a Protestant organisation back then and had very few Catholics! I was the only one in the 202 at that time. For this they made fun of me, but it didn't bother me. I really enjoyed the Boys' Brigade and whilst most of the pals I joined with dropped out, I kept going up until I left for Skye in 1977. A quick look on Wikipedia has just informed me that the BB was formed in Glasgow in the late 19th century. This I didn't know! I also went on to the BB website, but the 202 Company does not exist now. The 200 Company is still going though, and I have a faint memory of joining them when I was very young as they met at Colston Church.

Our Company leader – whose name I don't remember – was a very serious-looking guy, and the two officers that I remember fondly were Ramsay and Bob. Ramsay, who seemed old to me, must have been in his twenties as we attended his wedding ceremony in the Church near the bottom of Balgrayhill. We were his guard of honour and I remember when he was leaving with his bride he got into the car and us 'wee guys' were waiting on him throwing his money for the 'scramble'. It was funny because he opened the window and threw out a bunch of coins that we all 'scrambled' to collect but during this he jumped out and grabbed a fifty pence piece saying that he did not mean to throw it! He was a very nice guy, and I thought of him as being 'posh' because he had a 'proper' accent (unlike us). Bob was known as 'Uncle Bob' and he seemed ancient but probably was only in his forties! He was unmarried and quite religious but a very decent and patient guy. To be honest with you, they were superb role models for us and though we did test their patience, they treated us very well.

Most of us had nicknames and Ramsay had nicknamed me 'Roger' after Mr Moore, the then current James Bond. But he pronounced it in a faux upper-class accent! I didn't mind. The BB Friday night meets involved marching and parading. When we first arrived and donned our uniforms, we all had to stand to attention as the officers inspected us.

I did not have a full uniform so had to make do with an old belt given to me by someone on my street and a hat that I bought. I just wore a navy blue jumper. The belt was made of leather and the belt buckle a gold metal affair which we had to shine every week with Brasso. The officers checked to see if there was any white residue left over because of poor polishing. We had to make sure our shoes were nice and shiny, too!

During these inspections us 'wee guys' always behaved well but that could not be said of some of the 'big guys', in particular Steven Bradley from our street and John Porteous from Viewpoint! They along with others were always causing havoc and getting themselves into trouble with the officers! Steven 'Bads' Bradley liked to fart during assembly! We thought that brave and funny!

The Friday evening comprised doing 'classes' to prepare for badges that you collected and put on an armband! Then we would go to the school's sports hall to play five-a-side football and other sports. This I really enjoyed, though I was not particularly good at football.

On Saturday mornings the 202 had a football team and we would travel around Glasgow playing other companies. I loved this and nearly always got a game (if you turned up, you got a game). Our strip was yellow and blue, similar to the old Arsenal strip of the day. We had a couple of skilled players, the main one being a guy called Jim. He was our Captain and an excellent player who helped us win a lot of matches. I even scored a couple of times, mostly because he laid it out on a plate for me and I just had to boot the ball as hard as possible! It didn't matter the weather, I would always turn up every Saturday. I do recall a particularly wet day playing some team on a red ash pitch in Barmulloch that was half waterlogged and one big guy tackled me had and sent me headfirst into an enormous pool of dirty freezing water! Everyone laughed, except me. Ramsay and Bob would either be referee or linesmen!

The only part of the BB I did not like was the religious part. We had to meet at the Church on Balgrayhill and attend a 'Sunday school'; we also had to attend the Church service. This confused me as being a Catholic, I thought that I really could not go to a Protestant Church service. I also felt guilty that I did not go to Catholic Church. To ease my Catholic guilt, I ended up going to the service at St Aloysius first as it was earlier in the morning. Then I headed back up the road to attend the 'Sunday school'. After a wee while I thought to hell with the guilt and only attended the Protestant service.

One of the great things about the BB was the camping trips away. I really enjoyed these and always looked forward to getting out of the city and into the countryside. The first trip I ever went on was to a place called Corrie Grennan in Aberfoyle. This place was owned by the Forestry Commission. Our camping spot was beside a river.

For people on their first camping trip, they had to go through an 'initiation'. They normally carried this out on the first night of camp. The 'big guys' conducted this 'ceremony' in our company. The first-time campers, including me, were totally scared stiff as we had heard many horror stories about what they had done to people during 'the initiation'! That first night we waited in trepidation for the 'big guys' to come! And come they did! Luckily for me I got out of my sleeping bag quick style because their plan was to grab us newbies wrapped in our comfy warm bags and throw us into the nearby river! It might have been a warm summer night, but that river water ran freezing. They took several people to a spot that was shallow and dumped them in the water, in their bags! I was lucky and just got pushed off the bank into the water and I kept my balance so only my trousers got wet. Lucky me!

The weather must have been great because the next day I remember taking an airbed out on the river and swimming with it. The water was still Baltic, though!

Our last night they took us on a 'midnight walk' through the creepy forest. Ghost and murder stories told by the older guys filled our heads! I might not have shown it, but it scared me. They told us that body parts had recently been found in a nearby water tower and the killer was supposed to be hiding in the dense undergrowth. I sided up with a big guy just in case this 'murderer' tried to nab me! Nothing happened, and we returned to our tents to have nightmares. Great fun!

The other memorable trip for me was to an Island on Loch Lomond called Inchcailloch. It was the summer of 1976 we went there; this I remember as it was the summer that I did not go to Skye. Inchcailloch is a beautiful wee island in the beautiful Loch Lomond, and I really enjoyed it. No initiation this time, just fun. We had treasure hunts, swimming and BBQs! There is also a nice wee beach there which I remember as we had a late-night campfire joining other Island visitors. This campfire sticks in my mind because the non-BB folk obviously were rich judging by the size of their boats! We also did some swimming, but that Loch water was effin' freezing so we did not stay in too long!

'Uncle' Bob was a fantastic guy who gave up a lot of his free time for the BB. He would also take us on runs in his car, which was a not very big Fiat Super Mirafiori. Many of us would pile into that car and on more than a few occasions he would open the back seat and two or three of us would go in the boot with our heads sticking up behind said seat! You would never get away with that nowadays! We thought it was cool!

As previously mentioned, Bob was quite a religious guy (probably born again) and he did his best to save our souls! He would take us to various religious events which we showed no interest in as we just went for the car run and a laugh. I remember a bunch of us went to this church meeting, and the speaker was some guy who carried a full-size cross with him! We used to snigger at people who would randomly stand up out of their chairs and, with one arm in the air, shout that they loved Jesus!

I really enjoyed my time at the Boys' Brigade and often wonder what happened to all the company members after I left Glasgow in 1977.

Springburn Shops

Springburn was not a terrible place to live compared to a lot of other Glasgow districts. This was before demolition cut the area in two to make way for the bypass. Springburn Road had a wide variety of shops. For me there were only two shops that were of actual interest, one was Woolworths and the other was Cameron's the blue-painted toy and model shop, both at the bottom of Balgrayhill Road. For clothes we had Sellyn's which carried the latest fashions of the day, not that I bought much there as I preferred to go into the 'toon'.

Many people have fond memories of the Springburn Woolworths and recently I watched a rerun of an 80s Taggart TV show which featured the Woolies building as a butcher's shop! For us kids there was the Pick 'N' Mix, which allowed you to choose from an extensive selection of sweeties. Pay by weight, I think? The other great thing about the 70s Woolies was their record section. This is where we bought our singles. If you were lucky, you got an album, but it was usually one of them Top of the Pops covers LPs (not the original artists)! I think the last single from there was bought for me by my Dad, Big Gerry. It was 'Under the Moon of Love' by Showaddywaddy (I had to check the spelling on Google)!

For many Springburn kids (me included) Woolies was also the first shop that we shoplifted from) mostly the Pick 'N Mix, but as I was an Airfix model fan, occasionally I nabbed some small pots of model paint! This I didn't do often as a good thief I was not! In fact, I had been caught once before, but not in Woolies. There used to be tenements in front of our building, running along Springburn Road, and there was an Asian grocery shop run by two guys whose faces I can still see and who were very friendly to all. Unfortunately for me it was one of them that caught me stealing a McGowan's chocolate-covered toffee bar! He went mad and threatened to tell my folks! I apologised profusely through my crocodile tears and he never did shop me. I never stole from them again!

Woolies' own brand was Winfield and before leaving for the summer holidays to Skye in 1977, I got a pair of their 'Adidas Four Stripes'! They were white with four blue stripes and although I would have preferred an actual pair of Adidas, these were not too bad for jumping around in.

Finally, who did not love Woolies' Christmas adverts? We did, and in the 70s they seemed to be very long, populated with TV personalities of the day. You knew Christmas was on the way when these adverts played!!

 My brother, sister and I used to get 25p pocket money per week increased to 50p, and I spent most of my money on Marvel Comics (Spiderman in particular) and Airfix WWII model planes (bought from Cameron's) – the smallest scale, which was all I could afford. Initially, I would buy them then my old man would assemble them. Soon I was doing the glueing myself and occasionally trying to paint them. An artist I'm not. So most of them remained the grey colour they came in. Then Matchbox released models that were pre-painted so I bought them too! I would hang the finished articles by thread pinned to the ceiling of the bedroom that I shared with my brother Gary. They never seemed to last long though and most got destroyed pretty quickly!

Kay Street Baths

The swimming baths in Kay Street were Springburn's 'Cooncil' baths. And, where I learnt to swim. These baths no longer stand, but they served Springburn's great unwashed for years!

To one side of the building was the 'Steamie' where all the ladies laundered their clothes. Tenement dwellers, of which there were many in the 'old' Springburn, did not have decent washing facilities and only a few probably had a 'Twin tub' washer/spinner (like we had). I don't have any memories of being inside that part of the building at all.

Like many 'Cooncil' or 'Public' baths the pool was not too big and from the 'shallow end' of about three feet to the 'deep end' of just over six feet it was pretty standard for Glasgow and big enough for us. The tiled pool was surrounded by the changing rooms, which were a small cubicle with a wooden slatted seat, a coat hook or two on the wall and an unlocked door.

My old mind tells me that it was my Dad 'Big Gerry', who took me there first and got me confident in the water and as my confidence grew, I just naturally began to swim. What was good when the 'Big Man' took us to the 'Swimmin' was that he would take our feet in his clasped hands and sling us like a blood and bone torpedo over his shoulders! We would hit the water, go under and spring back up for more. Great fun!

The baths were to be one of the few play places in Springburn that we really looked forward to going. Luckily for me, my Galloway Street bestie, Mr Stuart Wallace, who lived in the newer tenements opposite – his dear old Dad George, was a British Rail train driver. BR arranged a swimming club every Monday night. It was from 7 to 9 and being pals with Stuart meant that I could go with him. This was great as during the day with the 'normal' punters it was always very busy and there was always the threat of a) getting a ducking or b) losing your swimming trunks!

There was no such danger at the Monday club, and the pool was not busy at all. Once changed into our trunks we headed to the corner near the deep end as that was where the communal showers were. Early on, probably up until the mid-1970s there was also a long slim bath that could hold a few people. This ultimately was removed to make room I suppose for more showers.

When we started at the club, both Stuart and I could swim. I remember the hurried excitement as we headed from Galloway Street down to Springburn Road; we could walk to Kay Street in about ten minutes or less! We rarely walked the length of Galloway Street and down Balgrayhill as we were out of our own 'bit' and there was a chance of being chased by person or persons unknown.

Excitedly we would pass through the turnstile without paying and quickly get changed. Before long we grew bored with the 'shallow end' and made our way bravely to the 'deep end', where we sat on the stairs and swam close to the edge. It would not take long before our 'deep end' fears disappeared, and we were jumping and diving in the water like professionals. We never returned to the shallows. I only have happy memories of that time.

The thing about the 'swimmin' was that it made you incredibly hungry and if we were lucky, we had some money to buy a roll and fritter or a roll and chips from Santi's 'Chippy' at the end of Kay Street. Santi's was famous for its deep-fried culinary delights and if you have never had a chip or fritter roll with salt and vinegar from them then you really have missed out!

Once satiated we would place our damp towels on our heads, pulling our trunks over the towel to fashion a 'Glesga' Arab head dress! Happily, we would walk up the road and if I was lucky, could catch some of The Sweeney on TV before my 10 o'clock bedtime!

Bishie Sports Centre

During the summer months and if we had enough money in our pockets, a bunch of us from Galloway would make the long walk along Colston Road into Bishopbriggs. Our eventual destination would be the Sports Centre. Once at the Cross, we would turn off to the left. Sometimes we would have a wee look around the shops at the Cross and I was fascinated with that wee river that ran close and had the creepy corrugated iron tunnel.

Walking through what we considered posh streets, it seemed amazing to me that one family could have such a nice big single house. Not a tower block in sight. After walking what seemed like hundreds of miles, the big Sports Centre came into view. Excited, we walked under the Golden Runner statue. Compared to Kay Street baths, this place was ginormous.

After paying our money, they would hand us a coloured rubber bracelet and a locker key. We thought this brilliant. The changing rooms were big and open, with plenty of showers. You would find your locker, open it, quickly get changed into your trunks. Close the locker and put the key into the wee compartment on your rubber bracelet. Then you would hit the showers. If you didn't have a quick shower, the attendants would send you back into the shower because you didn't look wet! Before the pools was a foot trough to make sure your feet got washed. This place was always busy with lots of screaming kids. I loved to play in the kiddies' pool first. This was a real novelty, and the water was always warmer. Then it would be on to the big pool and much colder water.

The swimming sessions lasted around an hour. Sometimes we would pay for a double session just so that we could make the fun last just a little longer. Up on one wall there were these coloured lights and when they shone and the colour corresponded with your rubber bracelet, it was time to get out. We would never leave on time, and it always took the swimming pool attendants so long to round us up and chase us back into the changing room. It was great fun. We would run riot in the changing rooms, not wanting to let our afternoon adventure end.

After handing back our magical rubber bracelet, we would never head home immediately. If – and this was rare – but if we had money left, we would go upstairs to the café and order a plate of chips. We were always starving after swimming and those chips tasted oh so good. Usually, we would pool what money we had and then share a plate between us. Then it was time to play some more. We would wander around looking over and down to the people playing tennis or badminton. For a while we would watch the big guys play five-a-side and then we would sadly start what would be our long journey home. I'm not sure how long that journey is in miles, but to a youngster it's effin' long. By the time we made it back to Galloway Street the only thing on our mind was getting our dinner as we were ravenous.

On a couple of occasions, we would jump on a Midland Bluebird Bus which you could get from the bus stop opposite our living room window on Springburn Road and journey to Kirkie baths. The exciting thing about this was that the Kirkintilloch pool had springboards for diving! Wow! Not that I was brave enough to dive from the highest dale, but I was a good enough diver to bounce on the lowest springboard. It was always busy though, and you had to be really careful. You could have someone dive on you or you could torpedo someone. The last time I was at Kirkie baths I was so hungry that I spent my bus money on chips. My only choice was to skip the bus or walk. There was no way I was walking from Kirkie to Galloway, so I skipped. The Blue buses still had conductors, so my two pals sat in the middle seats and I ran down the back. As soon as I heard the feet and voice of the clippie coming up the stairs I dived and hid in the corner. I was bricking it because I could not see what was going on. The worst thing that would happen was that he would throw me off. I heard him talk to my two pals and then there was a silence. Was he coming closer to me? I hid my head and waited for a big hand on my shoulder. It never came. Phew! I sat up with my pals and more passengers came on. The next time the clippie passed us he did not even bat an eye at me!

Fashion

The kids on Galloway Street could be cruel, especially about the clothes you wore and the shoes on your feet. We were very fashion conscious back then and peer pressure resulted in a lot of pleading with my Mum to buy the latest trousers or trainers. From a young age we became dedicated followers of fashion. I remember being desperate for the shoes that had the silver soles with moon terrain prints on them. In the heel was a compass. Finally, after a lot of crying, I got them and immediately sought some Springburn mud to see my shoe print. I also eventually got the shoes that had the animal footprint on them. I think it was a lion's print. My brother and I thought this was very cool. They also had a compass hidden under a flap in the heel.

When platform shoes were in, I needed to have a pair. The first ones I got from Gordon's on Stockwell Street. They were not particularly high, but I liked them. The only problem was I twisted my ankle in them on several occasions. I got another pair from Curtis that were pretty high, and I sprained my ankle really effin' bad with them. It didn't stop me from wearing them, though. There was a time that black and white 'spats' were the 'in' thing. Stephen Wallace had a pair, which I thought looked cool. I never got a pair of the black and white ones, but I have a memory of having the black and brown style. Or perhaps it was just a dream.

Who could forget 'weegens' or loafers as we know them around the world? I was desperate for a pair of those. I eventually got a pair of the cheaper ones with the loose lace tassel. I loved those slip-on fashion statements. Especially when you put segs on the heels. I also got a pair of the more expensive ones. Again, purchased from Gordon's. For the Christmas of 1975 I was desperate for a pair of black brogues. I had told my class pals John 'Mackie' McIntosh and Stuart McKenna that I was getting them, so I had to find a pair. I remember searching the town with my Mum. They cost £7.99 and when we got to Gordon's they only had one pair left which were a size too small for me.

Our last port of call was that shoe shop on the corner opposite
The Krazy House. Can't remember the name, but this place was
my last hope as it was getting near closing time. They didn't
have them, but what they had was supposed to be the next big
shoe thing. Bump top shoes! These were made of PVC had a
slight platform and the toes had a bump. They were in the style
of brogues, so I thought I would be ahead of the foot fashion
game. When we returned to school after the Christmas holidays
the first thing me and my two pals did was to check out each
other's shoes. Mackie was late coming in and we were all
standing saying morning prayers with Mrs Carr and as he
passed, he laughed at my shoes and showed me his shiny
brogues! It turns out that he took the last pair of my size from
Gordon's! We were too late! Bump tops never became
fashionable and the PVC split pretty quickly.

The last shoes I was desperate for was a pair of Major Domo
lace-up boots. Many people had Doc Martens, but only a few of
us had the Domos. Unlike the rounded toe of the Docs. Major
Domos had a square toe. I thought they looked cool. I wore
them my first day at All Saints, with red laces and I thought I
was the bee's knees.

Having the right pair of trainers mattered on Galloway Street,
and often I didn't have. As very young kids, we only had the
black slip on 'sanies' or sandshoes. As I got older my only desire
was to have Adidas trainers. I dreamt about them. It took me a
long time to get my first pair. I had to suffer a pair of Woolies
'Winfield' brand. These were white with four blue stripes. Then
I got a pair of Avon trainers, black with a yellow A on the side. I
got a pair of Gola trainers which were not bad, but it was Adidas
I wanted. I needed. Finally, I got a pair of Adidas Kick. These
were probably the cheapest trainers available at around £7.99.
Then I upgraded to Bamba, which was nice, but it took me a lot
longer to get my heart's desire Samba. I only got these when I
bought them myself with money I made from my first summer
job on the Isle of Skye.

Clothes were important, too. Flares and high-waistbanded
trousers were the in thing. There was a neighbour across the
street who made trousers to order, and she would make the

waistband with six buttons. Three either side. Some people had 12 buttons with six on either side. Denims were fine as long as they were wide bottomed and Wrangler or Levi's. My first pair of Levi's were a pair of cords that I thought looked cool. One time when I had returned from being on holiday on Skye, I had brought with me a pair of Skye style dungarees. I was so proud of these that the first day back I went out to play on the street wearing them. The only problem was that they were straight legged, not flared. All my pals made so much fun of my 'drain-pipes' that I ran home to change. Never to wear them again!

Three-starred jumpers were in though I never got one. There was also a polo neck jumper phase that we had, and I wore a red one. Bomber jackets were cool but out of my reach. Adidas T-shirts were in and I had one of them. The summer of 1976 saw me and my brother get a 'Snorkel' parka each. This was summer and we went out on Galloway Street with the Snorkel zipped to the top. We loved those jackets. I bought my first and only Army Shirt from Dee of Trongate. The year before I left Glasgow, I persuaded my mother to pay for a pair of made to measure black flares from Burtons. I left Glasgow in the summer of 1977 with a pair of black brogues. Yaas!

Mean Street

Galloway Street had a reputation in Springburn. It could be tough, but mostly it was no better or worse than other city streets. There were a couple of incidents involving my folks that I would like to mention. This first occurred around the mid-1970s, during the summer months. Our door was very close to the exit of A deck's corridor. There was a wall there that backed on to the area where the bin rooms were. At night 'big guys' from Galloway Street would hang out at this wall, usually with females around. On this particularly warm night there was a party going on in the Coogans' house opposite us. My folks were going, and they left the three of us in the house alone, occasionally one of them would come over to check that we were all right and had not burnt the house down. This night the 'big guys' were sitting on the wall. It was around 11 pm when I heard this loud thumping at our front door! Frightened, I ran down and saw that my Dad was inside with his shoulder to the door. It was obvious that the door was being kicked! I was terrified, but I ran down to help him keep the door closed. The kicker was Frankie Bird, one of our local 'hard men'. But why was he kicking our door? What had happened was, as my Dad came over to check on us, they exchanged some words. My Dad is big, but if there is a gang of teenagers you have to be careful. He cuffed someone who was being cheeky. And then the melee began! I was so frightened, but my Dad had only come back to get some more 'bevvy' and nothing was going to keep him from returning to the party. He had phoned over to the Coogans and told them what had happened, and a bunch of guys bailed out of the party to prepare for a street fight. There were some real 'hard men' at this party! By this time the teenagers had scattered and no fight happened. My Dad sustained a black eye! He did not seem too perturbed about it, but it really scared the hell out of me!

Frankie's younger brother John used to make fun of me, saying his big brother battered my Dad. I would just laugh it off, but inside it scared me. One of the partygoers had given my Dad a 'chib' in case anything happened later on in the week. I found said 'chib' under the sofa wrapped in newspaper. It was an effin' gigantic meat cleaver! Holy crap! That just made me even more scared! Nothing else ever happened, and the meat cleaver was returned to its rightful owner.

There was another night when my Mum and her friend Margaret McKeown were coming back from a night out and walking along the corridor back home. There was an incident of which I only witnessed the end.

Seemingly two couples who were drunk passed my Mum and her pal when one guy said something and drunkenly tried to kick them! My Mum lost her temper and walloped the guy with her handbag! We all know how heavy women's bags are. It probably weighed a ton! It knocked the guy senseless and cut his head with his blood spraying on the white wooden boards of the drying area! What I witnessed was my Mum's friend swinging her bag at the other drunken guy as he ran off. The head-injured guy's girlfriend pleaded with my Mum saying, 'He's drunk, he's sorry'! It was all over pretty quickly!

The next day I went to the drying area with some of my friends, proudly showing the blood that came from the guy when my Mum 'split his heid open' with her handbag. Don't mess with my Mum!

The Telly

The only inside entertainment afforded to us 1970s kids was the telly. If you were not outside on Galloway Street playing with your pals you were glued to the box. Our TV took pride of place in one corner near our living room windows. Until the mid-70s ours was a black and white job. The screen could not have been over 22 inches. My parents bought this TV magnifying contraption. This thing hung over the TV and made the screen look bigger. It was also meant to add some colour to your plain black and white, but I don't recall it being very good. The most annoying thing about that gizmo was that depending on where you sat, it might not have been in alignment with your eyes. Many arguments and repositioning took place nearly every effin' night – my parents always winning. Thank God it was replaced by a Radio Rentals (or was it DER?) colour TV.

For us kids our TV time was from when we arrived home from school till the six o'clock news. At the weekends it was ours all morning. I had to use Google to jog my memory of some of our favourite shows and there were a few. Crackerjack was a firm favourite with Michael Aspel presenting. Remember, there was a guy called Don Maclean whose catch phrase was when someone shouted 'Maclean', his reply was always 'yes I brushed them this morning'. Not particularly funny. Latterly the show had some very excellent bands on as guests. Dr Who was another favourite. Shown on a Saturday evening. I have vague memories of Patrick Troughton fighting the Cybermen, but it was Jon Pertwee who was my first real Doctor. Along with Jo his assistant and Bessie his car. His arch enemy the Master used to scare us to death. I missed Jon when Tom Baker took over in 1974. We soon learned to love him though, and I was an avid watcher until he left around 1981.

Both ITV and BBC 1 had some wonderful shows like Carries War, Children of the Stones and The Changes. Kids' game shows were popular, but the only one I really remember was Runaround. There was the creepy Sky and Tom's Midnight Garden, not forgetting The Ghosts of Motley Hall and Rentaghost. We had our fair share of Hanna Barbera shows and cartoons. My most favourite was the late 60s show The Banana Splits. Shown on a Saturday morning, this was essential kids viewing that included the cartoon The Arabian Knights and the live action Danger Island. Who can forget the Wacky Races and Dastardly and Muttley? I loved Inch High Private Eye, The Funky Phantom and Hong Kong Phooey. Scooby Doo was also a firm favourite. Recently they released a cartoon show called Mystery Incorporated, which my daughter loved. At first, I thought it was total rubbish, preferring the original show, but as I had no choice but to watch with her, I soon found it hilarious. More so than the original. The Harlem Globetrotters was cool and who remembers a show called Wait Till Your Father Gets Home? They showed this on a Saturday morning, and I was an avid fan. Not too long ago I bought the Here Come the Double Deckers DVD. Still love it.

Sci-Fi shows I really loved and in particular Gerry Anderson's stuff. I know they made most of these in the 60s, but they were often repeated throughout my childhood. Thunderbirds and Captain Scarlet along with one of my all-time favourite live action shows UFO and latterly Space 1999. We also had The Tomorrow People on ITV and Star Trek usually shown at night for the adults. Another personal favourite of mine were the American shows produced by Irwin Allen. Again, most of these were made in the 1960s, but they were often repeated. Lost in Space, Land of the Giants and Voyage to the Bottom of the Sea to name but a few.

What kid did not like Blue Peter? Or ITV's How? Another game show hosted by Michael Rod was Screen Test. This quiz show always showed clips of kids' movies. When we were desperate, we would even watch Play School and Play Away. I remember a lunchtime showing of the cartoon Mary, Mungo and Midge. So many shows have been lost to my memory, but some I have found with the help of the internet and continue to watch today.

Anytime we were off school sick, there were the 'For Schools and Colleges' shows on ITV in the mornings. Some were good, some not so, but we did not have much choice. In-between these shows they used to have a clock count down until the next show, and although it was just a minute, it seemed like an hour. One of my biggest favourites was a show called How We Used to Live. I really enjoyed this series when it showed life in wartime Britain.

Adult shows in the evening were also pretty good. Our bedtime was 10 o'clock, so we got to see the likes of The Sweeney and some un-PC shows like Love Thy Neighbour and Till Death Us Do Part. The repeats of Randall and Hopkirk were brilliant, and I loved Roger Moore and Tony Curtis in The Persuaders.

Thursday nights meant Top of the Pops, but before that was Tomorrow's World, which I really enjoyed. Funny now when you see repeats of old Top of the Pops shows how cheesy it was.

Big movies on TV were few and far between, and it was usually around Christmas and New Year that these got their first airings. The great thing about technology these days is that if you fancy most of these shows, a lot of them can be bought and downloaded for you to watch anywhere. Under my TV I have a home theatre PC and on it there are so many shows from the 1960s and 70s and when I'm in the mood, I will make myself comfy on the couch and watch them on my 65-inch Ultra HD TV. Brilliant!

Sister/Brother

Every time I hear the Bay City Roller Song 'Give a Little Love', I always think about my big sister Angela. She was a huge BCR fan. She loved them all. Two years older than me, she still works in the job that she started as a 'Saturday girl' when at school. After leaving, she joined my old man at the 'whisky bond' full time aged 16!

Angela is the Godmother to all my kids and for that I'm thankful. She has a heart that's big enough for two and is incredibly kind. She and my Mum hung on in Galloway Street until around 1988 when eventually they got a move to a lovely tenement apartment in the West End which ultimately, she bought. She remains there, and that's where we go to stay when we are on our holidays!

My big sister has had her share of difficulties in life but has a spirit and determination to get through no matter how hard it is. I only hope my daughter has some of her aunt's resilience.

Angela has a superb singing voice, and I used to love hearing her sing 'Your Good Girl is Gonna Go Bad', which we would occasionally get up and sing when we would go out drinking in the 1980s. Love her with all my heart.

My wee bother Gary was a very cute wee boy. Everybody loved him and he had a very outgoing personality, meaning that he wouldn't shut his geggie! He is smart and funny, and I often tell people that he was a lot cleverer than me. There was this one time when he and his pal John announced to me that they were going to our room to 'invent' something. I laughed. Sure enough, later they had designed and fashioned a way to turn our bedroom light switch off from our bed. The switch was just inside the door. They had made a pulley like system with string which ran across the ceiling and then hung down at the side of the room door. On the end of the string was a lead fishing weight and when you pulled the string by the bed the weight of it would bash against the switch and turn it on or off! Very ingenious and simple.

Unfortunately for him he has led a very colourful life which meant many poor lifestyle choices. Over the years he has driven us all mad and made us furious. For me the anger never lasts, and I'm pleased to say that for more than a decade now he has been living a relatively stable life. He has reconnected with our Dad and I'm proud of him and love him. He still talks too effin' much, though!

∽

Biker Boys

Back in the early 1970s we were oblivious to such a thing as stranger danger, and we could disappear for hours on end and not spark one flame of parental concern. It's different now with the internet's advent. We see child snatchers and paedophiles round every corner, but we are told the danger now is no different nor has it exponentially increased since I was a young kid growing up in Galloway Street. This innate fear we parents have nowadays severely restricts the playtime and places our kids play. Even though I like to think I'm different from other Dads and even though we currently live in a military compound, with many armed guards, in the Kingdom of Saudi Arabia, I worry if I leave my kid alone in the swing park right by our apartment block. We constantly complain to my 9-year-old daughter that she is going to end up with iPaditis (a recently discovered condition affecting children and adults), yet we don't give her the freedom to go outside when she wants! This has all changed post pandemic as my kids and wife are at our house in the beautiful Thai countryside. I miss them terribly but I'm happy to see them living a 'normal' life playing in the dirt.

The summer holidays of 1976 would be my last in 'Glesga' and although I was bitterly disappointed with not being allowed to travel to Linicro, at least I did not have to go to school! A few of us on the street had decided that we were going on a bike run to the 'sand dunes'. I know what you're thinking. Sand dunes in Glasgow? Bear with me!

This planned run was before I had saved up the money to buy my Raleigh Jeep from one of the Peebles boys opposite us. I ended up on the bike of one of the older guys' sisters. It was a red Raleigh, and it was one of those bikes that had the small wheels leaving you to pedal like a madman just to keep up with those whose bikes had normal-sized wheels! Still, it was better than nowt!

By early afternoon we were all set to head off to the mysterious dunes. This bike journey promised that there could be a chance of finding some nests of birds who make their home in sand. With a 'cheerio' to my mother, who did not ask where I was going, we got on our bikes and pedalled towards Bishopbriggs. The journey was not too far but as I had to pedal twice as fast to keep up with the rest of the gang, I realised it was going to be a very long day and a very long way!

We turned off toward the Bishie Sport's Centre but then headed out to what seemed like the countryside to me. It looked like we were going all the way to the Campsies!

The leader of our gang knew the route and after a good hour of pedal pushing, we came to an old quarry. Not exactly what I was expecting as the 'sand' in question – it just looked like dirt to me!

I suspect it was an old sandstone quarry; still, it was something new and exciting. And all that pedal mania had left me desperate for a rest! This old quarry contained several pools, no doubt created over the years by the Glasgow rain. The big guys warned us not to go too close to the water's edge as it was 'quicksand'! That was enough to put me off. I had seen the movies and knew it was impossible to escape a slow quicksand death if you got sucked under! I noticed that there were many holes in the 'sand banks' and this was where the birds hid their nests. Being an egg collector, I spent the next hour sticking my arm into various black holes in the vain hope that I would find a nest of eggs. To be honest with you, I don't remember seeing any birds around and all my searching produced not one solitary egg! In actuality, it was probably long past the nesting season for whatever birds made these holes, but that did not cross my mind. It soon became apparent to me that even if there were eggs hidden, the holes were far too deep for ma wee arms! So, it was time to give up. I noticed one hole that I had not tried, but it was very close to one of the water pools. I put on a brave face and tried to get close to it. The dirt beneath my feet gave way, and I descended towards the water. In a panic, I tried to 'swim' my way out of danger by doing a dirt crawl! This slowed me down, but both my legs went under and it felt as if they were being sucked by the dirt. By now I was panicked thinking I was caught in the 'quicksand' and my short boring life flashed before my eyes! It was then that both my arms got grabbed by a couple of my pals and these heroes pulled me to safety! Phew! Now, I don't know if the water hole was deep, and that I might have been able to save myself, but at the time I considered myself to be one lucky chappie!

Luckily the afternoon sun dried the dirt on my legs and troosers and by around four o'clock we were all ready to make our way back to Galloway Street. We were all starving too, but none of us had any money! After what seems like a cycling age, we crossed over the Bishie border into Colston, and Huntershill Street was a welcome view. I used the last of my energy to push that wee wheeled bike onto Galloway Street where it was returned to its owner safe and sound. My mother gave me what for when she saw the state of my breeks! All I could think about was the chips, eggs and beans that she was preparing for our evening meal. Yum!

Music Man

I suppose I have my old man Big Gerry to thank for my eclectic musical taste. Everyone on Galloway Street knew my Dad was a musician. Some made fun of the fact that he was a lover of

American Country, but a lot of the acts that he loved are often referenced by many rock legends as major influences. Hank Williams was my Dad's hero, and anyone who knows the story of this musical genius knows that he lived fast and died young.

Until 1976, the machine that we used to play music in our house was a massive reel-to-reel tape recorder that sat outside in the hall. A hole was drilled through the wall and a cable connected to a big speaker that sat in the corner of our living room opposite the TV. Big Gerry had loads of tapes. Where he got them from, I have no clue but his good pal John was also an avid tape listener, so they always swapped their music. Sometimes it seemed like a punishment for us kids to be forced to listen to acts like Hank Snow, Jim Reeves, Buck Owens and Mel Tillis but like any music that you hear day in day out you begin to like it. I still love a lot of these acts today. George Jones in particular. We were exposed to so many bands and artists it was obvious that these would shape our adult musical tastes. When you listen to acts like Dolly Parton, Porter Wagoner and Tammy Wynette they might have been singing about heartache or how the bottle let them down, but they did it with a catchy tune.

My Mum was not as big a country fan as my old man. She liked Charley Pride, though. She was more into The Beatles and The Everly Brothers. She loved Don Everly's solo stuff. My sister was the only one to have a record player which was a blue and white vinyl-covered mono player that she kept in her room. As the age of the 'Music Centre' began in the mid-1970s it was hoped that my old man would buy one but he did not. Instead, he opted for a relatively expensive record deck and stereo speakers. This was fine, but we were beginning to use cassettes and for us to make tape copies of records the only option we had was to place our mono cassette player in-between both speakers and hit record. Sometimes the hiss from the tape was louder than the effin' music.

Big Gerry loved rock music too. He loved the Eagles and Lynyrd Skynyrd. Gram Parsons was another of his favourites and he was happy to watch Top of the Pops and complain that a lot of the bands were 'shite'. Now we had a record player he would occasionally buy a Friday night single for us to play, usually from Woolies on Springburn Road.

My musical awakening undoubtedly began in the 'Glam' era. With the likes of Slade and The Sweet. If I had to choose, then it would be The Sweet. With classics like 'Hell Raiser', 'Blockbuster' and 'Ballroom Blitz' what was not to like? Govanhill's Brian Connelly was a brilliant front man with a magic voice. I only recently found out that Taggart's Mark McManus was his stepbrother. Brian died young at 51, but his music will live on. Slade were brilliant too. They wrote their own hits, and they had some crackers like 'Far Far Away', 'Cum on Feel the Noize' and 'How Does It Feel'. Noddy Holder and the boys were firm favourites with many on my street.

My sister Angela was a massive Bay City Rollers fan. She had all their albums. We pretended to hate them because they were a girly band, but actually I didn't mind the band and I still listen to them today. Two Christmases ago I bought a Greatest Hits CD which was signed by Les McKeown and I framed it for her. After my Granny Moore passed Angela got her old Radiogram and from her room, she would blast her beloved BCR records. I still remember watching John Craven's Newsround when they announced that Alan Longmuir was leaving the group and being replaced by Ian Mitchell. Immediately, Angela burst into tears. Gary and I just laughed at her.

That old radiogram might only have been a mono player, but it was plenty loud. The selection of good records to play on it were few and far between. She had a selection of those 'Top of the Pops' compilations that were sold at Woolies. Remember the ones that had people doing cover versions of the hits? Pretty crap. We also would have the singles bought by my old man. I remember Angela loving David Bowie's 'Sound and Vision'. I was also a big fan of Showaddywaddy and Mud. Who wasn't?

Big Gerry bought me 'Lido Shuffle' by Boz Scaggs, which I loved but didn't tell anyone on my street as I knew that they would make fun of me. By 1976 London's Pub Rock scene had morphed into the Punk Rock Scene and The Sex Pistols' 'God Save the Queen' was number one in the charts. I didn't get to hear it as the BBC had banned it, and it would be a few years later on the Isle of Skye when it first graced my eardrums. We were too young for punk and it frightened me a wee bit. I was in the town one Saturday on Renfield Street going towards the Odeon when I saw a bunch of teenage punk rockers. Girls and boys. Bright green hair. Loads of safety pins and the girls were wearing black bin bags for dresses. They scared me! The last song that I remember really liking before I left Galloway Street was Boston's 'More than a Feeling'. The next year I would get intimately involved with their debut album.

⌀

Evening Times

After having spent my 1975 summer school holiday in Linicro with my sister Angela the return to Glasgow saw me very unhappy and to make things worse everybody was singing that bloody awful 'Barbados' by one hit wonder group Typically Tropical. To add insult to injury, everyone on my street appeared to have acquired bicycles. I had an old scooter! It was August and Christmas was a long, long way off and there was no way my folks were going to ease my unhappy return to the city by placating me with a bike! What could I do? Apart from asking my pals for a shot of their two wheeled transport, nothing much!

Around September I had a moneymaking opportunity presented to me by my pal Stuart Wallace and his big brother Stephen. This could be the answer to my bike woes if I could save up enough cash. They had begun to sell the Glasgow Evening Times to the local inhabitants and there was a position for me in their small empire! Stephen took care of door-to-door deliveries, and Stu and I had to find a 'pitch' for our paper selling endeavour. He got the best spot. Standing outside the 'local' pub The Spring Inn. This was prime paper selling real estate. People entering and exiting the public bar ensured he sold out quick!

Me? I got a spot at the 45 bus terminus near Colston road! Not exactly a salubrious Evening Times selling pitch. In fact, it was pretty miserable as a Glasgow wet winter approached. My money-making venture started around 5 o'clock when I was handed my bundle of papers by Stephen. My routine saw me walk down Hunters Hill Street onto Springburn Road shouting 'Times' at any adult I encountered!

Heading to my pitch I had some regular customers including a couple of guys at the Esso filling station. Fridays always saw them giving me a tip!

The 45 bus stop had no shelter and my only respite from the elements was a garden wall that I hugged for some wind escape! As each bus stopped and the passengers decanted, I was there screaming 'Times' to all. If I was lucky, I would sell to all the passengers and the double-decker bus driver!

November nights were Baltic, and my garden wall offered me no hot love. This pitch looked onto a disused train track that was home to several 'Dookits' used by pigeon fanciers to keep their birds. Colston church in the near distance would have winter frost glistening off its black slate roof!

Once all my papers were gone, I could head home. Most nights I would have some unsold newspapers that I would return to Stephen along with my takings. I'd usually finish around 7.30 and if I was brave enough, I would cut through 'old' Galloway Street making my way home to 'new' Galloway Street. Unfortunately, in the past I had had my remaining Times stolen from me on the 'old' street and I'd have to pay for any missing papers from my weekly 50p (plus tips) wage!

As an anti-paper theft measure, I came up with a plan. I would remove my green 'snorkel' parka. Roll the remaining papers round my arms and put my winter jacket back on. Genius! When I walked down the dimly lit street, I not only remained theft free, I looked like I had body builder arms!

If I had had a bad evening with few papers sold, I would go to the Spring Inn. Usually, Stu had sold his allotted amount so I would stay there and try to get rid of as many as I could before surrendering to hunger. If Stu was still there, I would go to the

Talisman on Balgrayhill, and try my luck inside the public bar before getting thrown out. I would stay outside for an hour before giving up and going home. At the 'Tali' you were at risk of being jumped and relieved of your papers and your money, so you had to be careful.

I tried my best to give half my weekly wage to my mother, who saved it for my 'bike fund'! I spent the rest on Airfix models and Spider-Man comics!

It was a lonely winter with my only company the silent 45 bus stop! By December one of the Peebles boys opposite was selling a Raleigh Jeep. This had been customised by their Dad and had dropped racing handlebars. All for a tenner! Did I have enough money in my mummy bank? Yep, I had more than enough! The deal was done, and I owned my first bike. Not too long after that, I would retire from the newspaper business!

This bike would be instrumental in my leaving Glasgow and going to live on the Isle of Skye.

Losing My Religion

Being brought up as a (non-practising) Catholic and attending a Roman Catholic school was enough to put me off organised religion for life! That and the sectarianism that exists in my hometown. I have nothing against religion per se, but over the years I recognized that it would never be something that would be a big part of my life. When I tell people this, they automatically assume that I don't believe in God. Nothing could be further from the truth as I believe in God and love and every day I see God's love in the eyes of my children.

Attending an RC school meant that you were exposed to religion every day. Each morning began with saying prayers in class. Attending St Aloysius primary school meant that we were closely connected to St Aloysius Church (or is it Chapel?) which is situated just off Springburn Road. My class was pretty lucky in that we had the same teacher right up until we finished primary seven. Mrs Carr was a wonderful teacher with the patience of a saint. She would lead our prayers which always started 'Our father who art in heaven'. Kudos to Mrs Carr who, although probably a good Catholic, never went over the top with religion. The same cannot be said of the priests of St Aloysius! We had to regularly take trips to the Church, especially during our 'First Holy Communion' and our 'Confirmation'. The class would walk two by two and hand in hand down Springburn Road to the Church. I have little memory of the place other than the candles burning near the door and the big white castle-like altar.

What I have powerful memories of was the amount of 'confessions' we had to attend! We did not always need to attend the Church as the priests would come to the school to do these 'confessions'!

This was definitely one of the negative aspects of being an RC. They put the fear of God in us about sins and sinning. I still remember that I thought the soul was an organ of my body which was coloured white, and every sin I committed would leave a black mark on it! I could only wash these black marks away by going to 'Confession'! When we arrived at the Church, they separated us into lines outside a couple of confessional boxes. I vividly recall always trying to make sure that I was not in the line for Father John Meikleham's box! He was a particularly grouchy priest who doled out hard prayer penalties to us 'sinners'! Those of you who are RCs know the drill when you go into the darkened box you sat opposite the priest separated by a grill, leaving you looking at a rather creepy silhouette. You began with 'Bless me father for I have sinned. It has been X number of weeks since my last confession'. Then they would say something to you, and then you would rattle off all your 'sins'.

The thing about Father Meikleham's was that it seemed you could mention the most heinous of 'sins' e.g., murder, grand theft, starting a war et cetera, et cetera. and he would be relatively calm! However, should you mention that you missed

Sunday Service you would have felt the confession box shake and the heat radiate from his angry red face. He would then give you loads of prayers to say to absolve you of this terrible act! We were so scared, that after leaving the box and in fear of eternal damnation, under our breath we would say the multitudes of 'Hail Marys' and 'Acts of Contrition' in order to Persil away our black-stained souls!

Even though half my friends on our street were Protestants there was always a religious rivalry between schools. This could be detrimental to your health if you got chased by pupils from the nearby Elmvale Primary School. Also, for us walking to and from school, across the 'dump' you would have to dodge certain pupils from the nearby Colston Secondary School who occasionally would lash out at us wee Catholics!

Two examples of sectarianism still live in my mind quite clearly. I remember one day at four o'clock leaving the school and walking towards the 'dump' with some of my classmates. They lived closer to the school than me and they were going to head up the stairs home whilst I would turn left for the said 'dump'. At the bottom of the stairs there were several garages for the block opposite our school. As me and the boys walked past these, laughing and joking, from out of nowhere appeared three 'big guys' all wearing 'snorkel' parkas zipped up to the top! This was odd as it was summer, not winter! They then proceeded to run at us, and we scattered like wildebeest being chased by a hungry lioness. Luckily for me, they grabbed one of my pals and kicked him. This at least distracted them, and I took off across the 'dump' like the Road Runner! My friend broke free and ran away too. We sustained no serious injuries. The reason they did it was because we were coming out of an RC school.

The other incident was one afternoon walking home across the 'dump'. Halfway home I saw three older Colston guys approaching. I was not on high alert as they looked too old to bother with a wee guy like me. As I walked past, two of them stopped me and their pal who stood in the middle produced a rather large dagger from his waist belt! I had a mini heart attack and really thought I was going to get 'chibbed' or 'ripped'. I had already began imagining the number of stitches that my 'ripped' cheek would require. Fortunately, the dagger guy only produced it to frighten me (it worked). He and his friends laughed, and they let me go! Phew!

Thank God when I moved to Skye, I did not have to worry about getting chased by snorkel parka guys with knives!

When you were an RC in Glasgow, you supported Glasgow Celtic football club. I thought it was mandatory! I remember when I found out that a Protestant guy I knew supported Celtic! I could not get my tiny mind round this. How could a Protestant support a Catholic team? It truly was unbelievable.

My Protestant friends supported Glasgow Rangers! This was just the way it was on Galloway Street. Most of the time religious rivalry only amounted to calling each other names, but that entire experience left me not wanting to take part in any organised religions, ever.

When I first went to Portree High School (which was predominantly Non-Catholic). I remember a teacher telling me where the local RC Church was in Portree and that I did not have to attend Religious Education (R.E.). Yaas! That was the only time I was glad that I was a Catholic!

Park Life

The summer of '76 was memorable to me for three reasons. The first (and foremost) was that I did not go to Skye for the school holidays. It's hard to put into words how that made me feel and though the adults in my life tried to mitigate the hurt by saying 'there is always next year', I was inconsolable and as anyone knows the period of a year to an adult is the equivalent of ten years to a child!

The second '76 memory was that of the heat wave. Summer in the Glasgow city was hot! Once I got over the disappointment of not going to Linicro, I had to find ways to pass the long hot summer weeks.

The third life event was that I would leave the comfort (and joy) of Saint Aloysius primary school and be moving to the strange and scary world of first year at All Saints Secondary School.

Our street, baked by the heatwave, offered no fun, so my pals and I spent many a day on bikes in Springburn Public Park. With the green of the well-kept lawns and the view over to the distant Campsies, one could pretend that you were in the countryside!

Springburn Park in the mid-70s was very well kept and offered a world of adventure to us council house kids. Not only did it have swings, roundabouts and slides. It also had a rock garden, large 'hot hoose' conservatory, a putting green, acres of grass and its crowning glory a boating pond! To us kids the pond was loch sized and for the brave soul you could unsock your feet and paddle in it!

They had three different types of boats to hire. There was the double-handed, hand-cranked paddle boat, a foot pedal boat and a small two-oared rowing boat. A world of water adventure awaited those of us who had money in our pockets. With the 'taps aff' weather guaranteeing a busy park, you had to wait in line for your chance of boating mischief! Also, when it was crowded, you did not get to choose your boat – you took what was available. My favourite, though not the fastest, was the foot pedal boat. It was operated like sitting on a bicycle and pedalling like a madman to garner any kind of speed. If you were aboard alone, you could be fast, but if you shared your water ride, then the extra weegie weight slowed you down!

My pals and I would race the length of the pond, the winner securing bragging rights for the rest of the day. The oared boats had the most speed but nobody liked them. It was hoped that you could get one of the other brightly painted floating things with black numbers adorning each side. Park boating days were really great fun, only ruined by the boating pond 'parkie' shouting your boat's number and saying 'Yer times up'!

The pond contained some life and with a length of bamboo and a green net you could fish for minnows. The unlucky fish that we caught were often flushed down the toilet when it became too much trouble to keep them! We were told by the adults that they would reach the Clyde and be very happy river fishes!

Summer Sunday mornings saw the well-used paddle boats have a rest – moored in the middle of the oval pond – far out of reach for any naughty pirates like us!

On Sundays the pond was taken over by remote-controlled speed boat operators. We watched in wonder as the small petrol-powered speed boats zoomed around the large pond occasionally spraying us with wake water, and acrid petrol fumes would invade our nostrils. Great fun!

When not boating or playing at the swing park, my pals and I would zoom round the footpaths on our bikes getting shouted at and occasionally chased by the ever-vigilant group of grounds keepers or, as we affectionately called them, 'Parkies'!

In the cooler evenings we would go to the Balgrayhill entrance with a single roller-skate stolen from a sister, a piece of cardboard, and scoot down the hill sitting on our homemade skateboard. What a laugh! Injuries were not uncommon, and we wore gravel rash like a badge of honour. Ouch!

Before long the holidays would be over and unbeknownst to me, I would begin my last year living in the second city of the empire.

Around ten years ago I was working an agency shift at Stobhill Hospital and I visited the park to relive some memories before my shift began. Gone are the manicured flowery green areas and the 'hot hoose' is just a skeleton without its glass skin. Years of budget cuts and neglect have taken their sad toll on the once beautiful public park. The boating pond is now bereft of boats and the water level has risen high, flooding the surrounding footpath. Such a shame!

Still, I'm lucky to have seen the park in its heyday and enjoyed the adventures it offered us Galloway Street kids. I can say, hand on heart, that the 'parkie' did not catch me once when we caused our park mayhem and ran (or cycled) for our young lives dodging the grips of the green-fingered ground keeping security guards!

Record Sessions

The first girl I really fancied was one year ahead of me in St Aloysius. Her name was Audrey, and I don't think she ever looked at me … not once! Well, strictly speaking, that's not true. She looked at me once during a school performance that we did in the Springburn Technical College stage. We had a kind of ceilidh where I got up to sing solo, a song called 'East West Hame's Best'. Audrey was one of the Scottish Country dancing troupe and they would do a wee dance after each act and then sit round the stage. When it was my turn to sing, I stood on her dancing-shoed foot as I moved to centre stage! That was the only time she looked at me! I don't know what happened to her as I did not see her when I went to All Saints. In the first year I had a crush on this sporty girl called Claire who seemed too posh for our school. She did not look at me either!

Back in Galloway Street we organised small house parties called 'record sessions'. My pal Davie who lived opposite, was one of the first of our group to get a girlfriend! He was the same age as my sister, and he went out with this lassie called Jackie who was very pretty!

These 'sessions' involved taking records round to whoever's house and playing them and dancing! If we were lucky, there would be something to eat too! This would be where I got my first 'snog'. I think that the girl (whose name might have been Tracey) was a friend of Jackie's and although not as pretty as her, I did not mind! I had no clue what I was doing; I remember it was just four lips sucking air. No tongues!

My folks let me have one in our house and my Mum made up some sandwiches and provided crisps, nuts and bottles of 'ginger'. I got a new Adidas shirt specifically for the event. Dark blue with red stripes and logo. I loved that shirt. A bunch of us gathered to dance to 'Under the Moon of Love' by Showaddywaddy when an over excited dancer knocked over a big glass vase and it smashed to a million pieces on the floor! Luckily, it was not an heirloom or antique. As the hours passed the records got slower so that we could do a 'moonie' (slow dance} and hopefully get a kiss. Leo Sayer's 'When I Need You' got played quite a lot during these parties.

One thing kind of spoiled it for me, and it was something that was the sign of the times in 1977 Galloway Street. There were a couple of guys outside in our building's corridor who were 'glue sniffing' and totally away with the fairies! They knew we were having a party and stood outside my front door shouting through the letter box!

I will be honest with you and admit I was very frightened by this, but by the time our party finished the glue sniffing guys had gone!

After I left Glasgow 'sniffing glue' got popular on Galloway Street and there was a big article about it in the Daily Record as some wee guy from 'old' Galloway Street had died of it. The paper said that our street was known locally as 'Glue Street'. Thank God I missed all of that!

First First Foot

'Twas my last New Year of the 70s in Glasgow. 1976/77 to be precise. This Hogmanay would be different as my folks allowed me to go 'first footing' for the time! At the ripe old age of twelve!

It really was not too big a deal as I would only cross the street to the tenements opposite and be visiting my pals' hooses! Four of us had planned this well. We had pooled some Christmas money and had enough for a 'kerry oot'! So off we went to the Spring Inn and stood outside the 'off sales' pleading with anyone one old enough to buy us 6 cans of Tennent's lager! Luckily most people were in the season's spirit, and it did not take us too long to procure said alcoholic beverages!

We 'planked' them at the back of my pal's building, and as it was frosty, they remained in a chilled state! My folks would be at a party along the street, so everyone was relatively safe! We started drinking our cans by around ten (ish). One each and a few slugs of the extra tins! As most of us know, when you are young, lager is pretty gruesome and that bitter taste was an enemy to our young tongues, but as a 'guy' you pretended to enjoy the amber wet stuff! Tennent's is not that strong, but after one can we were all pretty steaming!

The bells saw us go up to the top flat of one of the 'closes' and take a lump of coal from the bunker outside the door of our first first foot! Ding dong and the door was open to a welcome heat and Engelbert Humperdinck crooning 'Ten Guitars'! Adult hands shook and wifey cheeks kissed we sat down in a lager daze! We got offered a soupcon of Babycham! In Glasgow this was a 'wuman's' drink therefore was suitable for minors! Has anyone tried Babycham? It's absolutely disgusting! We had to wash it down with a sneaky lager sip!

On to the flat opposite with the same piece of coal! 'Happy New Year,' we slurred. Totally Babychammed oot of our minds! More hands kissed and cheeks shaken! This time we got offered a minute amount of Warnink's Advocaat diluted with lemonade. This stuff had the consistency of vomit going the in way instead of out! We washed the yellow stuff down with a wee slug of Double Diamond 'Heavy'!

Advocaated, we stumbled 'doon' the stairs and to the next 'close' still with coal in hand, we made our last destination! A green and white house playing rebel songs! More hands and cheeks saw us deposited on the sofa. Each eye spinning in different directions!

Our last drink of the evening?

A tiny glass of Sweetheart Stout. A trifecta of spew-inducing material which would taste worse coming out than going in! Some dancing and singing about freedom and the obligatory I love you...no I mean I really love you...

We ended up on our street looking for girls to wish happiness to and the chance of a proper kiss! We found some older teens and drunkenly tried our moves on them with minor success! Who would want to kiss a spinning mess of a twelve-year-old? I of course persisted and embarrassed myself. This is something I would often repeat well into my adult life! I got a kiss on the lips though!

By about 3am Mr Sandman was shouting loudly, and I stumbled home. This I have no actual memory of and the next thing I knew my sister was waking me up the next day as I had 'conked oot' in her bed!

I awoke to a feeling of doom and an Advocaat aftertaste! I felt like I had been dragged through a succession of bushes backwards and forwards! I didn't spew, though! I made it to the living room with my folks, obviously hung over and laughed at my dehydrated state!

'That'll teach ye,' in stereo to more laughs!

If only they had been right. It didn't teach me at all! In fact, things got progressively worse and a hangover at New Year would become my new BFF!

Five Years

As documented in Skye Stories Volume 1&2 all you beautiful people know that between the summer of 1977 and autumn of 1982, I made my home in Linicro and Uig on the beautiful Isle of Skye. These five glorious years will be skipped here. What I wanted to say was that back then five years really was five years. A lifetime to a kid. Not like these very quick things we have now as auld adults that disappear in the blink of a blue eye. A year was a very long time to any kid aged 12 going on 13. Five years, man. That was long.

The thing is, had those five years not occurred it's highly unlikely that you would be reading these words as I doubt I would have written them if not for that half decade I spent in the highlands.

Had I spent those years in Galloway Street most probably I would have left All Saints at 16 and not stayed on to study for O'levels and highers. My guess is that I probably would have followed my sister and my father and started work for Slater and Rodger's Whiskey Bond. Perhaps it would have been a Saturday job that turned into a full-time job and who knows even some sort of apprenticeship.

Like many others of my age, I probably would have gotten married in my early twenties. With kids now in their thirties! It's weird to think about it.

I cannot understate the huge impact that such a short time had on my life. Personally, it was enormous.

So why did I leave Galloway Street and my family so young? What happened during those five years? I'm not telling you here. Read Skye Stories Volume 1&2 and enjoy.

For now, we have to skip to the early 1980s and my return to Glasgow.

September 82

Ali Aitken and I were on the Highland Scottish bus on our way to Glasgow's Buchanan Street bus station. We had spent a few days at his folks' place in Glendale after we finished our seasonal job at Uig Hotel.

It was a long, uncomfortable journey. These Highland buses were not what one could call comfortable. For me I had an unusual feeling in my chest, and I was not sure what it was, but it was there, nagging me. After having spent the last five and a bit years on the Isle of Skye, I was returning home. I had left Galloway Street a boy, and I was returning a man. It was weird. Something did not feel right. I couldn't put my finger on it, but something was wrong all the same. We arrived at the bus station, grabbed our stuff and got off the Skye bus.

Buchanan Street in 1982 was not the clean and covered from the elements bus station it is today. It was dirty, cold and smelly. With our rucksacks on our backs, we made for the 45 bus stop. This took us to Balgrayhill, and we walked to my parents' place on Galloway Street.

Our plan was that we would spend a couple of days in Glasgow to buy supplies that we needed for our planned big adventure. Over the summer we had decided to 'InterRail' over Europe. You bought this one ticket, and it allowed you to travel free on European trains. We said we would go for as long as our money lasted. We had no clue about anything, and it was exciting if a little scary.

I had arranged to meet Karen, who I had fallen in love with in Uig over the summer. She would come through from Shotts with her mother and I was to meet her in the town. I was unsure of myself and my feelings. We met up on Sauchiehall Street and when I saw her the thoughts and feelings of my first love came flooding back and I realised how much I had missed her over the past few weeks. I remember that she wanted to go to 'Das Haar' salon to get her hair done, so I went with her and spent as much time as the afternoon allowed. I think she missed me, but we were not in Uig anymore. We were back to real life and everything was up in the air.

I probably did not show too much emotion as we said our goodbyes and I told her I would call her when I got back from our trip. She looked sad. I felt sad.

A few days later we were back in Buchanan Street getting the bus to London. My Dad came with us and saw us on to the bus. As we sat on our seats, 'Tom Hark' by the Piranhas played on the overhead speakers. Ali had contacted an old school friend of ours, Sheila Khaliq, who was training to be a Nurse and she said we could spend the night at her place before we caught the train to Dover the following day. We arrived at Victoria bus station and it was busier, louder and smellier than Buchanan Street. It filled me with fear. Finally, after some time, we made it to Sheila's which was Nursing Student accommodation attached to a hospital. I have no memory of which Hospital it was but I remember the Nurses' home as it was an old building with single rooms and central heating. Sheila wanted us to go out for a drink, but I made the excuse that I was tired and just wanted to rest. The reality was it scared me to go out in this big city. Ali went out with her and I had a bath and went to bed. I remember looking outside the window and on a balcony opposite us I saw a bunch of guys sitting talking. That made me feel more uncomfortable. Ali returned from the pub and Sheila said her goodnights and went to sleep in her friend's room. I did not sleep that well, truth be told. The nagging feeling in my chest kept me awake.

From Victoria train station we got on the train to Dover. Getting off the train station we had a long walk to the ferry terminal and my rucksack was heavy and uncomfortable. It was an ex-army bag and not designed for comfort! Ali's was the same, and he had the added weight of carrying his faithful Yamaha acoustic guitar. As we walked along the terminal to our ferry, the signs were in many languages. This was the first time I had seen so many together on one sign! As our ferry departed for Calais, this would be the first time that I was outside of the British Isles. Fear and some excitement was all I felt.

Calais

We made it across the channel unscathed and we were walking towards the city. My first city in a foreign country. I knew very little French. Ali had some phrases remembered from school. I don't know what I expected, but it was not a pretty place. At least not what we could see as we walked in the evening light. Our destination was a Youth Hostel where we would spend our first night away from the country of our birth.

The hostel was almost empty. Late September was not high backpacker season. We checked in and dumped our stuff and went for a wee wander to have a look around and try to find something to eat. We found a nice bakery and bought some bread and then we went looking for a phone armed with the number of a friend of Sheila's whom she suggested we call and see if we could stay at his place in Paris!

Mr Aitken made the call, and the guy said yes! Great. This meant that we would save some money as we would not have to pay for a Youth Hostel there.

After a sleepless night we stumbled our way to the train station and boarded an SNCF train bound for Paris. What was immediately obvious to me was how much more modern the French trains were compared to British Rail. Very swish and comfortable.

Paris

Arriving at Paris Gare du Nord, we looked like two lost sheep in a giant pen. We had to find our way to the Metro and get to Vaugirard station. I loved the Paris Metro and their trains. I found it relatively easy to navigate and on our way there we were entertained by buskers who came on at one station, played a song and then got off at the next!

Outside of Vaugirard we had to find the flat on Rue Blomet, which was not too far. We were a wee bit nervous as it was a bit of a brass neck, two strangers just showing up at a door and asking to stay. The flat was in a typical Paris 'tenement' and it was on the top floor. I wish I could remember the guy's name, but I don't. He was Scottish with a French girlfriend and he was very nice. Also sharing the flat was an English guy and a Scottish girl. We thanked him profusely for letting us stay. Both of us slept on the floor in the dining room. We used our jackets as pillows.

We spent around a week there and although I was nervous about being in such a large city, I really enjoyed it. To me Paris is one of the most beautiful cities that I have ever been to and I only wished my French was better!

Most of the time we existed on bread and cheese, and we did our best to see some of the sights on offer. The flat was not too far from the Eiffel Tower, and that was one of our first stops. Even in September it was pretty busy, and we decided that we would just hang around watching people as opposed to climbing the tower's stairs or boarding the elevator. It was too expensive for our meagre budget.

We went up the Montparnasse Tower block, which was cheaper and gave you just as good a view. We enjoyed the Pompidou centre and the square in front of it which had many busking acts doing their thang! We spent more than a few days just hanging around there.

As mentioned, our budget was not what one would call big and I made a suggestion to Ali that we should busk at a Metro station. Over the summer we had learned to sing plenty of songs, so why not try and make a bit of money? He was not too keen on the idea. I'm not sure if it was nerves or what, but eventually he agreed, and we made a plan.

We made our busking pitch at Montparnasse Metro. Just outside of the turnstiles where passengers exited. Both of us were slightly anxious, but we gave it a go.

Every time we heard a train stop, we would sing a song. As people came out of the station some of them actually threw some coins into the soft guitar case we had lying in front of us! It amazed us to say the least! Our rather short set list included songs by Cat Stevens's, Neil Young, and AC/DC. With the money we made, it paid for our bread and cheese and the occasional big bottle of beer from the local supermarket. We busked each afternoon for about three days, then we would wander around aimlessly enjoying the Paris life.

My problem was with my heart. You have to remember that only a few short weeks before I was madly in love with my 'first love'. The more we travelled, the more my heart ached, and I did not know what to do. Never having been in love before!

Soon we were planning our next train journey, and we decided on Switzerland and in particular Montreux, obviously because of Deep Purple's 'Smoke on the Water'.

Switzerland

Having said our goodbyes and expressed our profound gratitude to the folks at Rue Blomet, we boarded the night train to Switzerland. On this train we had our own cabin, which you entered via two sliding doors. You could then pull down both sets of seats and it made into a double bed! My abiding memory was going to sleep and then being woken up by the Guard wanting to see our passport. It was very early morning, and I peeked outside the window and there was the Alps. Wow! Absolutely stunning. I had seen nothing so breath-taking in my young life.

After arriving in Montreux, we had to find the Youth hostel and get booked in. At this point I realised that I really was not a backpacking/Youth Hostel kind of guy.

On Lake Geneva, Montreux is a picture postcard type of place. It really is beautiful, and we just spent our days wandering around the banks of the lake enjoying the scenery. Everyone knows how expensive Switzerland is, so we could not do much else. Our diet of bread and cheese continued! I had suggested that we do some busking on the walkway by the lake. Try to earn some extra cash but for some reason Ali was not into it, so that was that.

Our last night there we splurged out and went to a pub and after a few beers we were suitably merry and made our staggering way back to Youth Hostel bed. The next day we were on our way to Italy!

Italy

I was not too keen about going to Italy. I don't know why, but we made the decision that we would travel to Bari at the foot of the country. The train journey was pretty spectacular as we passed the Alps into Italy and eventually, we ended up in Milan. Our plan was to find a train to Bari as soon as possible. Milan train station creeped me out!

I was a wee bit shocked about the condition of the Italian trains. Unlike the French, these trains were old and very grubby. We had a long journey ahead of us and instead of excitement I just felt dread.

After an excruciatingly long ride, we arrived in Bari mid-morning. I don't know what I was expecting to see, but it was not what I saw. Immediately I felt ill at ease and regretted going there. I'm not sure how Ali felt, but I was not happy. When I think back on it now that I'm a more experienced traveller, I realise that it was just me being stupid and lovesick. We could not find the Youth Hostel and no local took anytime to listen to our pleas for directions. I made the decision that I wanted to get back on the train and get the hell out of Italy! Immature I know, but that was how I felt. I don't remember Ali putting up much of a fight to stay, so he must have been feeling the same as me. He just wasn't lovesick!

That evening we were back at Bari train station, about to board another grubby train to Milan. At least we had our own cabin, or so we thought. We had planned to get some sleep and had pulled down the door blinds hoping nobody would disturb us. We were wrong. This massive, big guy slid open the doors with an unfriendly look and plopped himself down on the seat next to me! He was hairy faced and bespectacled and none too happy looking. After about 10 minutes, he tried to strike up a conversation with us. His English was as good as our Italian. He then spied Ali's guitar on the overhead shelf and seemed to cheer up immediately. Excitedly, he was saying something and pointing to the guitar. Ali thought he wanted a shot but when he brought it down to give him, he pointed to Ali to play. At this point he produced a bottle of J&B rare. I'm not a whiskey drinker, but I swigged it just to try and relax. Things got a little surreal. In his broken English he gave some chord instructions to Ali, who began strumming. This guy burst into singing 'It's Now or Never' in a concert hall loud operatic voice! He was fantastic. With more whiskey swigs and more songs being sung, I was pretty pished. The Italian guy was 'gien it laldy' in our cabin. We soon drew a crowd and at one point we had a chorus singing and a guy outside in the corridor playing a flute! Weird and a wee bit wonderful. It made the short Italy trip worth it just for that memory.

I will be honest with you and say that the next few days were all a blur of train stations, scenery and crappy railway food. We eventually ended up in Luxembourg!

Luxembourg

Why and how we ended up here I don't have the slightest idea perhaps it was something to do with the fact that I was a Radio Luxembourg fan?

The sun was shining as we tried to find the Youth Hostel. We got there early but could not get booked in and they told us to come back later. We found a nice piece of green grass to dump our stuff and lie in the sun. It was very picturesque with a stone viaduct in the distance. It didn't take long for something to happen that ruined the day for me. I laugh when I think back on it but then I was a naïve teenager with no worldly experience.

As both of us lay on the grass, a guy joined us. He had been to the Hostel and like us was told to wait. He spoke French and started up a conversation with Ali. He seemed to me to be overly friendly, and he lay very close to Ali. There were some French and English words exchanged then this guy did a bizarre thing. He had plucked a long grass from the ground and stroked the area of Ali's chest made bare by his unbuttoned shirt! WTF? Then he asked something to Ali and Ali said no and turned away from him. After we ignored him for a while he moved off. I asked Ali what he said and was told that the guy asked Ali if he was gay! After hearing that I went into a total panic. This guy is staying in the same hostel as us. What if he is in the same room as us? I was really crapping myself. I know what you're thinking, and I agree with you now but back then I had no knowledge of gay people and like most uninformed guys I immediately thought that he would try it on with me. Truly, I was petrified. It was enough to make me want to leave.

A crowd of people had gathered waiting to check in to the hostel, so we joined them. I monitored the gay guy and made sure he was nowhere near me! There were German boys and some Americans and these two English guys who showed up with no rucksack but two 'old ladies' shopping trollies instead! Strange, I thought. After we checked in my plan was to make sure we were not in the same dorm as the gay guy. It was all I could think about! When we got to the dorm both Ali, and I took the top bunks, and I was lucky to have a hulking big American guy below me. He would be my protection, I thought! I don't think I saw the gay guy again, so I felt a little more relaxed! What an idiot I was back then!

There was a decent group of guys in the hostel at that time and I should have enjoyed myself more, but I couldn't. My lovesickness was getting worse!

We had one good night out, though. Getting drunk in a pub. Playing Galaxian. A few days later we were on the move.

Belgium

I have no clue why we went to Belgium. Or why we ended up in Buizingen. I remember that Ali and I had a big argument, but I don't remember about what. I was not an easy person to travel with, so that probably had something to do with it.

Buizingen turned out to be pretty decent. It was cold when we arrived, and the Youth Hostel was empty. We dumped our stuff and went out looking for something to eat. If I recall the people in Paris told us the Belgians were not that friendly, but we found the exact opposite. As we walked down main street a guy was getting out of his car and we stopped to ask directions for somewhere (cheap) to eat. Thankfully, he spoke English and said that he was going to the restaurant across the road, and would we like to join him? He seemed nice, and we thought what the hell. Of course, I was slightly suspicious of his motives. That's what I was like back then. I'm the complete opposite now.

It was a nice wee family-run place, and the guy said that we could order anything we wanted. It was his pleasure to buy a meal for some tourists. We ordered steak and chips. Washed down by Stella Artois. I would later begin a long relationship with Stella. The guy was a local businessman who was well known to the restaurant. Sure enough, his motives were completely altruistic. He bought us another beer and paid the bill and said his goodbye as we drank the cold stuff. The kindness of strangers can be amazing.

Slightly merry we went looking for a pub which we found. This place was tiny but cosy looking. It had Stella and an odd-looking games table. At first, I thought that it was a small snooker table, but no. It only had one hole at either end with two bars on either side. It was a billiards table, and we wanted to play. There were a couple of local guys playing and they saw our interest and invited us to have a game. The Paris people were wrong about Belgians, everyone we met was really very friendly and kind. They spoke good English, and I told them what our Paris friends had said, and they agreed, but they said that the unfriendly Belgians were the French speakers. Here they spoke Flemish and they were the opposite of their other countrymen! We had a great night playing billiards and getting stocious on Stella! We staggered back to the Youth Hostel and spent a few frozen nights there.

We spent most of the time in that wee bar drinking and playing billiards, but our money was running out! We decided to go back to Paris and start busking again.

Paris (again)

The Rue Blomet residents were surprised to see us but welcomed us all the same. We told them of our money woes and our plan to busk and pretty much stay out of their way. As before, we wandered aimlessly and busked at Montparnasse station. I had purchased a tambourine to try and liven things up, but I was not particularly adept at playing it. My mind was wandering back to Scotland as I wanted desperately to see Karen. I spent an age looking for a special gift for her and found what I thought was a beautiful silver bracelet that I really could not afford. I bought it anyway, and I decided to return to Blighty.

We should have travelled more, but our money was running out and all I could think about was Karen. I had no choice. A train, a boat and another train later we were back in London. Ali wanted to stay in London our friend Sheila was called on again.

At Victoria bus station I purchased a ticket to Glasgow. We hugged and said goodbye and I boarded that National Express coach excited at the thought of seeing my love.

That was our Inter-Rail experience in a nutshell. Not particularly exciting, but with some excellent memories. I'm glad I did it and as time passed and I got more used to travelling abroad, I was less immature and learned how to enjoy myself.

✛

Returning Home

The only thing on my mind when I got back to Glasgow was phoning Karen and arranging to meet up. When I called her, I detected something in her voice that led me to think that her feelings towards me had changed. We made a date for the following Saturday and for some reason I thought it would be good to go to the afternoon showing of 'The Evil Dead' at the ABC on Sauchiehall Street! Big mistake! When she arrived, I immediately knew that something was wrong. Things had changed, although she said nothing. We went to the cinema and watched the movie almost like two strangers. Afterwards we talked for a while and she told me that she had met someone else. I was heartbroken. For weeks I was in a daze. First love was all-consuming and now it was over. I did all the usual things, like trying to call her and find out if it was truly over. It was. She had moved on and her life was on a different path and that really was it. A few more sad phone calls with me and one visit to her in Shotts showed me that there was no hope. No matter how much I wanted her back, she was gone. Love sickness sucks.

I had received a letter for an interview at North Lothian College of Nursing, and it was obvious that my future lay in Edinburgh. It was not an easy time for me and my emotions ran high those last few months of 1982. Somehow, I managed to get through it.

Music Magic

It's impossible to put into words the impact music has had on my life and how it has helped shape me. It's a beautiful thing, and I continue to feel its magic today. Especially when you discover something new and exciting. Even if it's not new and you are rediscovering a band or singer, there is no greater feeling than hearing special song for the first time. They can mesmerize and transport you to a place free of worries and care. Music is life. There is no doubt in my mind. I often thought that life would be so much easier (and better) if we lived in a musical. Wouldn't that be great? Whilst writing this book, I wanted to add my thoughts and feelings about what music I was listening to at the time and how it made me feel. It's a crucial part of my life story and I want to tell it in a way that's not too deep but gives you a wee idea of what I was listening to at a specific time in my life.

Unfortunately for me, the last months of 1982 I spent with a broken heart. There were songs that I found hard to listen to because it reminded me so much of Karen and sometimes it would bring me to big boy tears. The obvious ones were songs that we had listened to during the summer months. She had a couple of mix tapes that we would always play whilst we were smooching. One of these was a collection of the Commodores' greatest hits and even today when I hear 'Still' I'm reminded of her and the heartache I had. They have this brilliant song called 'Zoom' which has a fabulous strings section during the chorus. The sound is unbelievable, and I'm surprised that I have never heard someone use it as a sample over the years. You need to check it out.

Talking about 'Zoom' the Fat Larry's Band song with the same title was in the charts around the break up. Being and old romantic the lyrics made me think of her each time the song played on the radio...and it was played a lot! It was the same with Hot Chocolate's 'It Started with a Kiss'. We never listened to it together but after we broke up and she turned cold towards me the line 'You don't remember me do you' with its funky bass gave me chills of sorrow. 'Ten Years Gone' by Led Zeppelin also made me think of her especially when Mr Plant sang the line 'Changes fill my time, baby that all right with me. In the midst I think of you and how we used to be'. Sadness abounded for months with these songs. Slowly, into the New Year things got better, but not by much!

The Interview

In late 82 my cousin Bobby and I went through to Edinburgh for the day. That afternoon I would have my interview at North Lothian College. It was a grey Edinburgh day, and it was my first time to visit our nation's capital. To me, at first it seemed a strange place, and I wondered (and doubted) if I could make my life there. From the West End we jumped a bus down to Crewe Road and got off at the Western General Hospital. The Nursing College was at the end of the red-bricked Nurses' Accommodation block. Harry Needham and a female tutor interviewed me. Harry was a lecturer and Deputy Chief of the College. After a bit of small talk, we got down to the nitty gritty and they asked why did I want to become a Registered Nurse? I told them that I had originally fancied going into the Royal Navy and training to be a Medical Technician which gave you an RN qualification after three years but had decided that I want to stay on land as opposed to sea. I gave them all the usual fluff about wanting to help people and also pioneer being a male in what was a female-dominated area. In doing so, I hoped to encourage more males to enter the profession.

Interview done, they told me that I would be competing for a place in the February 1984 intake! WTF? Why so long I thought but did not say. Should I be successful, that was another year (and more) away. What the hell was I going to do till then?

Bobby and I spent some time looking around Princes Street and caught the bus back to Glasgow from St Andrew's Square. A few weeks later I received the letter saying they accepted me for the February 1984 intake and that was that. I would have to wait a year!

Glasgow late 82

I love Glasgow. I love going home and seeing my family. I love the city now, but I did not always feel that way. In the early 1980s Glasgow was pretty depressing. There was a lot of changes going on and the transition was not pretty. Springburn was being cut in half to make way for a new bypass. Buildings were being demolished everywhere and Galloway Street was dirty and unfriendly. Heroin raised its ugly head on many of our city's streets at this time. I was not what one would call happy. Add to that the fact that I was back, staying in my family home and I was sleeping on the living room sofa compounded my misery. I began 'signing on' at the local 'bru' down Springburn Road and it was soul crushing to say the least.

I was lovesick and the only friend I had was Bobby who had returned to his folk's home in Pollock. He was feeling the same as me, minus the lovesickness! Luckily, I was a part-time roadie for the band my Dad was in and that helped cheer me up. At least I got a laugh and a break from my personal misery. Three times a week we would be out playing, in and around Glasgow and sometimes as far as Manchester. I got on really well with the band, especially the drummer Davie, who saw that I was a little lost in the city and took me under his wing. Thank God for him and I will forever appreciate his efforts to get me out of my funk.

Davie and I would go into town and play snooker in the big hall near the bottom of Renfield Street. This I really enjoyed. It was he who introduced me to Glasgow's famous Dial Inn pub which put on various bands and where I would become a regular every Saturday. Jamie Barnes and Cochise were my favourite covers band and Pallas from Aberdeen were my favourite 'original' band. Unbeknownst to me, there was a 'Prog Rock' revival going on and Pallas were thought to be the next big thing. The Dial Inn is not that big a pub, but when Pallas played, they really put on a show. Lights, smoke and costumes abound. Their music was fantastic, too.

Shadows on Bath Street was another place I would hang out with Davie and also with Bobby. Both Shadows and The Dial Inn had good looking waitresses to look at as well! I might have been severely lovesick, but I was not dead.

Bobby and I had to do something about getting out and enjoying some Glasgow nightlife! Dressed in our best, we would go out on a Saturday night trying to pull a lassie (and failing). We would meet up in Shadows, then we would go to the slightly more upmarket Nico's on Sauchiehall Street. Our place to dance was the Ultratheque, just off Sauchiehall Street. There was a dress code, so you had to look a bit smart, or you would get a knock back at the door! Once down the stairs you entered this stereotypical 80s disco. It really was not our scene, but what other choices did we have? I don't think either of us scored – well maybe once – and that was at Christmas time with a kiss and cuddle at the Taxi rank! Something had to change. This was not the most enjoyable time of my life.

✧

Caramel and Country Pride

In the early 1980s my Dad Big Gerry was the bass player for the well-known Glasgow Country and Western band Caramel and Country Pride. Led by singer Caramel and her husband and singer/guitarist Gerry. The first time I met them they had 'wee Billy' on lead guitar, 'Billy' on steel guitar, and Davie on drums! They were a superb live band, and I enjoyed going to their gigs in the back of the van! All of them were hilarious, and I got on really well with Davie and Wee Billy! They played everywhere in Glasgow and the surrounding areas. Usually, social clubs and country music venues like Glasgow's 'Grand Ole Opry'! They took their country music seriously in this club that had been cinema at one time! My Dad of course knew everybody, and he liked to 'show me off' when I was in town! The Opry was always busy when the band played, and the audience was full of 'characters' who did then what is now considered fashionable and that is 'cosplay'! They would dress up as their favourite characters from the American west and during the band's break they would have 'gunfights' on the dance floor! They were hard-core fans; they did not use real guns…. or bullets, but very expensive replicas that fired loud blanks! They would dual and somebody would referee! It was fun, if a little surreal!

The band played a lot of 'standard' country and Western songs and, depending on what type of gig it was, would play a couple of rock numbers. Wee Billy, who had a magnificent voice would sing these! His songs were The Eagles 'Peaceful Easy Feeling', The Stones 'It's All Over Now' and a well-known standard 'High Heel Sneakers'. My Dad had a couple of numbers too! Big Gerry was a great singer (and I'm not just saying that because he is my Dad). He had a classic country crooner voice and, if he had been born in the US, might have had a notion to try his luck in Nashville. He had the pipes that people in the country scene love, but Dad was happy with his beer and extra pocket money in Glasgow! He would sing 'The Tennessee Waltz' and 'How Can I say Goodbye to a Girl like You'. I loved to hear the big man sing.

Caramel had a great Irish sense of humour and would often make fun of the audience! One of her common quips would be to shout out to the audience 'stop talking while I'm performing,' or 'I go to your house and talk when you're performing'! If any balding guys, particularly those with 'comb overs' would walk by she would often shout 'hey mister there's a hole in your wig'! She had a really great 'show band' voice.

Davie the drummer had an excellent sense of humour and he would always have me in stitches. He was also a brilliant drummer and could play any type of music. He just had a great feel. As mentioned, he took me under his wing, and I would help him carry his drum gear to and from the van! Billy the steel guitar player was just mad!

I don't have any rhythm in me, but during the sound check I would often get up and bash away at the drums! On a couple of occasions wee Billy, who could play any riff, would start playing Black Sabbath's 'Paranoid' so that I could do the drum bit at the end! Great fun! He liked to partake of the 'wacky baccy' and I remember one gig at Glasgow's Cladda club, another converted Cinema, had a high stage. Billy had been puffing in the back of the van and I got a 'contact high'. During the gig Davie the drummer got me to sit up beside him and wow did his drums sound loud and proud! What a laugh I had that night – and many others – as I did my roadie duties for the last months of 1982

Wee Billy has passed, but I will never forget him and his guitar playing. I will always be grateful to Davie for his company and the kindness he showed me and the rest of the band who gave me such a laugh.

Annan

After his divorce, Derek Graham, one of my old Uig Hotel bosses, had moved to Annan in Dumfriesshire. It was a relatively small market town on the Solway coast. Even though I had told Mrs Graham I was not in contact with him during the previous year, he occasionally phoned me. I think he was lonely, and he wanted to hear any gossip from Uig. He had my parent's number and in early January 1983, he called me up. He had bought a villa and was planning to renovate it and make it a small fancy Bed and Breakfast and he wondered if I would be interested in helping him? There would be no salary until the business was up and running, but it would be rent free, and I could at last get off my parents' sofa and away from Galloway Street and Glasgow. I asked if I could bring Bobby, and Derek agreed. I had not asked Bobby, but I felt sure he would go for a wee while. Anything was better than living at home! He agreed and at the beginning of February we were on a bus to Carlisle to be picked up by Derek who was still driving his over-the-top mustard yellow Chrysler Charger.

As we passed the historic Gretna Green and made our way to Annan, I thought that this was more my style. Lots of greenery, lots of farms and not a big city. If only it had some hills, but no, it's quite flat. We turned down the Hecklegirth Road and made our way towards our new home.

Solway Bank

Just after we passed a strangely placed factory building and under a wee bridge, we turned into Solway Bank House. This was a red sandstone villa that had uninterrupted views across green fields and across the Solway Firth. It looked very nice. We parked at the side near the garage and entered the house through the back door. Once inside, we saw that it was very outdated and needed a major refurbishment and we would help bring the old building back to life.

It was not a massive place, but it was bigger than any house I had ever stayed in. There were four rooms on the ground floor. Three bedrooms upstairs. There was also what I presume would have been a housekeeper annex at the back. The two ground-floor front rooms would be where the guests would be entertained. The main lounge and the dining room led to a sizable kitchen. There was another living room at the back. This would be our bedroom for the next couple of months. Derek had bought two single beds and placed them up against the wall. There was a fireplace and some comfy chairs. With a colour TV this would also be our living space. It was fine, but a bit cold. The entrance hall was rather big with nice parquet flooring which led to an enormous staircase leading to the bedrooms. On the staircase landing there was a door which led to the housekeeper's accommodation and a back stair to the kitchen, the utility rooms and a cellar.

The villa was surrounded by a sizable garden and as you would have read in Volume 2 my career at Uig Hotel began with me working in the garden with Derek who always seemed to be in a bad mood so I guessed at some point I would have to resume my green fingered work with old sour puss Derek when the weather got better. It could be worse I suppose, well at least it got us out of Glasgow.

Derek had already begun having work done on the place and over the coming months we got to know the plumbers, electricians and plasterers pretty well. Bobby and I were general dog's bodies and would help anyone and everyone. We got on well with the plumbers and had a real good laugh with them, apart from the time they grabbed me and rubbed bitumen on my nethers! They installed central heating all over. We fixed the roof. All the bedrooms were renovated and given their own ensuite bathrooms. They redecorated every room except our living room and the kitchen. The kitchen had a new cooker and new equipment installed. It took a few months and a lot of cleaning to get it ready for furnishings.

Night Out

I had been to Annan before with my Dad's band, Caramel and Country Pride, who had played at the Ex-Servicemen's club. Even though Bobby and I were on the dole, we wanted to see what Annan offered in the way of nightlife and a Friday night was our night out! Annan has one main street, which is the High Street, lined with shops, cafes, hotels and pubs. It was a fair effin' walk from Solway Bank to the town centre. The first pub we went into was the bar at the Queensberry Hotel. It had some kind of Wild West theme but was not exactly jumping! We made our way into the small lounge bar where at least there was ladies to look at. Being fresh faces in a new (small town) most people ignored us. From there we walked towards the red sandstone council office building with its clock tower, and just before the bridge over the River Annan we found the Blue Bell Inn. They had a poolroom, so we bought our beers and sat round the table waiting for a game. The Blue Bell would become my local, and it was relatively friendly. There we found out that every Friday they had a 'Disco' in the function room of the Corner House Hotel.

Drinking up, we walked towards the Corner House and went into their lounge bar, which also had a pool table and a jukebox. This seemed to be the place where the young folk drank, and then we paid our money and went into the 'Disco'. It was a typical function room, surrounded by tables and chairs. A bar and in the far corner a DJ had set up his double decks and PA with some flashing lights. Cheesy, but at least there were more ladies to look at and occasionally we got up to dance!

For the next couple of months, this would become our routine every Friday. Trying in vain to score and failing miserably. Bobby was the first to meet someone and through her I met a girl. It was all pretty casual and nothing very serious. At least it made us look as if we fitted in and most people were friendly enough. I did not mind the place at all and was becoming quite fond of Annan. It was as good a place as any to spend time until I had to start my Nursing course the following year.

No More Bobby

After a few months Bobby got itchy feet and planned to leave to join his sister Flora in Shetland. I was sad to see him go because it left only me and Derek in the house. All the big renovation jobs had finished, and it was now time to fill the place with furniture. To be honest, it was not really my scene then, but if I had the choice now to do what we had planned for the house, I would jump at the chance. I was a 19-year-old teenager and had other things on my mind. I was also very lazy.

By this time, we had made the old housekeeper area at the back into two small single rooms, one of which was mine. I also had my own shower room. Derek stayed up the stairs in the back bedroom. It must have looked odd to people, this old guy driving down Annan High Street in his Charger and this skinny pale kid sitting next to him in the passenger seat. Most people thought I was his son!

Derek's brothers stayed on the outskirts of Annan and were farmers with lots of land. They were all super nice to me, but they must have thought it strange as well. Derek enjoyed having me around as it reminded him of Uig Hotel, which I know he missed.

Some people would no doubt think that he was a wee bit eccentric, and he could come across as being a bit of a snob, but he could also be hilarious and lived an eventful life. He had been a pilot during World War Two and then got into commercial piloting. At one stage in his career, he had been the head of Sudan Air in Khartoum. How he and Gracie Graham got together, I will never know. To me, they were polar opposites.

Both Derek and I would go round local auction halls and buy up antiques at low prices to furnish Solway Bank. I enjoyed that and got to learn a thing or two. He also bought some expensive reproduction furniture like the massive dining room table and chairs. We would go to Carlisle a lot and just outside of Carlisle there was this wee village called Brampton were there was this old furniture restorer. This guy was highly skilled and very interesting. His work was top-notch, and I always enjoyed going to see him at his workshop.

Derek would let me buy some old wooden furniture that I could renovate myself and I really enjoyed that. I had a wee room at the back of the kitchen and could sand and stain to my heart's content whilst listening to Pink Floyd's 'The Final Cut' and Marillion's 'Script for a Jester's Tear'. Both of which helped me through the dark days of lovesickness!

~

Script for a Jester's Tear

Still suffering serious love sickness from the previous Skye summer, I found solace in several albums as I settled into Annan life. Marillion's debut album was released in March 1983 and having read about it in Sounds, which I read religiously every week, I did not fancy it. Many people likened them to Genesis when Peter Gabriel was their front man. I only knew Genesis with Phil Collins as a singer, and for some inexplicable reason I had decided that I didn't like the band with Peter Gabriel. This then tainted my view of Marillion as just being a Genesis sound-alike. I had no desire to buy the album. Not until I heard the single 'Garden Party'. I loved it and immediately went to John Menzies on Annan High Street and bought the cassette. From the get-go, I was hooked. The title track I related to my love hurt situation. The song starts with 'So here I'm once more, in the playground of the broken hearts'. This song really touched me, and I could relate to every word sung by Fish. I love every song on that album, although it took me a while to warm to 'Chelsea Monday' and 'The Web'. Fish's voice I thought beautiful and his complicated, storytelling lyrics were something new to me. I played it to death whilst working around Solway Bank. Today it still gets played and its songs transport me back to that lonely time of my life. There is no doubt it helped save my sanity. It would not be the last time Marillion saved me emotionally.

The Final Cut

Also released in March 1983, Pink Floyd's last album with Roger Waters got me through some bad days and nights. I know many Floyd fans don't rate this follow up to the massive 'The Wall' but for me it's one of my favourite albums of all time. Roger Waters' lyric writing is brilliant. This album sounded very personal for him, with the themes of war and loss. It is safe to say that it's not what one could call a 'happy' record. The title track touched my bruised heart, and every word meant something deep for me. I had heard that my ex had a new boyfriend and for me that truly was The Final Cut.

Hello, I Must Be Going

Phil Collins, second solo album after 'Face Value' is a total cracker. Released at the end of 1982 it was made for me it seems. There were sad songs, joyful songs and with 'I Don't Care Anymore', defiant songs. 'Like China' was what I wanted to sing down the telephone line to my first love. 'I Cannot Believe it's True' and 'Do You Know, Do You Care'. Were songs I lived daily. His cover of 'You Can't Hurry Love' was fun and offered us lovelorn folk hope of redemption.

Genesis

This self-titled album remains a classic for me today. Released in October 1983, it reminds me of a much happier time of my life. I had met a new girl and life was looking up as I would soon move to Edinburgh to start my Nursing course. The weird and wonderful 'Mama' was a breath of fresh air. 'Taking it all to Hard' and 'That's All' are beautiful and 'It's Gonna Get Better' offered all of us old romantics hope and redemption. I love all the songs on this album and thought the fun song 'Illegal Alien' should have been a big hit. It wasn't. It remains my favourite Phil Collins Genesis albums.

On My Own

With Bobby gone, it meant that I had two choices on a Friday night. Either stay in or go out by myself. I chose the latter. Having recently opened an account with Top Man in Carlisle, I had a couple of brand new 80s outfits to dazzle the female population and I thought that I looked hot! I was on the tail end of my long lovesick episodes with some days better than others. The good days began outweighing the bad!

After dinner, around 7 o'clock I would walk up that long road and visit a few pubs on my own. Usually, I would end up at the Blue Bell, where at least I could play pool. I didn't go to the Corner House Disco as I was slightly self-conscious of standing there like a lonesome serial killer.

It was through playing pool that I met some friends. There was this one guy who came to the pub every week with his wife, and we would play pool together and I got on well with him. He was a good guy, and we ended up becoming great pals.l. All these years later I'm still in touch with my old mate George Hurst and I'm godfather to his first daughter Megan. Through George I met his brother Willie and got on well with him too. It was not long before I would plan to meet George minus Irene, his lovely wife at the time! He would take me up to the Ex-Serviceman's club and there we could play pool and snooker. Occasionally with him and Irene we would go to a dance there. I liked it as I was used to seeing my Dad's band playing in social clubs.

Soon enough I was introduced to James Cochrane and Andrew Dalgliesh, who were best pals. Through a love of pool, snooker and beer, I got friendly with them. It took them a wee while to warm to me and they later told me that they used make jokes about my accent and hinted I might be gay! Their joke was that Raymond was 'fair smashing' in an effeminate voice. I promise you I didn't have that type of voice and never once said 'fair smashing'. I got on well with both of them in particular Andy who had a great sense of humour and was just a brilliant guy. I also got on well with James who had a girlfriend called Maria who later became his wife and is now Andy's wife! It's a long story and not mine to tell. Suffice it to say that I'm still friends with Andy and Maria. They made me the godfather of their gorgeous wee daughter Georgia and to me those two are a real shining example of an exemplary couple who are still madly in love with each other after all these years. They are my role models.

Getting ahead of myself there! The point I'm trying to make is that I now had friends who I could meet up with and go out drinking with and have a laugh with, so I was feeling pretty good as we headed into the summer of 1983.

Andy lived with his folks, and he owned that luxury item known as a video player. I believe it was a Ferguson. Home video renting was taking off, and it was the era of the 'video nasty'. Great fun. After a night of beer and pool he would invite us back to his place to watch a late-night movie. We took turns choosing the video from the rental place opposite The Blue Bell. I had the misfortune one night to choose a real duffer called 'Night of the Bloody Apes'. It was a terrible dubbed Italian movie about a guy who turned into a cross between an ape and a werewolf! The special effects were total crap, and it was only saved by some gratuitous nudity. They never let me forget that movie and both Andy and James had nicknamed me 'Nights Of'. We still laugh about it today.

New GF

Life was looking up in Annan. I was not constantly thinking about my old love and had a hope that I might meet someone new now that I was going out with a bunch of mates. With this new air of confidence, it did not take me too long to catch someone's eye. I had seen this blond girl before in the Corner House, but this time I noticed she was looking at me. I was there with the crowd and I didn't stand out like a sore thumb. Near the end of the night, I chatted with her and we seemed to hit it off. Her name was Etta, and she lived with her folks close to the Corner House. I being a gentleman offered to walk her home, and she accepted. It was a warm night as I walked the short distance to her house. As we reached her street, I saw a guy coming directly towards us; I thought he looked a wee bit odd. As he approached, it was obvious he knew Etta and as it turned out was her boyfriend. He was pretty upset about seeing her with me and she quickly made up the excuse that I was a cousin from Glasgow. I had no clue what was going on but felt it right that I should retreat. He was giving me daggers as I left, walking back up towards the High Street and home. In the distance I heard what I thought was a loud female laugh and for a microsecond I imagined it was Etta and her boyfriend laughing at me trying to 'get off' with her. Confused, I walked all the way home and kind of just accepted that I would not see her again.

The following week I met her again in the Corner House and she immediately apologised to me about what had happened. I told her I thought I had heard her laughing as I left; she replied that it was not her laughing but her screaming as her boyfriend had slapped her face! WTF? Done in a fit of jealousy and rage at her ending their relationship. He had tried to apologise, but this was the excuse she needed to get rid of him once and for all. From that night on Etta and I were an item, and it was not too long before I would fall in love again for the second time!

It was not the end for me and her ex-boyfriend, though. Two weeks later I was out in the Corner House with George, James and Andy. Luckily Etta had something else on so I wouldn't see her till the following day. There I was standing at the edge of the dance floor waiting for one of the boys to bring me a drink and looking at the people dancing. Suddenly, like the parting of the red sea, the crowd separated, and this angry-looking guy rushed towards me, intent on harming my personage. It all happened so quick that as he came close to me, I caught him with a solid punch on the side of the nose. He kind of fell into me and we started to scrap. Blood was coming from his nose and before too long the bouncers came and grabbed each of us. By this time, I was angry and trying my best to kick or punch him. I was wearing a light, capped sleeve t-shirt and a St Christopher necklace given to me by my sister Angela. As the bouncers pulled us apart, his hand ripped off my chain and the t-shirt off my shoulder. What a sight I must have been. They dragged me out to the lobby, and I was saying it was not my fault I was just defending myself. To no avail. They were chucking me out! I noticed that my shirt and arms had blood on them. Not mine, thankfully, and I asked if I could go to the toilet to wash. They let me clean myself up before escorting me off the premises. They didn't even let me get my jacket. There I was, standing outside, waiting for my pals, ripped t-shirt flapping in the warm night wind. They threw him out too and it was then I realised how drunk he was. He came at me again, but this time I got him in a neck hold and I told him I did not want to fight. He swung some more punches, and I pushed him away. He fell on his backside as my friends came outside with my jacket. This time he tried nothing again. We laughed about it all as I walked along the High Street. I was not hurt and, if I'm honest I kind of felt a wee bit sorry for the guy. He had just lost his girlfriend. To me!

Moving On

The rest of that summer in Annan was great. Etta and I became more serious, and we always wanted to be in each other's company. I was going out a lot more and coming back drunk as a skunk. Derek had this effin' burglar alarm system installed and if you did not make it quickly enough to the kitchen cupboard and disarm it then the thing lit up like a funfair and twice as noisy. When you're drunk your hand eye coordination is not great so the entire system would sound off until I eventually could silence it and then rearm it. As Etta stayed with her folks, I had to sneak her into my place. Then she would have to walk home in the very early morning and sneak up to bed without her folks hearing. There was a lot of sneaking going on!

My relationship with Derek was fraught as I wanted more freedom and basically did not want to work every day at Solway Bank. How it all went down is unclear, but we ended up having a massive fight and I packed my stuff and left. Luckily, I did not have that much stuff to pack! Mostly my cassette tapes. Where was I going? Where would I stay? I was just so annoyed that anywhere was better than being in the house with him. I walked up to Standalane where George and Irene lived and asked if I could stay in their spare room for a few days. A few days ended up being a few months!

Standalane

I spent the last few months in Annan at 100 Standalane. My friend George and his wife kindly put up with me and treated me like one of the family. That chest-nagging feeling had all but disappeared and I was determined to enjoy the last few months of freedom before my course started in February 84.

Etta and I were going strong and life, as they say, was rosy. I was signing on again at Annan 'bru' and the fact that George and Irene were providing me with rent-free accommodation and feeding me as well was a sign of just how good they were to me.

I spent most of my days playing snooker with James at the Ex-Service, and I spent my nights with Etta. I got into a lot of reading at night. Annan library was my supplier of books and I discovered Joseph Heller's 'Catch 22', one of the best and funniest books I have read. I slept late and woke up late.

Etta still lived at home, so I had to meet her parents. Her mother was sweet to me but her Dad, George was more reserved shall we say. The poor guy had all daughters, and I'm sure his experience dealing with Etta's older sister's admirers had jaded him somewhat. At least he would always say 'how do' if I passed him in the Ex-Serviceman's. That was all he said. They had this scary Alsatian dog who looked like he felt the same way as George did. Anytime I visited he gave me the evil eye! They also had a Mynah bird who spoke a lot. He liked me. I think!

Me and the boys had another fight incident one night, which began at the Corner House. James was at the bar when some young guy banged into him and spilled his drink. The youngster got a bit lippy, and I think James swatted him like an annoying fly. The guy and his pals were giving us looks all night. Nothing happened inside the disco, but later we all headed towards the Chinese Takeaway for some late night eats. As we arrived James noticed that the guy from earlier was inside with his pals. George went in to have a word with him. Not good. I prepared for the worst as I watched from outside of the glass door. George spoke for a few seconds and the next minute all hell broke loose! The fighting started inside and as I rushed to help, a swathe of bodies ended up on the pavement. Some guy grabbed me, and we struggled with each other. I might have landed a punch or two before George ran over and grabbed him off me with a fist to his face! Some bloke was wrestling with James and George went to the rescue. He's a wee guy, George, but he's wiry. Andy was half chasing some other teen who kept saying 'I don't want a fight'. Andy relaxed, and the guy threw a punch at him! People who we did not know were fighting. It was a Friday night melee! Soon enough the police came in a big van and started throwing bodies in the back. We all moved away and did our best to look innocent. The last thing I remember of that night was a lone takeaway lying on the pavement and a girl asking had anyone seen her boyfriend. He had apparently come out to watch the fight and was thrown into the police van. Minus his meal. Poor guy!

They reported the incident in the Annandale Observer. And the Police were quoted as saying that the fight was started by person or persons unknown. A couple of guys got charged with breach of the peace!

It was getting close to December by now and Etta, who worked in a travel agent in Carlisle, informed me that she had taken a job in Edinburgh and would start soon. I did not even know that she was looking for a job. It was great though because by that time we were mad about each other. She left Annan before me and found a room in a Leith Walk flat. A few weeks later I would leave Annan and join her as the flat had another room to let. I had officially moved to Edinburgh. It was near Christmas 1983.

Edinburgh

Leith Walk

I miss Edinburgh and as I'm typing this; I find it hard to believe that I have spent more time living in Saudi Arabia than I did in Auld Reekie!

From Annan I went home to Glasgow for a few days to pick up some stuff and get ready for my new life and new accommodation. The top-floor flat in which Etta had found me a room in was just opposite Pilrig Church. The owners were a young couple called the Flanagans. The rent would be 80 quid a month and they knew initially I would be 'signing on' and claiming rent allowance until I started working in February.

I arrived at St Andrew's bus station on a freezing winter night to be met by Etta. We jumped on a bus at York Place, which took us almost to my new front door! There was no intercom. We got a key for the main door. In Edinburgh tenements the front door could be opened by a lever placed on the wall of the landing in between the two apartments. This saved you walking all the way down to let in friends. Out of breath, we made it to the top, and opening the flat door I was shown into my new room. Before I had time to settle, I had to meet 'the landlords' they took me into their living room to go over the 'house rules'. Basically, just telling me that the only place that was 'off limits' was their living room! They also asked me to be respectful if coming in late as both of them worked! They were fine with the fact that for the next few months I would claim rent allowance from the council as they knew I would have my first pay by the end of February. It was a spacious enough flat that had three double bedrooms, a bathroom, a kitchen that had two box rooms off it. One was used as a dining area the other had a shower unit in it. My room had two single beds and looked onto Leith Walk! The Flanagan's bedroom was one side, and their living room was the other side, all looking onto the Walk. Etta's room was a twin-bedded room at the back! They knew that Etta and I were in a relationship and they were fine with that. That first night we were meeting up with Etta's roommate and her boyfriend for a night out at the Haymarket bar! I had only been to Edinburgh twice before, so it was all new to me! I remember it being freezing and it was a Friday night. The girl's boyfriend was from Edinburgh and he was a die hard 'Orangeman' and I think at that time the Haymarket was known to be a 'Protestant' pub nonetheless I settled in quickly enough.

Claiming housing allowance, I had to have my room inspected, and I remember the afternoon when the guy from the 'Social' came. He checked everything but kept asking me if I shared the room with anyone? I said no, but he persisted. I asked him outright, 'why do you think I'm sharing a room'? He looked down at the floor under the bed and he pointed to a pair of shoes? He said, 'I'm wondering why there are ladies' shoes under the bed'? Cheeky bastard, they were my shoes, and they were very fashionable at the time!

Skye's Neil McLennan and Duncan McDonald were staying near us in the fancily named 'Clifton Hotel' just off the Walk. This was a large townhouse that rented out all of its rooms and shared a bedroom. It was a bit of a flea pit, but it was great having them close.

With Etta working she wanted a room of her own and she found one in a big, shared flat on London Road! Her new flatmates were cool, and I spent most of my time there with her. It was great for me because they had a video player in their living room, which most of her flatmates rarely used She began in a twin-bedded room which was absolutely freezing as they had no central heating! Later on, to save money, she moved into a cosy wee room in the 'loft', Accessed by a wee set of stairs in the flat's lobby. I really liked that room as it was nice and tidy and did not feel as cold as the rest of the flat! In the better weather you could access the building's flat roof area to do a bit of sunbathing!

Those first 8 months in Edinburgh were a real blast and there was plenty of drinking done! I should have been less selfish with Etta as I spent a lot of time out with the boys! The Stage Door was our local as it was near to Etta's flat, there I drank a lot of Tennents and Tartan Special!

Around the spring of 1984 the Flanagan's flat on Leith Walk housed Ali, Neil, Duncan and me. All of us refugees from the Isle of Skye. Duncan and Neil shared the back bedroom, and they had a black and white portable that we used to watch Top of the Pops and The Tube! Both essential to us young yins! Duncan had this record player that would not always play, and you would have to tap furiously near the rpm selector to get it to work. Over time, it got worse, and I used to use my Denim deodorant bottle to bash the crap out of it so we could sing along to 'American Women' by Krocus! The flat owners told us that they were selling up and had bought a house in Cambridge Avenue, which is off Pilrig Street, close to our current abode. It was a terraced house on a street that none of us knew existed! They said that there would still be two rooms for us to rent, so we thought, why not? We helped with the 'flit' and as a reward Mr Flanagan who for some reason I was referring to as Flannagenie took us out to the pub and paid for the drink all night! Yaas!

Neil did not move to Cambridge Avenue, only Ali, Dunc and me! The house was OK, but the bedrooms were smaller! Dunc was on his own, but Ali and I still shared a room. The only bonus of the new place was that it had a basement and Flannagenie had installed a snooker table! It was not full size, but it was of an excellent quality, so we spent a lot of time there playing snooker!

Etta had moved to a small flat above the Volunteer Arms on Leith Walk, which along with the Golden Lion became our 'local'.

In the 'Volley' you could get a game of pool. I became good friends with a couple that moved into Etta's old London Road flat. The girl was a nurse (whose name escapes me) and her boyfriend was an Australian named Steve. He was some bloke! Very personable and well-liked by everyone he met! They eventually moved to a flat near the New Kirkgate at the bottom of the 'Walk'. They invited me to attend their wedding reception and the standout memory of that was a very drunk Steve who was kitted out in a kilt, flashing his tackle to his mother-in-law! The look on her face was truly priceless!

Peter Gabriel 4/Security

The first time I heard this album was on a tape made for me by one of Etta's flatmates when she lived on London Road. It was not the full album as it cut out halfway through 'Lay Your Hands On Me'. I was unfamiliar with Mr Gabriel's solo work and had only heard 'Games Without Frontiers' a few years earlier. I still had heard none of his work with Genesis. Released in 1982 this album had not registered with me at all but once I heard it everything changed. I was totally hooked and ended up having a real obsession with his music. A watershed album that saw him move in a different direction with the use of a Fairlight sample machine and a lot of electronic gizmos. From 'San Jacinto' to 'The Rhythm of the Heat' this album sounded like an electronic tribal extravaganza. I love the touching 'Wall Flower'. I spent months trying to do the hand claps along with 'The Family and the Fishing Net'. My musical taste buds got a new education with this record. I did eventually buy it and got to hear 'Lay Your Hands On Me' in full. I loved it. I love it still.

Selling England by the Pound

The reason I did not hear the full version of PG's 'Lay your Hands On Me' was because Etta's flatmate had also included this Genesis Album on the same tape. This was the first time I had heard Peter sing with them. It was love at first listen. Hard to believe they released it way back in 1973. 'Dancing with the Moonlit Knight', 'I Know What I Like' and Phil Collins touchingly sung, 'More Fool Me' just sucked me into the world of Prog rock. I'm not saying I love all of PG's Genesis albums, but I love the guy's voice. His lyrics. His gift for telling a story that can move you to tears. The man is an effin' legend.

Can't Slow Down

Already a big Commodores fan, it did not take much for me to fall in love with Lionel Ritchie's solo album. Who the hell does not love the song 'Hello'? Neil and Duncan, my then flatmates, bought me this for my 1984 birthday. Thanks, guys. 'All night Long' and the Eddie Van Halen riffed 'Running with the Night' along with Lionel's brilliant voice have made this one of my favourite solo albums. Ever.

First Day at College

At the beginning of February, I was poised to start my Nursing career at North Lothian College of Nursing and Midwifery, which was attached to the Western General Hospital. Back in the 1980s, they trained student nurses at their hospitals and paid a salary. The training would take over three years to complete and comprised theoretical work in the classroom and then actual work in the wards. The longest period of classroom time was about to start for me as I left my Leith Walk flat, hopped on a maroon bus to the West End and from there jumped on another Lothian bus to Crewe Road and the Western General Hospital. I was nervous but also excited. I had been waiting nearly two years since my application and interview.

I walked towards the then Nurses' accommodation as the College occupied one wing of this at the far end. Later on, a purpose-built College opened on Crewe Road near to the Royal Victoria Hospital. The February 84 set gathered for the first time in a classroom. The class was quite big, with over twenty females and three males (including me). The first day was taken up with orientation and stuff like that. The other two guys, Colin and Neil, and I got to know each other. Colin was a 'mature' student and a former carpenter who decided to retrain. Neil was fresh out of High School. Both were from Edinburgh.

They had given us guys the keys to an empty bedroom that we could use as a locker room. For those who remember the old building, our room was down the stairs opposite the TV lounge. It only had a bed and a sink in it, but that's where we spent our break times after lunch, and any other free time.

Most of the girls were around the same age as Neil. Most had recently finished High School although a couple like me had applied in 1982 and had to wait!

We spent approximately 12 weeks in the classroom, as I remember, and it was pretty intense. I always sat at the front of the class and soon reverted to type when I became the class joker! What I remember most was taking loads and loads of notes, none of which I ever used when studying!

At lunchtime we would all go to the Hospital cafeteria and, as this would be my main meal of the day, I always ate a main course and a dessert. I was very thin at the time and some of the girls in class asked me if I had been ill? I told them that I had only been lovesick! Smoking was permitted in the lounge section of the cafeteria, but as I was trying to quit, I would only sit there occasionally and ask someone for a 'drag' or two. Colin smoked and occasionally I would cadge a fag from him when we were in our 'room' but generally throughout my Nursing career I tried not to smoke as I did not like to face the patients smelling of smoke!

Many times, in our wee 'locker' room I would have a nap until afternoon classes would resume.

It really was just like being back at school again. Most of the tutors were female, and nearly all of them had no sense of humour. One of the tutors was Harry who had interviewed me. At least he had a sense of humour! I think it was during that first 'block' of classes we met the equivalent of our 'form Teacher', Muriel Webster. She was a short lady with frizzy hair and a warm smile who named our set 'Fab Feb 84'. She was a brilliant teacher and advisor and as a bonus she had a wonderful sense of humour! Over our training years she attended some of our class 'nights out'! Thanks for being a great tutor, Mrs Webster!

Near the end of the 12 weeks, we all had to don our uniforms and go into the hospital to learn how to make beds. Us guys had these three-quarter length 'Dentist jacket's' and I remember feeling a bit of a knob as we walked through that long corridor in the hospital, with many eyes looking at the 'fresh meat'. I believe we went to an empty room in the Radiotherapy unit to practice our bed making skills. Having worked at Uig Hotel for three seasons I was pretty experienced in tucking sheets under mattresses. How serious we all were when the Clinical Tutor was explaining about draw sheets, counterpanes and blankets!

I got on well with most of the girls in my class and I remain in touch via Facebook with a few till this day, but I lost touch with Colin years ago and ultimately Neil dropped out of school. Our classroom time was almost up and according to our schedule half of us would be distributed to Medical wards and the other to Surgical wards either at The Western, The Northern or The Eastern General Hospitals in Edinburgh. My first ward was to be a surgical ward in The Western.

D1

I was incredibly lucky when I was assigned to Ward D1 in the Western General. I could not have hoped for a better first ward. How that experience helped me through more challenging future experiences is difficult to express in words, but it really helped save my nursing career!

My first shift was a late one from 1pm till 9pm. I was still living on Leith Walk and sharing a room with Ali Aitken. Ali had a ten-speed bike which he let me use, so every day my journey began by cutting across Leith Walk and on to Pilrig Street. I pedalled all the way to Queensferry Road until I hit the Crewe Road roundabout, then it was down Crewe Road to the Western. They allowed you to store your bike under the Paderewski building near the hospital's entrance. This building is also where they had a sewing room, and you could go there to get your uniforms altered. Strange when I think about it now, but I have absolutely no memory where I changed out of my grey 'joggy' bottoms bought from Top Man on Prince's Street. I remember the nervous walk to D Block finally to D1 where I entered and took a deep breath.

D1 was a male surgical ward specialising in the likes of Crohn's disease and other inflammatory bowel conditions. It was a typical 'Nightingale ward' with around eight beds on each side separated by a communal dining table and a small nurse's station. At the far end were the toilets and bathrooms, and to one corner was the sluice room, which I would become intimately familiar with!

As you walked into the ward on the right-hand side was 'Sister's' office, which is where I stood to announce myself. The Sister was a tall slim lady probably in her late thirties to early forties named Sister Annis. She was a bit posh and quite stern. The second thing she said to me after saying hello was that I should not be wearing slip-on shoes to work. I had no choice as the only black shoes I had to go with my black trousers and white Dentist jacket were a cheap pair of slip-on's purchased awhile back from Curtis Shoes in Glasgow. I explained to her that I planned to buy a fresh pair of laced shoes with my first salary! She looked me up and down and then called a Staff Nurse to show me around.

D1 also had a nice sun lounge for the patients which had a pool table in it. Cool! There were three Staff Nurses in D1: Karen, Joan and the other (whose name slips my mind), were incredibly kind to me and really helped me settle in. Their three faces are clear in my mind's eye today.

Sister Annis was tough but fair and I think that she secretly liked me. She never showed it though. The main tasks of Student Nurses were to make the beds, wash the patients, feed them and do the 'obs'- meaning check their pulse, BP and so on. Sister would check the beds and give her nod of approval if they were made to her high standards.

'Mr Moore,' she would call. 'Would you care to check the corner of this bed that you have just finished making,' she'd say. This meant to make the bed again, but this time do it right!

Being a 'bowel' ward, we dealt with a lot of poop! Well, when I say we, I mean the most junior student dealt with the poop and that student was me!

We collected faecal fat collections over days. The patients would leave their 'gift' in a bedpan that had their name on it, and I would have to place this in a specimen bag and transport it to their container, which looked like a paint tin. There was a load of bed pans to be cleaned (by me) every day! Luckily, we had an automated bedpan washing machine that did a decent enough job. Once cleaned I would rack them to let dry and then they were ready to use again! We used a fair bit of bowel prep (preparing one's colon for surgery) too, and in particular one called 'Picolax' which was basically bowel dynamite! Sometimes the results were splattered up the toilet cubicle wall and it was up to me to clean it up! I constantly had the smell of poop in my nose. Great fun!

Sluice duties did not really bother me, in fact I did not mind any of the jobs they tasked me with. I can still picture the first patients I looked after as they were ward regulars, I even remember some of their names!

About halfway through my stint on D1 there was a planned closure of D2, which was the female ward opposite! They would transfer the female patients to D1 and distribute the males to the upstairs ward like D4 and D6. As I was the only male Nurse on the ward, I was asked if I wanted to work upstairs in the other male wards. I did not want to leave my Staff Nurses, so they allowed me to stay and help look after the females. We really had a brilliant laugh with the ladies, and most did not mind a male looking after them – even if this involved helping to give them a bed bath! I will never forget being told by this elderly spinster (who was on morphine), that in the evenings, outside her window, there was a naked man showing off his undercarriage! It was so funny to hear her talk about it and we did our best to let her know that although we were on the ground floor; the windows were not accessible because of a basement floor beneath us. I don't think she believed me!

Another 'Student Nurse' job was to go round at night before shift's end and serve hot drinks from a trolley. Apart from tea, we would also serve 'Camp' coffee. They allowed certain patients a wee tin of 'Sweetheart Stout'!

Patients who had planned bowel surgery had to be put on a 'low residue' diet. This type of diet left little to anything in the bowel and by that, I mean poop! Those on this diet had the option of iced water flavoured with 'Krusha', this was a low residue fruit flavoured powder.

D1 was the unit that I saw my first dead body. It was of an old guy who I did not know very well and who I had not looked after. He passed away in his sleep. I was taken by one of my Staff Nurses and we did my first 'Last Offices' which was preparing the body for collection and sending to the mortuary. Dead bodies never really bothered me throughout my career. What was important was to comfort those who were on the verge of death.

My three-month stint in D1 passed very quickly, and then it was time for my evaluation. We received an 'Interim' evaluation about halfway through placement and then a final evaluation at the end of the three months. You could fail the interim evaluation without too much pain but if you failed the final evaluation, they put you back a class! If you failed again, then you were off the course! Luckily, both my interim and final evaluations were extremely good. The Staff Nurse evaluating me documented my first Cardiac Arrest and how well I had done with assisting during it. They however neglected to mention that in my nervous excitement to bring the 'crash' trolley, I had also brought the light source for the rigid colonoscope! What use that would be during an emergency, I have no clue! I was sad to leave Sister Annis and D1 but happy that it was a really positive experience (not all of my clinical placements would be so good).

As a treat, the Staff Nurses took me out to the Pear Tree after our early shift and we all got drunk into the night! I have a vague memory of staggering to a bus stop and getting back to my Leith Walk flat just in time to watch 'Alien' on the black and white portable TV we all shared.

❧

First Gigs

From the fourth year at Portree High School, I had been a big fan of Ali Aitken's music after he surprised me that not only could he play the guitar but that he also wrote and sung his own stuff! It was very cool! On a Friday afternoon in fifth Year, even though Ali had left, we used to get together with him in a room in the 'Boys Hostel'. There would be Ali, Duncan, Jimmy and Neil and I. We would have 'jam session'. I would just sit there and sing along to the choruses. I had written this simple song called 'You're a Friend' and Ali had made it into a very nice wee ditty.

My favourite memory of that time was late one Friday afternoon we were all in that wee room and we were graced with the presence of the lovely Maggie Gunn and Lorna Cormack. Both sang the chorus of my song with Ali. It was pretty moving, and we caught it on tape, which I have, but it's in a box with other demos and with my brother in Glasgow. It was getting close to 4 o'clock and all our buses were beckoning, but we kept jamming. Neil put the 10-watt guitar amplifier on his shoulders, still plugged in and pretended to leave the room. It remains a beautiful musical memory.

Before I became a band manager, I had orchestrated Ali's first two 'solo' gigs. Through a friend of mine in Uig who had heard a tape of some of Ali's songs, I managed to get him a spot at a 'folk club' at the Skeabost Hotel on Skye. It was a winter's evening when we arrived at the venue. Cold and dark! It was a small intimate setting and Mr Aitken was very nervous. I was also nervous for him! He got up on stage and he played a few of his songs and one of mine. The crowd realising it was not strictly 'folk' gave him a warm reception! I know afterwards he was glad that he done it. There was a West Highland Free Press contributor there to review the night and her remarks about Ali were all positive and she described the set being finished by the song 'a poignant' 'You're a Friend'. He was pleased, and I was proud.

Fast forward a couple of years when Ali and I shared the room in the Flannagenie's Leith Walk flat. I was always pushing him to do some 'solo' gigs. We did not have a proper demo tape, just a recording that he had made at home himself. I took it to a few pubs, hoping they would give him a chance. It was difficult, but eventually a small bar on the High Street called Clowns gave him an evening spot in their wee back room. We were all excited about it. A flat mate of Etta's had made a laminated poster which had a black-and-white photo that I had taken of Ali under a bridge in Glendale. Why? I don't know. It might have been the only hard copy we had!

I had asked Etta's flatmate to put on the poster 'Ali Aitken' underneath that, 'The Word is Out'. There was a space to write the venue name at the bottom and we stuck a few of them up in the pub and around about Edinburgh.

Clowns was a tiny bar that had an even smaller gig room! They did have a small P.A. though, so that was cool. Few people showed up to the gig. Only some friends and the Flannagenie's! Ali did a great job entertaining us as the rest of the world ignored him and his excellent songs. Even I got up and did a couple of 'numbers' with him! The only one I remember was a drunken version of Peter Gabriel's 'Biko'!

By the time we got back to Leith Walk, we were all 'steamin'! The Flannagenie's invited us into their living room and the husband broke out a bottle of his homemade red wine. Which we all drank! I had to work the next day and remember that I had a stinking hangover throughout my late shift.

Soul Mining

We were at a party in the Marchmont flat of our old school friend Archie McGhee when he played The The's Soul Mining. Heavily under the influence of beer and smoke, I could not take my ears off it. When Jools Holland's piano solo kicked in on 'Uncertain Smile' it memorized me. I was gone, man. It was music magic. 'That Sinking Feeling' and 'This is the Day' were the icing and the cherry on the musical cake. It was a beautifully wondrous aural experience. I mean it, man!

To Skye

Etta and I made one trip to Linicro when we were together. I think she enjoyed it. We stayed in the caravan with my cousin Bobby. The weather was decent, so I got to show her the sights and most evenings we spent in the Ferry Inn.

It was from the Ferry Inn that we three got invited to a party in Glen Conon, and it was full of the usual faces. There were some doobies being puffed and as I was drinking, I gracefully refused. As we were leaving, I was handed something small and was told to smoke when I was sober! By the time we made it back to Linicro it was early Sunday morning, and we crashed out. We were all hung-over the next day, so there would definitely be no drinking on the Sabbath.

It was in the evening that I remembered the small parting 'gift' I was given, and I fished it out of my pocket. It was a blackish substance that was malleable. I showed it to Bobby and asked if he knew how to doobie up? He did, but there were no papers. He said he had a pipe and produced this soap stone pipe in the shape of a penis. Yep, you put the burning stuff in the ball sack and sparked up. This we did, and I took a few puffs. I was totally inexperienced in such things. After everyone took a puff, we just waited to see what would happen. What happened was the worst night of my effin' life! I felt absolutely awful. I was in the vice like grip of 'the fear' (as experienced by I in the cracking movie Withnail and I). My heart was pumping ten to the dozen. Bobby was zombified but calm. Etta looked out of it but ok. I got up and immediately fell on to our fold down bed. My heartbeat was that strong that I thought that it was making the whole caravan shake. All I could do was wish for it to end! What the hell was that stuff we puffed? I raised my head and saw that Etta had disappeared. Where had she gone? My mind was racing. I had this deep fear that she had walked over to the wee hoose and was talking to my Aunt about life, the universe, everything! It panicked me. I pleaded with Bobby to go and find her. He staggered out the door and after a few minutes returned. I asked, 'did you find her?'. He said yes. I asked where is she and he said, 'I don't know'. My heart began running again. I was convinced she was in talking to my Aunt and I believed Margaret would see that she was out of her mind! Please make it all stop. I prayed. Eventually Etta came back in and had told us she had just went for a walk on the road. At least with her in my sights I felt a wee bit better, but not much! Man, it took hours for the effect of that stuff to wear off and for my heartbeat to return to normal.

Never again I said although I laugh about it now!

John Martyn

Did I just say 'never again?' This first gig I went to in Edinburgh was to see Glasgow's John Martyn at the Queens Hall. I'm more a fan of him now than I was back then, but it was a night out with the boys. Along with me, Ali and Neil had tickets, and we were meeting my classmate Colin in the Queens bar.

As we made ourselves relatively presentable someone had sparked up a doobie (and I don't mean brothers). I was not particularly experienced in the way of the weed but as I smoked cigarettes; I took a puff or two (maybe three). Big effin' mistake! Everything was going fine. We were walking to the bus stop on Leith Walk and we hopped on a bus to the Southside. We had just sat down upstairs when I felt 'the fear' come over me (again). Not being used to smoking, I had what was commonly known as a 'whitey'! I felt bloody awful. Totally panicked. Being a guy, I did not want to show this to my friends who were having a lot better time than me. I went from fear to paranoia and back to fear as if on a mind roller coaster. Hiding my 'whitey' from my pals was making it worse. Every single bus stop till the Queens Hall I wanted to get off to try to calm myself down. I couldn't though. I gripped the metal bar of the seat in front of me and tried to ride through it. The bus finally stopped, but the site of the crowds going into the Queens Hall amplified the fear. Someone had turned it up to 11. I was up for running all the way home and hiding under my bed, but I soldiered on bravely. It was not easy. We made for the bar and I thought that a couple of drinks would calm me down. We met Colin there and started on the beer. I think I was chatting with Colin for about half an hour, not hearing one word he was saying. My brain was at war with the whitey. My heart pumping piston like and about to chest burst. It was time to be seated and our chairs were right in front of the stage. This made me feel worse. I sat down and breathed. The band came on and as soon as the music played, the fear I was feeling for the last hour slowly dissipated. The music won the whitey battle for me. I was Zen calm and really enjoyed that whole concert.

In the bar after the gig, I was back to normal. I had to admit to Colin that I really had no clue about what we talked about earlier because of my condition. He just laughed.

Ward 6

After another classroom stint, my second placement was Medical, and I was lucky to get Ward 6 Male medical at the Eastern General Hospital on Seafield Road. This was my first time at the Eastern, but it would not be my last and mostly I really enjoyed all my placements there. At the Eastern I learned to love smaller hospitals, although compared to my current hospital in Saudi Arabia the Eastern General was massive!

I was still riding my borrowed bike and would bomb down Leith Walk, turn towards Leith Links and then onto Seafield Road. We had a locker room that was in one outbuilding close to the main Seafield Road Entrance.

When originally typing this I could not for the life of me remember the name of the Sister of Ward 6 who had short fair hair and glasses. I can see her clear as day in my mind. She was quiet but very nice. Recently I joined a Facebook 'Edinburgh Memories' group and was sharing some thoughts about working at the Eastern. My post got a lot of rseponses from former Eastern staff. I put out a plea for Ward 6's Sister's name and I got the answer...Pat McGhee. Thank you, Sister McGhee.

Ward 6 was a general Medical Unit, and it shared a Cardiac High Dependency called 'The Link' with the Female Ward 7. The link had four cubicles and Ward 6 had around 20 beds. The Sister's office, where we would get our reports, looked on to Seafield Road and the Firth of Forth beyond. Outside the office there were three beds that were reserved for those patients needing the most observations. Going towards 'The Link' there was a room with about six beds, and these were occupied by patients who needed the most nursing care – usually, those who had had strokes. Going the other way passed the office was another four bedded bay. You then went out the door towards the stairs and there was a two bedded room, which was mostly kept for terminal cases. A six bedded bay right at the back and furthest away from the Office was meant for patients about to be discharged home.

All the Staff were very kind to me in Ward 6 and and I enjoyed my time there. Most of the hard work was done in the bay with the stroke patients. I swear I can still see the two Georges. One bedridden the other semi-mobile both having had bad strokes. I remember the frustration we nurses would feel with the semi-mobile George as we thought he could physically do more. We would spend a significant amount of time trying to stop him from going back to his bed. His wife was also frustrated with him too. I understand now that the stroke really changes your personality, and it was not all George's fault. In fact, I see things similar with my Dad, Big Gerry, who had a dense stroke. So George, if you're out there in the ether, I'm sorry for getting on at you so much all those years ago. We had another stroke patient who took the place of the bedridden George when he passed. The bed was almost still warm, such was the number of strokes in Scotland.

The face of the new patient I can still see. He was a Lothian Bus Driver who had a very dense stroke and who was completely paralysed down one side and unable to talk, but he would try his best to help you with anything. Whether it was having a bath or just sitting up, he would always try to assist you.

Ward 6 was the first Ward that I had to do mouth to mouth resuscitation and CPR. This was exciting, if a little nerve-wracking. This was when we really did mouth to mouth without a barrier! It was also one of the few times that I saw a patient who had 'arrested', successfully resuscitated, and who ultimately was discharged home.

The Eastern had a few characters who worked there, one being Miss Reid who was a rather serious (and slightly scary) looking 'Nursing Officer' in charge of the Medical Wing. She would often do rounds and grab a student who would then have to give her a verbal report on the patients that they were looking after. Many a time I would hear 'Mr Moore, come tell me about your patients'. She looked scary but had a very good heart. Her comment about me to the Sister McGhee has always stuck with me when asked to give some feedback about my verbal reports she described me as 'pale but interesting'!

One thing I learned and put to good use in all the hospitals that I worked was to be nice to the cafeteria staff (also to the housekeeping staff, the porters and the storemen)! It was no different at the Eastern where the staff knew me well and I would always have a laugh with them. They all thought that I was far too thin, and my portions of food were always very generous. Out of all North Lothian Hospitals the Eastern served the best food! I'm not saying it was restaurant standard, more akin to school dinners. But it was the best, and I always left with a full stomach!

A very special 'one off' type of event happened in Ward 6, which was very special. When I think back, I'm amazed that we pulled it off. In the two-bedded side room we had this very special old lady who was terminally ill. She really was a beautiful soul who faced her last days very bravely and with a sense of humour! It turned out her son was a well-known composer of film and TV music (I had never heard of him) and his kids were all musicians. He came to me and asked if there was any way that we could arrange a wee 'concert' for the patients? I thought this was a brilliant idea and suggested we could use the back room, which had no patients. I went to Sister McGhee and told her of the offer and to my surprise she immediately agreed. The grandkids came in the early evening and set up their gear in the back bed bay. They had keyboards and guitars and a small PA. We gathered as many patients as we could find from the both the male and the female ward, and the grandmother took pride of place in the middle! It was a truly magical, if slightly surreal experience having this three-piece band do a set in the ward.

The music was not loud and the look of pride on their Granny's face made it all worth it. The Nurses enjoyed the music more than the patients, I think! Imagine trying to get permission to do that now? The grandmother passed away peacefully, surrounded by her loved ones a few weeks later. For me, her face and her family will never leave my mind!

I would soon leave the Eastern General to go back to class to prepare for my next placement, which was geriatrics, split between the Northern General and The Royal Victoria Hospital. I would return to the Eastern a few more times during my training, though.

1984 was ending, and I had been very fortunate to have had two excellent experiences in both Surgical and Medical wards. Some of my class were not so lucky – and I wouldn't be so lucky in other placements! The fact that my first year had been so positive gave me an inner strength that I was to call upon during more challenging future placements. I have all the staff and patients to thank for these memories and although their names might be long gone from my brain, their faces are not.

∽

Heartache No 2

Since my arrival in 'Auld Reekie' I had really enjoyed myself. Going out with the boys, getting drunk, all that good stuff. I was really 'into' my course at college and was doing well. Life was peachy, as they say. But as the end of the year approached, things between Etta and I went awry. She had a change of heart and I don't blame her. I behaved very selfishly throughout our relationship and many times treated her not particularly well. During our time together I often behaved like a single guy and did what single guys do. I was too immature to be in a relationship and she suffered a lot, so it was no surprise that things changed regarding her feelings towards me.

She had begun her Psychiatric Nurse training and was staying at the Nurses' accommodation in the Royal Edinburgh Hospital. She had new friends and was enjoying her course which I totally understand now but back then it was all 'me me me!' Two funny things happened that I want to share. Though they were not funny at the time. One night I had been trying to call Etta. I suspected that she was seeing someone, so with no answer to my calls I made my way to her Royal Edinburgh accommodation. Someone let me in the main door and as I went to her room, I fully expected to find her inside with another guy! She was not in. Where could she be? It was getting late, and I had a decision to make. Wait for her and miss my bus back to Cambridge Avenue or just go home. I should have gone home. I sat in the TV lounge and waited and waited. I eventually fell asleep on the sofa and woke up around 6 AM. Immediately I went to check on her room and she was still not back. She probably spent the night with the guy, I thought as I sheepishly made my way out of the Nurses' home. Walking towards Morningside Road who should appear in front of me but my girlfriend. She looked shocked and surprised to see me! She told me she had been out clubbing with her friends, which I chose to believe. I had used the same type of excuse with her many a time before. The writing was definitely on the relationship wall.

Another night someone had told me that all the nurses go to this bar opposite the Hermitage Bar on Morningside Road. Now called 'The Waiting Room' I thought Etta would be there with her new beau, so I planned to go and confront them! It a long bus ride from Leith Walk to the bottom of Morningside Road. During that ride I went over in my mind what I was going to do and say! I must have looked like a crazy person sitting alone on the top deck. Eventually I got off and walked towards said pub. I was all puffed up and ready for action. The bouncers would not let me in the front door! I pleaded with them. I told them I was meeting my girlfriend inside, but no was their answer. I asked if I could go inside just to give her a message. Another big no and I was told to eff off! She might not have even been in the place, I just guessed. Crestfallen I sat, a lonely soul, and bussed back to Leith Walk and my empty room!

The Northern

I can't say that the Christmas of 1984 was a particularly joyful time for me. My relationship with my girlfriend was, as Neil Diamond sang, 'on the rocks'! I had also begun a placement in a long-term care of the elderly ward at the Northern General on

Queensferry road. I would not say that the staff were not nice to me, just that they were not as warm as my previous encounters in other hospitals. My mood was very low and the work each day was very heavy. It was a large unit with probably 30 beds and most of the patients were bedridden and incontinent. I spent most of my time doing toilet rounds and feeding these unfortunate elderly ladies and gentlemen.

I'm not saying that it was totally horrendous and there were some highlights but cycling in the dead of winter from Leith Walk to Ferry Road was not what I would call fun and each shift produced very little respite for the nursing staff.

On a positive note, during the morning bed baths and bed making, they allowed us to have a radio on the 'back trolley' which we tuned to Radio One with Simon Bates. We all liked to hear his 'your song' segment, which contained a sad story sent in by a listener and a song at the end which had some special meaning. One story brought me to tears (I was emotional because of my failing relationship). In a nutshell, the story was about a young couple who had been trying to conceive for a long time with little success. Eventually they got pregnant and had a baby. Not long after the birth, the father was diagnosed with a terminal illness and ultimately passed away. It was the wife who had written into Simon with her story and the song played at the end was Cliff Richard singing 'Daddy's Home'! I was in floods of tears after that! Every time I hear that song, I'm reminded of that cold winter morning in the Northern.

Six weeks of back-breaking work could not end fast enough for me. There was however one other incident that happened that was pretty funny. We had just served the evening meals and were preparing to feed our patients when there was a power cut. Emergency lighting came on, but it was hardly bright! It seemed to be an age before the lights came back on and when they did it revealed utter chaos. The patients who could feed themselves had tried to eat their dinner during the 'blackout', most were unsuccessful in their endeavour and there was food absolutely everywhere except in their mouths! We spent the rest of the shift cleaning up! I was happy to leave that Hospital, never to return during the rest of my training.

The Vickie

I had spent some time at the Royal Victoria Hospital's geriatric assessment unit in early 1985 and I was to return there for the summer working in the Psyche/Geriatric unit. This was to be my only experience caring for 'psychiatric' patient's during my training. Most of the patients had dementia but had behavioural problems which made them more difficult to monitor! By this time I had moved out of the Cambridge Avenue house and got a room at the Royal Vic's Nurses home.

This was a decent place by Nurse's accommodation standards with sizeable rooms and not too many people living in the building. Unfortunately, I really only have terrible memories of there as by this time Etta and I were pretty much finished. We had tried a couple of times to make a go of it, but I think she was just trying to let me down easy. The last night we spent together was at the Victoria Nurses home, but the evening did not start well as we had not planned it. I laugh now when I think about it, but at the time it was the opposite of funny.

This night I had been out with Colin from my class for a couple of beers and was waiting at the West End for a bus to Crewe Road. I can't remember the name of the pub right beside the bus stop, and it probably changed many times over the years, but then it was like a fancy 80s 'wine bar'. As I waited for my bus who should walk out of this bar hand in hand with a guy? Yep, my girlfriend! I was in shock. I did not know what to do. She did not see me, and I nearly let her go but didn't. I confronted both of them and nearly got into a fight with the guy. Etta eventually told the guy to go and came back with me to 'talk' about where our relationship was going. Soon after, we broke up for good.

Later on, in the summer I met up with her, and her new boyfriend, named Ray! We had a good night and by then I realized that I was over the heartache. We saw each other sporadically throughout the 1980s and then lost contact. We reconnected through Facebook and I'm happy we did. We remain in contact till this very day.

At the time everything was more than a bit depressing! At least I did not have far to go to work. The unit staff were OK if not overly friendly. This unit was 'locked' to stop patients from wandering off. To make matters worse, the food in the cafeteria was the worst I had ever experienced. Ever.

Unhappy with my life and with my work that summer I was not at my cheeriest (it had a happy ending, though). Only two things of note happened that I wish to document. This was the first (and last) place that I looked after a patient who received Electro-Convulsive Therapy (ECT) and unlike 'One Flew over the Cuckoo's Nest' it was done with care. The patient was an old lady with a bi-polar disorder that had slowly gotten worse over several weeks! Nearly every morning I would be greeted by her fully dressed and ready to leave as she told me that she had to 'go to a funeral'. When I asked, 'whose funeral?' She would say, her own. She would not rest and did not sleep. They gave her ECT during which we sedated the patient and after a few zaps she was returned to her bed for monitoring. It was quite incredible the difference in her condition. She was back to her 'normal' self. I used her as my course 'case study' (which I passed)! Again, as with many of my former patients I have no memory of her name, but I can see her face very clearly.

The only other thing of note was 'Live Aid'. This concert took place on a perfect summer day and I was working a late shift! The unit had a TV lounge, and I did tune in to try and see some of the concert, but every time I left to do some work, when I came back someone had changed the effin' channel. The lounge also had a 'music centre', with a radio and cassette recorder. I had brought a blank tape and as the Live Aid concert was being broadcast on the radio, and I recorded it. I returned to the nurses' home to watch the last of the show on the box in the shared lounge, alone.

After finishing my placement at the Royal Victoria, I had to move out of the Nurses' home and move to the Western's Nurses' home. Where thankfully all my memories are good ones. Neil McLennan came to help me shift my gear, which comprised some clothes in two plastic bags and a record player belonging to my ex. We carried all of it on foot to my new room on the third floor of my new accommodation.

Fugazi

My heart was broken again when Etta left me. My life was pretty bleak for a while, housed in that room in the Royal Victoria's it felt like a cell and I was a prisoner of love (gone wrong). One of my saviours was Marillion's second album, Fugazi. How many lonely nights the songs on this record got me through? Many is the answer! 'She Chameleon', captured my feelings completely. 'Assassing' and 'Incubus' are epic, and the album is completed with the desperation of the title track. This is still a standout musical work, and it sounds fabulous today.

Peter Gabriel 1/Car, 2/Melt, 3/Scratch

Those lonely weekends feeling sorry for myself were made much more comforting by these three friends who soothed my aching soul. I was obsessed with Gabriel and his lyrics. 'Modern Love' and 'Humdrum' helped me through some bad days. 'Here Comes the Flood' and 'Dolce Vita' got me through the long nights. 'White Shadow' is effin' awesome. 'DIY' and 'On the Air' great to sing-along to. And I'm not ashamed to admit that I cried to 'Flotsam and Jetsam' and 'Home Sweet Home'. I realised that fear was the 'Mother of Violence'. From 'Scratch', 'And through the Wire' offered me hope with that rocking Paul Weller riff. 'No Self Control' and Intruder' comforted me once more. 'Lead a Normal Life' made my eyes moist. Peter Gabriel's first four solo albums are just so damn important to me and my life. They are akin to living organs. My organs. And I'm not donating them to anyone!

Home for Nurses

I shifted accommodation from the Royal Victoria Nurses' Home to the Western's Nurse Accommodation at the beginning of September 1985. Life was looking better after spending the last six months feeling sorry for myself and being lovesick. My new room was on the top floor of the main building and comprised a bed, a bedside table, some cupboards and a sink. Along the corridor to one end were shared toilets and bathrooms. There was also a wee room that held a fridge freezer! To the other end of the corridor was the kitchen and right at the end was a coin operated telephone. It was not much, but it was warm and did not take much effort to keep clean. On the lower ground floor there was a TV lounge and a table tennis table. I seemed to be the only person making use of the TV. I soon decided that I wanted a TV in my room, but as I didn't have a lot of cash, I opted to 'rent' a 14-inch colour portable from 'Radio Rentals'. Life was good! I was the only guy on my floor, and I think at that time there were only two or three guys in the entire building. Initially, we all had a front door key. Later they introduced a new electronic lock which accepted a 'key card'.

One night, not too long after the installation of the electronic lock, I came home a wee bit tipsy only to realise that I had left my card in my room. I think there was a bell which I rang and above me a night housekeeper opened the window and asked me what I wanted? I told her that I wanted in to go to my bed. She did not recognize me or believe that I was a resident and thought I was the boyfriend of one of the female students. I showed her my room key, but she suggested that my girlfriend might have thrown from her window. I then told her to check my room number and to see my name there. After about ten minutes, she came down and let me in. The irony being that in a home full of young women; the place was a den of iniquity. I was the only one behaving myself!

Ali Aitken returned to Edinburgh after spending time on Skye making a cassette album with Derek MacLennan in Broadford. It was called 'Moth to Light' and had some superb tunes on it.

He came to stay on my bedroom floor until he could find more permanent 'digs'. I think most of the Nurses' home residents thought he was my boyfriend!

It was around this time he purchased a Carlsbro PA speaker system and amplifier and a new electric guitar from a music shop in Stockbridge. These new toys stood proud in my wee bedroom corner for a good couple of weeks. Whilst he stayed with me, we had to go out and get 'pished' a few times and I'm sure I really annoyed many people when we got home as I would play records on the Garrard deck via my Wharfedale speakers very, very loud. Selfish I know but we were young and drunk!

One night we came back from a late night at Sneaky Pete's in the Grassmarket, the worse for wear. We both crashed out pretty quickly. In the morning I noticed a paper note slid under my door which read something like 'if you were the two guys who have just come into through the front door, we would like to invite you to our room'! It had the room number etc. Damn! We missed out! For months I tried to spy who was in the afore-mentioned room and I never found her, and the offer was not made again!

There was one other night I was in alone when one of my neigh-bours came by slightly under the influence of alcohol after just finishing her mid-course exam. She was wearing her night-clothes and not to put too fine a point on it made me an offer. She was very attractive, but by this time I had just embarked on a new relationship with a certain girl from Point of Sleat. I declined the offer and told her that I had to study! It would not be first or the last time such offers were made to me and I declined them all!

After a month on my floor Ali Aitken, Duncan MacDonald and Neil MacLennan moved into a big ground-floor flat in Gilmour Place. Portree's own Mr Jimmy McLeod would soon join them!

Assessment

Student Nurses on clinical placements had to complete an interim assessment and a final assessment. This would be given to you by your preceptor who would be a ward Staff Nurse and a Clinical Instructor with feedback from the Ward Sister too. If the final assessment is not passed you were 'put back a class' and if you failed again, you were off the course! My problems started when I worked in the Radiotherapy Unit at the Western. This is where I did my first night duty shifts along with early and late shifts. I really did not enjoy working there but tried to make the best of it. Some staff were very nice especially the Staff Nurse that I did my nights with, but some of the other staff did not take a shine to me at all. This is fine. I know that I can rub some people up the wrong way. I won't hold it against them but for someone to go out of their way to make life difficult for me is unforgivable. This is what happened on this placement. When it came to the interim assessment, it was given to me by a Staff Nurse with whom I rarely worked with and who was in no professional position to provide a proper assessment of my work. She failed me and this was compounded by the Clinical Instructor who did not seem to like male nurses! She had never worked with me either and she failed me too. It was not the easiest of times and I felt that I'd been unfairly treated. I was on the verge of leaving my course. However, things eventually worked out and luckily, I never had to return to that unit.

Who's That Girl?

It was 1982. I was in 6th year at Portree High and I hung around with Jonathon MacDonald from Broadford. At lunchtimes we would skulk about the town, not doing much but managing to fill the lunch hour. Usually, we would go for a coffee, Twix, and try to cadge a cigarette off someone. The big man and I did not have many classes together, but there was one afternoon we were hanging out at the wall, staring blankly across the Blaes. I saw this couple walking hand in hand across the pitch coming towards us. I did not know them personally, but I knew that both of them were a couple of years below me. As they passed, I remember saying to Jonathan that the girl was pretty, and he accused me of being a baby snatcher! There was only two years' difference. Not like she was in the first year or something! Anyway, I made a joke by saying she will be really nice when she grows up. We laughed and then that was that!

Fast forward into the near future. 1985, to be precise. I was living in the Nurse's Home of the Royal Victoria Hospital. Feeling lovesick and sorry for myself. I particularly remember a lonely night spent trying to sleep as I was on an early shift and the Festival Fireworks were banging away above the castle! Being enjoyed by all except lonely me. I could not even be bothered to have a look out the window and just pulled the blanket over my head, hoping the noise would end soon!

A week or two later I was waiting for a bus at the West End, and I bumped into Angus 'Gibbon' Maitland an ex-classmate. He was just about to jump another bus, and he handed me a ticket to his 21st Birthday party celebrations in Grindley Street Student Union. I took the ticket and thanked him, but the way I was feeling I thought that I probably would not go.

A week later I was feeling more positive and decided to get my dancing clothes on and head to the 21st birthday bash and I'm really glad that I did. The place was full of former Portree High Schooler's and it was great to catch up. The night was going really well when I saw this girl that I recognized from school but did not know. I really wanted to go and speak to her, but she was with a bunch of people, most of whom I recognized as pupils from the years below me. As the evening went on, I was planning to make a move, but my courage was lacking. Then the DJ played a slower song and Angus was dancing with her, having a laugh. It was now or never! I dashed on to the floor and said excuse me to 'Gibbon' and took the girl by the hand and drew her close. I introduced myself and she told me her name was Beth.

154

I realised then that this was the girl from school who had been walking hand in hand across the football pitch and the one who I had said would be really nice when she grew up!

As we danced, I told her this story, and it made her laugh, and I was getting positive vibes. What a wonderful feeling it is to meet someone for the first time and know that they like the look of you as much as you like them. She obviously thought I was funny too! We spent the rest of the evening chatting, drinking and dancing until closing time! Someone was having an after-birthday party, party in a flat in Polwarth and I asked Beth if she wanted to go? She said yes. Inside I said Yaas! She was a student in Aberdeen, with a plan to go to Edinburgh College of Art. We spent most of the party in each other's arms, canoodling. After the party broke up, we exchanged phone numbers and she went off with her friends. I returned home to my room in the Royal Victoria that suddenly did not seem so depressing!

I was also finishing the placement in the ward that I did not like and had moved into the Nurses' home at the Western, so things were definitely on the up and up. Beth and I began to see each other regularly and we became a serious item for several years. I never got to thank Angus for the invite that led me to Beth. Better late than never, so thank you, boy!

Aberdeen

Beth's and my relationship began long distance. She was up north in Aberdeen and as soon as I could, I went to visit her. This would be my first time in the Granite City. She met me off the bus and as we made our way to her Nelson Street flat. I was struck by how grey the whole place was. Unlike Edinburgh's red sandstone tenements, all the Aberdeen building are built using granite. At first, I was not impressed, but after visiting her a few times I grew to enjoy the place.

Her flat was in a grey tenement that was full of students. I was surprised to see that the stairs up to her top floor home were made of wood. I was even more surprised to see that they had an outdoor toilet on the landing before her flat. This wee water closet was shared by four flats. The apartment was small but nice. Two bedrooms, a small kitchen and a living room. My first visit she made a bed up for me in the living room. And that's where I slept my whole time there. Honest!

We had a really brilliant time and she showed me around the city. We ate at her favourite restaurant called Radars. Not fancy but it had decent student food. We found a bar near the water that had live music and I wish I could remember the name of it because it became our place and every time I visited we inevitably ended up there. This is where I developed a love for Newcastle Brown Ale. Still love it.

Beth had arranged a party in her wee place, and it was very well attended. The music was good, and the beer flowed. Being in the first flush of our blossoming relationship was absolutely brilliant. She was beautiful, funny and artistically gifted. I knew that weekend that our relationship was going to last. On the bus back home, I had that warm glow that you get when you know you're in love. Returning to Edinburgh, I was very happy. I could not wait for my next visit.

By my next visit winter approached and Aberdeen was effin' freezing. Beth's flat had no heating and this time around I was not sleeping in the living room! It was so cold that at night if you needed to do more than a pee in the bog you had to boil a kettle and take it down with you to melt the ice in the pan! Waking up with a bladder full in the middle of the night was a torture. Too lazy to get dressed, I would throw on my big charity shop overcoat and sprint down the freezing stairs.

It was during this longer visit that I declared my feelings to her. With the help of some Newkie Brown. When she reciprocated, I was over the proverbial moon. They had planned another party for Nelson Street and this time some of Beth's friends from her year at school came. I knew them by sight, but not to talk to. Gordon and Jim, I got on with really well. Gordon was staying at the flat, so we got to know each other better and I really enjoyed his company. I met him a few times in Aberdeen and a couple of times in Glasgow. A funny and genuine person. We recently got in touch through the Something Skye Facebook page. All was going well with the party. People were dancing and laughing when I went outside to go to the bog. Outside the front door were stairs up to the loft. It was from there I heard a roar and crackling sound and smelled smoke. I looked up the stairs and the loft was engulfed in flames. I just about shit myself. My heart sunk. I ran back into the party and shouted, 'Fire. Everyone needs to get out'. The crowd looked at me in disbelief, but soon the smoke was inside the flat. The place emptied at supersonic speed. Gordon and I were the last to leave, ensuring everyone was safe. On our way down we knocked furiously on every flat door, trying to make sure nobody would get trapped. Most of the occupants had been at the party. My major concern was the wooden stairs. Thank God that there was a fire station close to Nelson Street. The Fire Crew were there very quickly and managed to get the blaze under control before it did too much damage. The cause of the fire was unknown perhaps faulty wiring? Beth's flat suffered a small amount of water damage and the loft was charred but not compromised. We let the flat air for one day and stayed with some of her friends. Nobody was hurt and we all had a good laugh about it later, but it was super scary.

Being young and in love, I visited her as often as I could, and we would spend our days in bed and our nights out drinking. We would visit charity shops and it was with Beth that I developed a liking for buying their cheap second-hand clothes. Now when I go home to Glasgow, Janya and I always visit the many charity shops in the West End and Dumbarton Road to pick up bargains. We usually buy a lot of toys for the kids to play with whilst at my sisters and before we leave, we donate them back. Soon enough Beth moved to Edinburgh in a flat near Warrender Park Road. Her course at the Edinburgh School of Art began in 1986. Our relationship would go from strength to strength. At least for a few years, anyway.

Misplaced Childhood

For Marillion's first two albums I had been lovesick for their third, I was not heartbroken. I had started a new relationship, and all was well with life. Living in the Western's Nurses home was pretty good too. One of the senior students who lived on the floor below me let me borrow his copy of Misplaced Childhood and I was blown away with it. A concept album which I totally related to. An album based around Edinburgh. Love and loss. Regret and redemption were the themes that struck a chord in my heart. There were also a few catchy tunes like 'Kayleigh' and 'Lavender'. 'Heart of Lothian' filled me with Scottish pride and Bitter Suite resonated loudly with me. The album's last track was the rousingly positive 'White Feather'. I soon purchased my own copy and played this to death. For a while it was the soundtrack for my life. This classic is my totally favourite concept album of all time.

Surgical at the Eastern Part 1

Regarding failing assessments, I do have to report another failure, I'm afraid. This occurred during my senior surgical placement, which was at Ward 14 at the Eastern General Hospital. A colourful character ran this male general surgical. Sister Jeffries was well known throughout North Lothian Hospitals. She was quite rotund, wore her Sister's cap high on her head and liked her lipstick. She looked tough and talked tough, but underneath it all she was just a kitten. I liked her! Many a time she would take me and one of her Staff Nurses on break with her to the WRVS café in the long corridor of the hospital. I believe she suffered from high blood pressure and sometimes would feel dizzy on the way back to the ward and would ask you to steady her by feeding your arm through hers! I 'supported her' on many corridor occasions!

Mostly, I was enjoying my stint there and thought I was doing well. One of the Staff Nurses was pretty tough but did not treat me any worse than the other students. I was so sure I was doing fine until the Clinical Instructor visited me. I recognized her from the Western as she used to be a Sister in D Block. From the get-go she took an instant dislike to me, she complained that I walked around like a 'half shut knife' and was too 'familiar' with the patients.

I had an issue with my 'aseptic technique' when doing dressings, and although I agreed that I could do better, I was not doing any worse than most. Between her and this Staff Nurse (who did work with me a lot this time) they failed me. I was even more shocked than the first time, and bitterly disappointed! Again, I could not hold back my tears but this time I had no complaints as both the Staff Nurse and the Tutor had spent a considerable amount of time working with me! I just did not agree with their assessment. In particular, nobody said anything to me for six weeks until this interim assessment was due. Surely if you knew someone was not performing well or their technique was bad you would correct them as and when it was observed? That's what I would do. That's what I do now. Again, I felt like packing it all in but managed to get a grip of myself! I did everything that I was told to do and was observed many times doing dressings with the Clinical Instructor peering over my shoulder. Eventually I was doing aseptic technique the way she wanted me to do and scraped by during the final assessment!

All of this must have been around Christmas time because I do remember working an early shift on Christmas Day 1985. The reason this is stuck in my mind is that the Staff Nurses forced me to dress up like the Ward Sister and hand out the Christmas gifts with one of the House Officers dressed like an elf!

Not only did they make me wear makeup, I also had to wear tights and high-heeled shoes. Some newer patients did not recognize that I was a guy in drag. They thought I was the Sister!

I really did not like the feeling of nylon on my legs! It was a pleasant way to finish my senior surgical placement and later on I would get some revenge on that Clinical Instructor!

Surgical at the Eastern Part 2

The Eastern's Operating room is where I did my 'theatre' placement and although I did not enjoy it much, I didn't hate it. Most of the Staff Nurses were OK, but there were a few that were not easy to work with. The Sister was not overly friendly towards students. Luckily for me at that time my spirits were high as I had gotten into a new romance and this placement only lasted six weeks. There were only two theatres and for the most part student nurses just observed. Occasionally we had to 'scrub' for a minor case. This I hated!

The guys that made the time go by quickly and who liked a laugh were the Operating Department Assistants and Theatre Technicians. They were all decent, and I had a brilliant laugh with one guy named Billy. On nights out he was great fun to hang out with. His father lived very close to the Hospital and had been admitted to a Medical Ward and was on an intravenous (IV) drip when he was reported missing. They called Billy and it turned out his father took a wee trip home just to check that his house was OK. With his IV drip attached to his wheeled IV pole!

The only other thing that sticks out from that time was one case where the patient was not anesthetised enough during a gallbladder removal and they sat bolt upright on the table. Overstretching all the IV lines and endo-tracheal breathing tube. Not to mention giving everybody an effin' heart attack. They quickly increased the anaesthesia, and they helped the patient to lie back down!

Surgical at the Eastern Part 3

In our last year as a student, they allowed us to request a unit to work in. Surgical or Medical. I chose Surgery at the Eastern but instead of Male Surgical, I requested Ward 15, which was Female Surgical. Its Sister being an amiable lady called Sister Gardener. At the college they thought that it was a strange choice and as far as I know no other male Nurse had ever worked the female surgical ward before. They approved my request. Ward 15 was opposite Ward 14 and, as I had asked for this unit and passed all my surgical courses, the Clinical Instructor would not visit me. She was still at the Eastern and would visit our unit to see other students but not to work with me! My revenge? Walking in front of her like a 'half shut knife' and when she was in the Ward, I was very over familiar with the patients. By this point I'm not even sure that she noticed, let alone cared!

I really enjoyed working in Female Surgical and had no problems with patients allowing me to care for them. I would always ask if they minded me looking after them and there were few times that they said that a female was preferred. This was fine by me, and it was rare. It's funny, but even here in Saudi Arabia I get called to look at patient wounds to give advice on wound care. Most of these patients are Saudi females and who, for the most part don't have a problem with a 'Western' male inspecting their body parts. We give them the choice of course but to date I've had zero refusals.

Ward 15 had Kathy, an enrolled Nurse who had worked there for donkey's years and who knew everything that you needed to know about surgery at the Eastern! She was very cool and liked a laugh! She also liked to smoke and in the back of the Ward they had a small 'locker area' which was referred to as 'Mrs Brown's'. If you were going for tea and a puff you were going to see Mrs Brown. The Ward Sister did not smoke, but she had no problems with those of us who did.

Ward 15 was my final surgical unit as a student. I really enjoyed my time there. All the Staff were so good to me, and the female patients were very supportive of having a male looking after them.

Last Ward

After passing our finals, our final ward placements were for supposed 'management' experience. I ended up at a geriatric ward in the Eastern. This was an assessment ward but had several 'long stayers'.

Prior to attending this placement, the Western's Nurses' home manager had informed me that if I was not working at the Western, I could not stay there. I would have to get a room in the Eastern's Nurses' home. The previous home manager was very relaxed. She didn't bother which hospital you worked in as long as you were relatively well behaved you could stay! The new manager was not quite so forgiving. I tried my best to stay as long as I could, but she was always on my case.

It turned out for the best. Rather than move to the Eastern's accommodation, I began looking for a room in a shared flat. All the guys from school were living close to the city centre in a flat in Gilmore Place and my girlfriend Beth was living across the Meadows in nearby Warrender Park, so I wanted to be close to them.

It ended up that I only looked at one rental, which was a box room in a big flat on Bruntsfield Place. This place looked across to the green lawns of Meadows and was close to my pals. It was a decent sized box room that had a window looking on to the main road with the only downside being that the room was accessed from the living room. If people stayed up late, the sound of the TV and their voices would keep me awake. It was cheap, though. Eighty quid a month! So, I took it and moved all my stuff in the 'oner' via a taxi! Most of the time I was spending at Beth's anyway. She had a nice double room and my cousin Bobby had moved into her flat's box room.

The biggest downer was the journey to the Eastern ... still using my bike! It was fine going there as it was all downhill but coming back was a total nightmare. Many times, I would almost walk the length of Leith Walk and onto Princes Street as I was too knackered to pedal.

This journey was the only time in all my bicycling years that I had an accident. There was an enormous villa that was being renovated near Leith Links, and I always liked to look at the progress as I cycled by. One late shift, I was too busy gawping, and I hit the back of a parked car! Unfortunately for me the driver was still in the car and although the car was not damaged and I was unhurt, he got out and gave me a mouthful of expletives! Soon after that I had given up with the bike and was taking the bus.

Although it was a geriatric ward, I really enjoyed Ward 16 and as I had passed my finals, I did not have to worry about anything. The staff were all nice and they had this really brilliant wee wiry Sister who liked me a lot. So much so that she was doing her best to convince me to apply for my first Staff Nurse Job there. I did seriously consider it because I liked the Eastern, but life had other plans for me.

The end of my training was all a bit of a blur, but I do remember that we had a certificate ceremony at the new Nursing College on Crewe Road. Many of the girls turned up with their families. I was on my own! It only sticks in my memory because most of my class were all dressed up to the nines and I turned up in jeans and a denim jacket. The shirt I wore I only ironed the collar and the front and left the rest creased. When I was called to collect my certificate, the head of the college said 'congratu-lations' and 'I see you made an effort with your clothes'!

It was April 1987 and I had survived over three years of nurse training. After all the trials, both professionally and personally, I had earned the right to the title that I still have today. I'm proud to be a Registered Nurse (RN). I worked hard for it and over thirty years later, I'm still working as a nurse. Albeit in a different country and as a Manager of a Central Sterile Supplies Department (CSSD) with no patients to look after and only technicians to manage!

Bruntsfield Place

Sometimes I think I'm still living in Bruntsfield Place, even though I left that flat in 1997! My life there spanned two decades. It's weird, it feels like I left a piece of my heart and soul there.

My flat was on the end of a tenement row, just opposite the Meadows which is a large park area behind the Royal Infirmary of Edinburgh. It was on the first floor and had an intercom system. It was a good-sized apartment. Needing some decoration, but clean; there were two double bedrooms, a large kitchen, bathroom, large living room with big windows looking on to Bruntsfield Links. My box bedroom contained a single bed and a wee cupboard. As the flat was on the end of the block, my room had a window which gave it the appearance of being large and roomy.

My first day, I sat in the living room and was introduced to the other occupants. One room had a couple in it, the girl was a Nurse and the other had a single female student. They all seemed nice, and I was relatively happy to be there. The only thing that I was not too keen on was the access via the living room, but it was cheap and close to all my pals.

I set up my old Garrad deck and amp on the floor beside the windows. Also, my ever-expanding record collection had room to breathe. I told my flatmates they were free to use my deck and LPs anytime. Thank God they had a video player in the living room and I immediately joined Azad Video Rental on

Bruntsfield Place and another wee video shop in Tollcross. I was and still am a total movie freak.

I did not spend that much time there as I was with Beth. On the occasions that I slept there, I didn't like the box room. I found it too difficult to get to sleep. Luckily, the single girl soon moved out . Yaas! That meant her double room, which was at the back of the building, was up for grabs. I contacted the landlady and agreed a price of 100 quid PCM. This was dirt cheap for the location. I was extremely happy. Soon the couple who shared the other room decided they wanted to be on their own, and they moved to a flat oppositee on Crichton Place. This left me in the flat all alone. But not for long!

Bobby jumped at the chance at getting the front double bedroom and he and his then girlfriend Catriona from Sheader in Uig moved in. Not too long after that Beth moved in as well and we really had a very nice setup for a while.

Point of Sleat

Beth's parents lived in Point of Sleat on the Isle of Skye. Sleat is in the south of the island whereas I had lived in the north. Little did I know how isolated it was. I soon found out on my first visit! The single-track road ends and you have a long walk on a rocky path to her house by the shore. I was lucky to visit there a few times and though too isolated for my tastes, it's an exquisite area. Both in winter and summer. Her folks, Georgie and Roger, welcomed me with warmth. That first visit I slept on the living room floor! I moved to a bedroom later as our relationship developed. There was no mains electricity for the house (so no TV). They had a wind generator that charged a bank of car batteries and Calor gas powered their fridge. Book reading was a big part of the Bidwell's life and they had an extensive selection of books.

Beth took me all over to check out the local sites. There is a beautiful wee sandy beach which is yours for the day as it's so remote. We visited the lighthouse too, and the views across the sea are fabulous.

Her father was a sailor, and he had a cracking boat called 'Kit' (I think). One summer's day he took us all the way round to Armadale and although I really enjoyed the journey, the sun bouncing off the sea burnt my face something rotten.

When pouring a bath, it was strange to see that once the tub was full, the water was totally brown from the peat! I think it was good for your skin. Her Dad was a far braver man than me as one sunny day we walked towards the large stream near the house when he suddenly threw off all his clothes, soap bar in hand he went for a natural bath! That water was icy, but he soaked with pride!

The funniest thing happened one night after we had all gone to bed. I was reading on the floor of the living room when I heard footsteps upstairs. I then heard what I thought was the roof window being opened. The next minute there was the crack of a gunshot? WTF? The window closed and the footsteps came downstairs and out the door. I thought perhaps her dad was scaring off a fox. In the morning I found out that as he was looking out his bedroom window, he spied a deer. Quick as a flash he grabbed his hunting rifle, hung out the Velux window and shot the beast with one shot! Wow! That visit we ate a lot of venison, which I really love!

I met with Beth's sisters Emma and Mo and I always felt at home everytime we visited. Apart from the long walk down the rocky path I loved staying at Point of Sleat.

D.C. Desouza

By late 1985 Ali Aitken was sharing his Gilmour Place flat with our former school buddies, Duncan, Jimmy and Neil. Having played gigs as 'Rakantanut' on Skye with Duncan, Jimmy and Derek MacLennan earlier in the year, Ali was looking to form another band. He had amassed a fair number of songs that we all thought were brilliant, so I was excited and keen to help.

We had a drummer in Jimmy. Duncan was on bass and through an advert placed in a shop window we met multi-instrumentalist, the very talented if slightly eccentric Dave Watt. Neil and I shared 'management' duties. We booked rehearsal space in the West End. The rehearsal rooms previously functioned as a recording studio and my memory tells me it's where the one hit wonder 'Japanese Boy' by Aneka was recorded. The band worked on getting a set together. Neil and I would go to the rehearsal room and hang out and check on their progress.

The band still had no name and one evening in Gilmour place we were throwing around potential monikers, none of which we liked or could agree on. I had recently worked with a Doctor whose family name was DeSouza and I suggested using that. I thought it was different and had a 'ring' to it. I would not say I was 100% sold on it but it was better than the other names we had come up with. Neil suggested adding D.C. at the beginning which I really liked and as we could not think of anything better D.C. Desouza was born. I really like the name now but felt less confident about it at the time.

Neil and I being 'managers' only meant that we were the ones who would have to find the band gigs. Before that, though, we needed a demo to give to venues where we hoped to play. We had a lot of fun at Gilmour Place, but one thing we did not have was money! I was the only one who was getting a wage, so I ended up being the band's financier. I didn't mind as I probably would have just spent the money on beer!

I can't remember the exact amount of cash we had to make a demo, but I think it was less than three hundred quid. Probably nearer two hundred! Neil and I got on the phone and started phoning studios. We were pretty green, and we soon found out our budget did not buy much studio time. We settled on Craighall Studios, which gave us a day to record and mix. We were all excited about going into a 'professional' studio. This studio's clientele was normally not 'rock' bands. They recorded more 'highbrow' music such as classical and chamber. Recently, I discovered that my sister's favourite band, the Bay City Rollers, had recorded there in the early 1970s. The engineer was up for it and we had a few songs ready to be put on tape. The main song for that demo was 'Shake It All About'. We recorded a couple of other songs, but time has taken their names from my memory.

What I do remember was that near the end of the day the engineer said that we still had some time and tape left and did the band want to quickly record another song? Thank God he did because what we recorded next was, and still is, a brilliant song 'Almost Blue'. They recorded it in one take with only Dave on piano and Ali singing. It was studio magic!

Being young and naïve, we thought that we had the best band in Edinburgh and definitely the best demo tape! This was the 1980s and Ali's brand of 'rock' was not fashionable back then, but we had belief and enthusiasm!

Next on our to-do list was to make copies of the demo and to punt it around venues in the vain hope of someone offering us a paying gig. This was not easy. Neil was far better at finding the band gigs than I was. We tried all the Student Union's in Edinburgh and most of the pubs. We soon found out that not everybody would be a fan of D.C. Desouza. We caught a break though, there was an American girl who was part of one of the Uni's Student Association and she liked the band and I think she enjoyed chatting to Neil and me. They were planning some events, one of them taking place in the Meadows. She booked the band to play on a trailer near Middle Meadow walk. I was working in a Paediatric Unit in the Western, this I remember because one patient came along with his parents to support the band. The day was overcast and cold. The band and Mr Aitken in particular were nervous about their first gig. The set was fine. It was by no means perfect and few people stood by to watch, but it was fun, and we had the first gig under our belts. It was obvious though that the band needed to rehearse more!

Neil and I jokingly called ourselves 'Big Bad Music Management'! We even got a banner made that said: 'D.C. Desouza presented by Big Bad Music'. We sent the demo to anyone and everyone all across the country, trying to get gigs. It was a slow process. The first gig they did in Glasgow was at Jordanhill College. Not a well-known venue on the circuit. We might have been the first (and probably the last) band to play there. The gig went well, but the punters were not really into it. We enjoyed ourselves though – probably a lot more than the students. More gigs came our way, playing at some local 'festivals' in Edinburgh.

A gig that I really enjoyed was at the Bandstand in Princes Street Gardens, beneath Edinburgh Castle. Organized by the American girl from the Student's Association. The festival was called 'Rock against Fowler'. The Fowler in question was a Tory Minister at the time. The government was planning financial cuts to students. In fact, to everyone! It was a decent weather day in the Gardens, and I thought the band played excellently! We got some brilliant photos from that gig too. Taken by the lovely Beth Bidwell.

We entered the band into a 'Battle of the Bands' contest at The Jailhouse in Edinburgh. Run by a local band manager and promoter called Gordon Gooch. He became a big fan of the band and loved their first demo. He still does, and I'm in touch with him occasionally today via Facebook. A couple of A&R guys from London based record companies were to judge the contest. It was exciting. We thought, in our innocence, that the band would get signed immediately. The night of the gig, Duncan our bass player was late, and we ended up asking the bass player from Edinburgh band 'The Alice House' (whom we competed with) to stand in for him. I think the guy played a few songs before Duncan arrived. I can remember being very annoyed, but you couldn't stay annoyed at Dunc for very long.

He played the last couple of songs, but the night blurred under the haze of beer! D.C. came third, and we got some record company interest. They all really liked 'Shake it', which I thought would make a great single. Ultimately, nothing happened with any of these companies, but the band attracted some fans and gained a reputation of being a band that might make it!

We continued to organise gigs and arranged one in Glasgow at Shadows bar in Bath Street. Once a favourite haunt of mine. The bar had its own in-house DJ, who was the guy that booked us. It was not a busy night, but the DJ said to me that he thought that the demo was one of the best he had ever heard, and he had heard a lot of demos! My Mum and my sister Angela came to the gig. In the 'List' magazine the listing read: Shadows. D.C. Desouza. Thankfully, the TV is pretty good on a Thursday night! Funny now, but we took it personally back then!

Meanwhile, I had sent a demo tape to a guy in London who had advertised for bands in Melody Maker. He was looking to put out a record, and he loved our demo. Simon Haveland worked (and still works) in the TV and Movie field. He came up to visit us and stayed with me at Bruntsfield Place. He was a great guy who I got on with well and whom I remain friends with up until now. Unfortunately for the band he did not have much money, but he was willing to pay for a rerecording of 'Shake it All About'. The band had done a few other demos by this time. All of them paid for by me from my meagre nursing student's salary, but the reaction from the 'business' was lukewarm to say the least! I still believed in the band and in Ali's talent as a singer songwriter. By this time Neil had bowed out and was doing his own thing. We still gigged as much as possible, playing in Edinburgh's Music Box and Negociant's. I also arranged what I called D.C. Desouza's 'Highland Fling' with gigs in Inverness and on the Isle of Skye.

The band featured in a radio documentary on Radio Scotland. Archie the presenter was cool, and he liked the Skye connection with all of us. I was included talking nonsense and some of the band's parents were interviewed. This included a funny quip from Duncan's dear old Dad and a very serious assessment by Ali's father. We also attracted the attention of Runrig's manager Marlene, who was always very supportive of the band and was available on the end of a phone to give some advice.

The biggest venue the band played was at the Aberdeen Capitol. The boys were on the bill for a night of music for a charity called 'Oil Aid'. Aberdeen was big in the North Sea Oil business back then. Top of the bill was Runrig. Wet Wet Wet were a no show (before they were famous) and Goodbye Mr Mackenzie (who I love) played. This felt like the big time. We even got to stay in a hotel for the first time. The reality was the venue was only half full for most of the bands, including us. But we had a great time and a very drunken after party!

We kept on keeping on and through Neil we had made a friend in Chris Rainbow who lived in Broadford and who had produced Runrig's last couple of albums. Chris was great for advice and for fun. He stayed with the boys in Gilmour Place on a couple of occasions and slept on their (smelly) couch!

We ended up asking Chris if he would produce the rerecording of 'Shake it all About' and he agreed. Only if we could come up with the money! Through Simon we had a budget of a few grand and Chris gave us a sizable discount. The studio was a well-known one outside Edinburgh. The budget allowed for two songs only. These were 'Shake it' and a new song called 'Living in a Bubble'.

I was working of course but managed to get out to the studio on the last day of mixing. When I heard 'Shake it' I was totally shocked and disappointed! The song had its tempo speeded up. Jimmy the drummer was replaced by a Linn drum machine and Chris sang backing vocals. It's not that it was bad, far from it, and if you had never heard the original version, you probably would have thought that it was very good. When Simon heard it he was very depressed. Having spent all his money and not getting what he expected. There was one saving grace though and that was the second song 'Living in a Bubble'. Everyone really liked it and it helped us get more record company interest. I made my peace with the new 'Shake it' and actually ended up really liking it just was not as much as the original cheaply made recording. The original had a raw feeling, and the slower tempo worked better with Ali's great riff.

Simon and I made the rounds of semi-interested record companies in London, but nobody made any offers. This was probably early 1987, and it just was not the music that was in vogue or in the charts. It was a shame I really believed in Ali's talent. So did Simon. We kept on plugging away, but I suspect the rejection was playing on Ali's mind a lot which he did not verbalize.

Look, I loved Ali like a brother, and he was always a wee bit of an eccentric, but he acted weird, and the truth was it worried me. One afternoon I turned up at Gilmour Place and Ali had shaved his head bald. It shocked me! He had a good head of hair! This all put a strain on our relationship, but we still believed in the music. Jimmy had left the band and our regular drummer for the last year was my mate, George Jeffrey. 'Big George' to us although he hated that name! What an effin' character he was and through him I met other musicians and bands that he was working with. He was an excellent drummer too and he recorded some demos with D.C. Desouza.

More gigs were played, and we did a repeat 'Highland Fling' playing in various bars culminating in a few gigs back on our beloved Skye. I had hired a 'portable' video recorder from 'Radio Rentals'. It was still the 80s so portable meant it was huge, sitting on your shoulder eye-spying through a very small view finder. It took full size VHS tapes, that's how big it was! I was filming everything from a gig at the Hebridean Hotel in Broadford to a great gig in the Skye Gathering Hall. Most of the times I was drunk, so it's a miracle that the camera never got trashed. We also took it up the Lump in Portree and filmed various scenes that we 'might' use for a planned promo video. That whole trip I had a good laugh with George, but there was something not right with Ali. On viewing a lot of the mostly unusable video footage, it was clear that he was not in a good state of mind. Unlike our first trip to Skye, he hardly laughed at all and got annoyed if you pointed the video camera at him!

In the words of Spandau Ballet 'to cut a long story short' I got involved in projects that George was working on and eventually I parted ways with the band. Ali and I had a falling out, which was unfortunate. We were young and immature! By 1990 Ali had formed 'Rootlove' with Derek MacLennan on lead guitar. Jimmy and Duncan also played. They were excellent with some brilliant songs, I just had nothing to do with them and had moved on to other musical projects!

By the late 1980s early 90s I was working mostly as an Agency Nurse and involved in several music projects. I had met some fantastic people who I got on well with and that wanted me to work with them. I really enjoyed my time with D.C. Desouza, and I'm really proud of the music that I helped them make!

Penultimate Paris

After finishing my training, I claimed back the 'superannuation' that I had paid over the years as a student. It was not a vast amount, but I decided that I would take Beth to Paris. It was wintertime and there were a lot of good, cheap 'package' deals to the city of love. To save some cash, we took the train to Calais via London and got on a Hovercraft across the channel. I was really excited about the channel crossing. I think Beth would have preferred to fly. I was slightly disappointed with the Hovercraft. I thought it would be bigger. The noise from it was ear shattering and there were fuel fumes filling the cabin! It was an experience, I suppose.

We stayed in a cheap hotel opposite Gare du Nord station. It was a basic bed-and-breakfast affair. The room had no shower or bath. That was shared in the hall. The room had a toilet bowl hidden behind a shower curtain. Not what one would call luxurious We did all the tourist things, and the trip was enjoyable. We even visited Rue Blomet, the street I had stayed at with Ali when we went travelling.

One evening we were out and had been drinking on an empty stomach and we had a big fight. I don't remember what it was about, but we were outside a restaurant and we did not know where the hell we were and of course I decided I would be the one to find a Metro. Beth and I could be loud with our arguments! She was crying and shouting when this French couple came out the restaurant and thought that I had hit her. They went to console her and looked at me with daggers. Through her tears she told them we were lost and also that I had not hit her! This very nice couple gave us a lift to the nearest Metro and from there my great sense of direction saw us back home safe in our cheap hotel.

The last night we had out in Paris was the most memorable. We were in this student bar sitting drinking when the guys besides us spoke to us. They were all really friendly and wanted our opinion on the meaning of some Pink Floyd lyrics. Well, as you know I'm a Floyd expert! We had a brilliant evening with them and at the end one guy offered to drive us back to the hotel. We were drunk and he was not far behind us and we asked if he was sober enough? He said 'Oui'. He drove a two door Fiat and Beth and I happily got into the back seat as one of the other guys in the group sat in the front. We did not know the exact address but asked him to take us to Gare du Nord. No problems. We were all fine and happy until suddenly we were surrounded by two or three police cars. WTF? I thought it was a bit much for a suspected drunk driver, but as the police exited their vehicles, they all drew their guns! Holy sheeeeit! They opened the two doors and manhandled both the drivers out on to the street and searched them. They ordered Beth and I out too. I was bricking it. I was drunk and I got my leg caught on the front seatbelt and nearly fell on my arse. Guns pointed at us as they asked questions in French. Our French buddies told them we spoke English and they asked to see our passports. We did not have them on us. By then the mood had lightened a little and they had let the French guys go. A terror related incident had just happened and a car similar to the one we were in had been identified! They let us go with a smile and did not ask our driver if he had been drinking! Nervously, we laughed about it all the way back to the hotel.

Sheep

A few of us made our way to Skye. It was the late 1980s and Neil MacLennan had secured us jobs as stewards for the Isle of Skye Music Festival in Broadford. He had worked that last couple of festivals and promised us we would have a drunken laugh! Crossing the ferry, you would think it was the middle of winter as opposed to summer, the weather was atrocious. It was blowing more than a gale and the rain was pelting down hard. Some of us stayed with Karl Ross in Broadford, but I got lucky and was housed at Neil's family home just outside the village. Both his parents were super nice and welcomed me warmly. Even though I had known Neil for years, this was the first time I met his folks. His father was the local vet and a bit of legend around the Island.

The night before the festival we attended a meeting in Broadford Hall as it looked like the festival was in doubt because of the foul weather which still raged outside. Afterwards we all retired to the Dunollie Hotel for a few or more drinks. Both of us staggered home, drunk and soaking.

Waking with brutal hangovers we saw that if anything, the weather was worse. The rain was coming down in sheets. Neil was going to the Hall to find out what was happening. He left me to my hangover. Later, I planned to join him. As I was about to make my way to Broadford Hall, the call came in that they had called off the festival. It was just too dangerous to have that much electrical equipment exposed to the Skye elements. Slightly miffed, I refused requests to join Neil in the pub to drown our sorrows. The thought of a drink turned my stomach. I settled in for a lazy day.

After a pleasant meal with his folks, I sat with Neil's old man who was partial to a wee dram and loved to tell a story. I'm glad I stayed in that night because his story which I'm going to try and recount verbatim made the whole washed out trip worth it. With his weather worn ruddy face and eyes twinkling, he began. I can't promise you that this is true, but it is what he told me to the best of my recollection.

It was very late, actually early morning one Sunday when his phone rang. Not an unusual occurrence for an always on call local vet. When he answered it was the Police calling him from the Broadford station asking him to come immediately as they had a 'situation'. Intrigued, he donned his tweeds and deer stalker and made his way to Broadford in the family car. On arrival he noticed a sheep grazing on the grass in front of the Police station. A rope tied to a fence secured the beast. Into the station he went where he was greeted by a pair of local Police who invited him to sit down and have a strupag. Confused, he sat down, and the story was told to him.

The Police had been out cruising the roads, no doubt on the lookout for inebriated drivers. On a lonely piece of tarmac, they had noticed a small blue van parked at a 'passing place'. Taking a mental note, they drove on. Later on their return they saw that the van was still there and decided to take a look. Their thought was that it was a local sleeping of the effects of a Saturday night drink. They drove past slowly and spotted that there was no one in the driver's seat. They drove on thinking the driver parked it because they had run out of petrol and were now on the hunt for fuel. They circled back along the single-track road and as they did, they saw a guy get out of the back and who appeared to be buttoning up his trousers. It now clicked with the Police that it was someone with their female friend, getting it on. The guy noticed the approaching Police car and a look of panic took over his face. He fiddled with his breeks just as the boys in blue stopped beside him. He suspiciously closed the van's back door and fidgeted nervously. His nerves got worse when the Police asked him what he was doing. He stuttered and could not seem to find any words of explanation. One officer exited the vehicle and walked over to the back of the van. The guy tried to block his view of the back window. It was then the officer heard something move inside and he bent down to peer into the van's back. Expecting to see a married woman, he was ever so slightly shocked when he saw the eyes of a black face sheep staring back at him. 'What the hell', he thought when it dawned on him what was going on! This guy was in the back of the van being very 'friendly' with the sheep. They asked the driver to accompany them to the station.

He sat in the back of the Police car and one officer drove him whilst the other accompanied the sheep back to base! Neil's Dad was shocked but still was not sure what he was there for? They explained that they wanted him to check the sheep for signs of 'abuse' and see if there were any incriminating 'samples' to collect! He said he would do his best. After his examination of the beast and with the samples taken, he thought that was that. He gave a report and handed over what he collected. As he was leaving the Police asked if it was possible, he could take the sheep home as they could not leave it outside the station. Having only the family car, he said it would be difficult. However, Neil's Dad was a good guy and eventually agreed. He lined the front seat with black bin bags and moved the sheep to the front seat area so he could hold with one hand as he drove back to his croft. By this time, it was morning and Broadford was awake and the rumour quickly spread about some guy being caught 'sheep shagging'! Driving through the village at a snail's pace, many of the locals who were gossiping about the sheep perp saw the local vet pass them with a smile on his face and a sheep at his side! I don't have to tell you what they thought.

With a slug of his dram, he laughed and said to me, 'what do you think of that, eh'? I could not stop laughing and as I tried to sleep, I kept seeing his face in the car with the sheep, waving to the locals as he drove by! Classic. Made the entire journey to the wet and windy Isle worth it!

Funnel Vision

It should be obvious by now how important music is to my life. It has been my comforter and my constant companion. Helping me navigate the bad times and allowing me to dance through the good. All my Skye friends in Edinburgh were musicians, and it was natural to be around creative people. Ali Aitken, Duncan Macdonald, and Derek McLennan. It was not only friendship I was actively involved with all their musical projects and did my best to get their songs in the ears of as many people as I could!

Roundabout the end of 1987 there was a birthday party being held in a downstairs pub opposite the Odeon cinema on Lothian road. They wanted a band for the party and I'm not quite sure how it came about but we decided we would form a covers band and play our first gig there. I was on vocals, Derek, lead guitar; Duncan on bass and an Edinburgh-based drummer named Mike. We knew him as he played in Bluefinger, a local blues band alongside Dunc.

We needed to practice, and we organised a quick couple of sessions at the 'Wash House' rehearsal rooms in Edinburgh. Many local bands practiced there and several bands that I was working with also used these rooms. I knew the guy who booked the rooms, and he gave us a good deal. We quickly got a set together which was an eclectic bunch of songs from Peter Gabriel's, 'Here Comes the Flood' to The Monkee's 'I'm a Believer'. We also did some covers we had no right to try and play, the likes of Talking Head's 'Once in a Lifetime'! We managed two or three full band practice sessions, then I spent time with Derek practicing at his flat near Meadowbank. I also had to learn loads of lyrics in quite a short space of time, which was not easy. We needed a name and the only one that stuck came from Mr Macdonald and that was 'Funnel Juice'. It had no meaning. It loosely referred to drinking (a lot) of alcohol. We all thought that it was funny, so we stuck with it.

I will admit to being nervous the night of the gig, as I had had little recent experience at singing in public! The bar was pretty small, but there was a decent birthday party crowd that turned up. After a few Dutch courage beers, it was time for us to hit the floor.

What you have to remember is that we had had only a few rehearsals and I had to learn a bunch of song lyrics to sing live for the first time! That and the copious amount of alcohol being consumed made us sound not too bad! Some songs were more successful than others. I know I can sing well enough for a pub band but when you can't hear yourself it's easy to sing off key.

Happens to the pros all the time! That's my excuse and I'm sticking to it!

We had a fantastic time, even though we were a bit on the rough side. It was a party after all, and people knew that we had just gotten together so they got into the spirit of things and danced the night away.

With one gig under our belts, we had thoughts of doing some more, after we'd had the odd rehearsal or two.. We set our sights on Skye. We ended up going to the Island twice, once purely as Funnel Juice, and the other was with Derek's 'serious' project, The Bridge. After his set, we changed line up slightly and did a FJ set.

We took D.C. Desouza's piano player, Dave Watt, with us as he had an old Post Office Commer Van for the gear. We laughed all the way from Edinburgh across the ferry to Skye.

I consumed a lot of beer on both trips, so forgive me as I'm going to lump all the Skye gigs into one and try and tell you what I remember. We played at the Hakin bar in Kyleakin to a small audience who were not overly impressed. We had a laugh, and our old mate Chris Harley was there to give us support. He understood that we were dodgy as a band, but he knew that the individual musicians were very good.

To Broadford and we played four gigs in total there (over two visits). We all stayed in Karl's flat. Karl was very generous and a decent bloke, albeit a wee bit on the eccentric side. My memories of his place was the smell from his beloved old dog. Friendly it might have been, but its personal hygiene was questionable. Karl loved that four-legged furry friend. It was Karl that helped to get us the gigs in Broadford. I wonder what became of him? Karl, that is, not his dog.

In no particular order, let's start with the gig at the Broadford Hotel. The hotel was a bit more upmarket than other gigs. Ordinarily we would never have been booked there in a million years. They had booked this gig as a thank you to a bunch of Territorial Army soldiers who had come to Broadford to build an adventure playground for the local kids. We set up our gear in one corner of the hotel's wooden floored function room. The place was busy, but the ratio of guys to gals was probably 5-1. There were a lot of drunken soldiers about. I was not what you could call sober either. I had a great laugh, making fun of the soldiers who all seemed to enjoy the nonsense that was emanating from my drunken mouth. We played quite well that night and we really had the crowd on our side. We even had a few people up on the floor trying to dance. Alcohol and soldiers can be an incendiary mix, especially when these soldiers were fighting over the small number of females available. There were a couple of scuffles on the dance floor and during the break I went to the toilet only to be confronted by a few guys fighting outside the bog. Nervously I approached and to my surprise they stopped, and like the red sea they parted to let me in and then they carried on their fight! We really had good fun that night. Well, I did anyway.

The next night they booked us to play the bar at the Hebridean Hotel and we all were suffering from the effects of the previous night's drinking. My voice was pretty rough due to the fact that I did not have a good singing technique. It makes a difference; you know. You need to sing from your stomach! I sang from my throat. I had asked Duncan and Derek to share more of the vocals with me and I had to apologies to the punters, most of whom had been with us at the previous night's gig. More beer was drunk to banish the hangover and we ended up having a fantastic laugh and going down well. When we sang 'Here Comes the Flood' I could hardly do the chorus as my throat was that sore.

Our other two gigs in Broadford we played at the Dunollie Hotel and then at the Broadford Community Hall. The hall was not as busy as the hotel, but fun was had and Ali Aitken, who was now with us, got up on the stage and joined us for a few numbers. Dave Watt also joined in and my memory tells me we had a good gig.

We played the Skye Gathering Hall twice. The first time was a school dance for Portree High, which gave us the chance to catch up with Mr Nichol, one of our old teachers, which was cool. I'm not sure the kids knew what to make of us, but they got up and danced. This gig was probably the soberest we ever played. I do remember a young Peter Macinnes from my favourite Totescore family being in attendance. The second time we played was on a Friday night and involved quite a lot of beer.

Derek and his band played the first set and by the time we went on as Funnel Juice the place was full of drunken folk shouting requests for songs. I'm not sure how we sounded, but from the stage I thought it was good. The strongest memory I have of that night was lying on the stage floor as we played a (very rough and ready) impromptu version of Led Zeppelin's 'Whole Lot of Love' and we ended the night with a (very) long version of Queen's 'We Will Rock You'! Both these songs we did not rehearse (and it showed). At the end of the Queen song, we sped it up into a riff rocker with me making up the lyrics! We may or may not have played another unrehearsed song by AC/DC's 'The Rocker'. My schoolboy dream of playing on the Gathering Hall stage, fronting a rock band, with Derek playing lead guitar came true. Yaas!

Our other Portree gig took place in The Tongadale Hotel and I know I had a laugh that night. We had a visit from our old school chum Christine Murray who used to go out with Derek and who I had a huge crush on in the 4th year. It was great to see her. That night the band stayed in the Hotel and they even gave us breakfast the next morning.

Our last fling on Skye was in an Armadale bar, but I don't remember its name! I think it was because we had free drink all night. I'm not sure how well we played or sounded that night. All I remember was having a really, really good laugh and getting paid for it. We seemed to go down well with the audience. I have to mention 'cheese bastard'. It's a total 'in' joke that was not particularly funny. We got free food and I ate a huge cheeseburger and changed the name of it! I still laugh at thought of that night afterwards we all stayed at Derek's family house in Isleornsay.

So that was the Funnel Juice story of playing on Skye in a large nutshell. As the band members played in other bands we had less and less time to rehearse, plus we were not actively looking for gigs. An agent from Inverness booked our last venue. He got us a gig at a hotel in Aviemore. We were looking forward to it as it was somewhere different, and they were giving us bed and breakfast. The place was busy, and the band went on without me and launched into The Talking Head's 'Once in a Lifetime'. I was still changing into a pair of ripped 'stage' jeans and eventually got out to the band and sang! That song is hard to pull off, and we failed miserably. I, no doubt, was singing out of tune, and the band hadn't rehearsed in a long while! I remember we played Bowie's 'Let's Dance' and Peter Gabriel's 'Modern Love' when a guy came to the side of the stage and told us to finish up! WTF? Were we that bad? Probably! He told us we were not what he was expecting and that we would not be doing a second set. They paid us and let us stay the night. I was hugely disappointed! I don't think the rest of the band were that bothered, really. That was our last gig. Being taken off the stage mid-set sucked, but it wouldn't be the last time that it happened to me!

Don't Stand Me Down

I totally missed this Dexy's Midnight Runners album on its release in 1985. I was a big fan of their first LP with the classic 'Geno' announcing their arrival on Top of the Pops. Kevin Rowland might have been a bit of a dick at the time, but I respect him and what he tried to do. The copy I purchased was a promo copy and I found it in a wee second-hand record shop next to Bennet's pub in Tollcross. The album cover intrigued me as the last time I had seen them on the TV was during their 'Come On Eileen' days. This time they looked like they had been dressed by Top Man. It amazed my ears when I heard the likes of 'This Is What She's Like' and 'The Occasional Flicker'. All the songs on this album are musically wonderful. On its release it was completely trashed by the critics, but over the years it has become one of the 1980s classics and given the respect it was long overdue. The band broke up after this, but

I'm glad to see that they have reformed and are playing shows again. Rowland's voice remains brilliant and is one of the most distinctive singing voices in music. Ever. Download it. Blast it. You won't regret it.

The Fight

Throughout the late 1970s and 1980s, Ali Aitken and I were very close. I loved him like a brother, but with my departure from managing D.C. Desouza, our relationship, which had already started to become strained, deteriorated further. It was a real shame. There was not one big thing, just a culmination of little things. Also, I had moved on to work with other bands and this caused more friction in our shared Bruntsfield Place flat.

The Tex Fillet Five, one of the new bands I worked with would hire Ali's PA on a regular basis. One afternoon we had an argument over the microphones or cables or something stupid that turned into a physical fight outside my bedroom. Like our first fight way back at school in the late 1970s, Ali was still a lot stronger and could easily have pummelled me. We went smashing into the bathroom door, shattering glass to smith-ereens. Somehow, we both ended up on the bathroom floor with Ali pinning me down. Our flatmate Coune had to come and separate us. Nobody got hurt, but our relationship went downhill faster after that.

We ended up not speaking to each other for a fair amount of time, which was pretty awkward. It was also totally puerile. It made living in the flat a veritable nightmare, and poor Coune was in the middle of it all. When I think back on it, I kick myself because if we had just talked it through our relationship might have survived.

Ali ended up leaving Bruntsfield, and I did not see that much of him for several years. I went to Rootlove gigs as I loved their music. We met up in the bar of Edinburgh's Assembly Rooms in the mid-1990. Jimmy, our old D.C. Desouza drummer, was playing in a band who had a gig there. We apologised to each other about how things went down and, as Ali was now living in Glasgow, we loosely arranged to meet up. We never did. Luckily, as previously reported through the magic of Facebook, we have reconnected. Recently Rootlove played a reunion gig and there is talk of them getting back together to play some gigs. I hope that the internet allows me to see that if it happens.

$$\sim$$

Boonierats

When Jimmy McLeod left D.C. Desouza we had to advertise for a new drummer. The second demo we recorded – which was 'Razor Love' and 'What Is It All About' – at REL Studios and was not cheap. The drummer was a guy who had one of those electronic drum kits that looked cool but sounded very 80s. He did not play any gigs with the band, though. George Jeffrey was drumming with Edinburgh's 'The Alice House' and working on many other musical projects. The Edinburgh scene was small, and we got to know him. He joined the band for the third demo, recorded at Newtown Studio's and included 'If Your Friends All Hate You' and 'Some Boys'.

George was an excellent drummer, a wee bit eccentric and a very decent guy who I got along with very well. Around about 1988 he was telling me about his other project, a band called Boonierats who were recording an EP at Pier House Studios. Incidentally, the engineer at the studios was a guy called Ian who used to do 'sound man' work at local gigs. He was doing sound at the Southern Bar when a little-known American rock band who were playing at The Calton Studios did an 'acoustic' set as part of a charity gig for Edinburgh's Sick Children's Hospital. The band and Ian got on well. They asked him if he would be interested in working with them which he ultimately did and he became their monitor sound mixer guy. The band? Nirvana! A Google search has just informed me that Ian now works with The Foo Fighters. Cool.

George had landed a pressing and distribution deal with Backs Records in Norwich, which was part of the UK Independent Record Distributors 'The Cartel'. I was very interested in this and asked if I could help. He invited me to one of the Boonierats' gigs Shady Lady's in Victoria Street. A venue that had many floors and stairs that appeared to descend into the underworld. I knew very little about the band or its members. Someone had told me that in order for the band to get 'psyched up' for a gig they would watch clips of 'Platoon' and 'Apocalypse Now'! The reason for this? The Boonierats sung songs about Vietnam and war. They dressed in fatigues and with camou-flaged painted faces, looked quite menacing! The gig was not overly crowded when the band came on to a backdrop of dry ice and green and black. In fact, for the complete set, there was only one guy dancing. It was obvious that they could play. They had two guitarists, a double bass player, a singer and George on drums. I was not that keen on their music, though.

Boonierats had an alter ego, the aforementioned Tex Fillet Five. This band was all the Boonies except Andy, the lead guitarist. They were essentially a busking band who would play on the streets and in pubs. The money they made financed the Boonierats.

Slowly I got to know the band who were Davie on guitar, Andy on lead guitar, Les on double bass and the singer Glen. I got on really well with Les, who remains my closest friend to this day. Les was, and is, naturally hilarious. To think that he was just a funny guy with a quiff would do him a huge disservice as he is also a very talented songwriter. We would go on to make more musical memories as the years went on.

Eventually the 12-inch record was pressed, and we received our copies. Called 'Messing' it might have appeared that it was just an inane collection of songs about Vietnam, but actually it was really about the colonial leanings of the US and the UK and how we effed everything up by our 'messing' in other countries business. I really liked the cover artwork as it was subtle and classy.

It soon became obvious that I was doing management work for the band and I ended up spending a lot of time working with them trying to get gigs and to promote the EP, which, by the way, was universally panned and did not sell many copies.

It took a wee while for me to get into the four songs, but eventually I liked them. I still think that 'Incoming' and 'Flag Day' are brilliant songs! The overall sound of the EP tells the listener that it was recorded on a budget, but I don't mind the primitive production, I think it gives it character. I went onto the Discogs Music Database and Market website and bought a copy of it a couple of years ago and got it sent to me here in Saudi Arabia. I recently purchased a record player, so I dusted down my 'Messing' copy and blasted it through my speakers. I still like it and have grown fond of the two other tracks, 'Leech Reef' and 'Tiresome'. I was talking to Les on a video call recently and he reminded me of a story back when the record first came out. He gave his Aunt Margaret a copy, and she immediately put it on her record deck. As it was a 12-inch single, she thought the speed would be 33 1/3 RPM. Her first listen was of the song being played at the wrong speed and she said to Les that it sounded 'bloody awful'. He told her to change the speed to 45 RPM, which she did, and her comment was 'it sounds even worse now'! I still laugh when I think about it.

Soon I was busy trying to arrange gigs to promote the record. This was not easy. I also got involved with the Tex Fillet Five as we needed their money for Boonierats' stuff!

Trying to book gigs for unknown bands is not easy and I hated phoning people and pleading for a gig. It was almost as if you were begging them to play in their crappy venue for hardly any money! I spent a fortune on sending demos to 100s of venues. I spent another fortune trying to phone them to get to speak with whoever booked the bands in the hope that they had listened to the demo and wanted to book the band. It could be soul-destroying, and we had little hope of finding an agent to do this work for us. The Boonierats did not play many gigs. Their music was an acquired taste.

I booked 3 gigs down south, culminating in a gig in Norwich where the record distributer was based. I hired a van from

Arnold Clark, and we packed up our stuff and headed off to Newcastle to play our first ever gig in England, a student union. We ended up having a really good laugh and discovering that Newcastle was effin'g freezing! The boys went into the town centre to busk as the Tex Fillet Five but to be honest the passers-by were not particularly interested, and we never made much money! Any money we did make was put into the petrol tank of the van. After the gig I was a wee bit under the influence of the drink when went to a 'nightclub' in the town centre.

Not my kind of place really, but it was a late and we all wanted more bevvy! It was there that I saw the biggest indoor fight that I had ever witnessed at a club. All those swinging punches were female! It was wild and took a fair few bouncers to break it up. We stayed at the flat of one student who had booked and who was Scottish.

The next day we got up, hung-over like hell and fell into the van, taking us to Middlesbrough and another student union gig. We got drunk again and ended up at a party on a street that looked like Coronation Street. We then got invited to sleep on the floor of one of the partygoers and my last memory of Middlesbrough was staggering through the terraced streets, wrapped in my sleeping bag. The next day we made our way to Norwich, which was quite a road trip in the back of a van with a bunch of hung-over smelly guys!

We had arranged to meet the people from Backs Records in a pub called The Red Lion and that's where we parked the van. We would be sleeping in the van for two nights. The gig was at an Arts Centre the following night. We ended up getting stocious and being invited to a party that took us ages to find! Glen and I were wandering about like nomads trying to find the party venue, gripping our carry out in plastic bags. Something weird happened as we walked up a steep hill road in the wee hours of the Norwich morning. A guy sped past us like the proverbial bat out of hell, zooming down the hill on his wheel-chair. Very surreal! I was drunk; I admit it, and I don't know if we ever found the party! We tried to sleep as best we could in the van, but it was not exactly comfortable and when the pub opened; we used its toilets for our morning ablutions. We spent the day milling around the city centre until it was time to go to the gig. A local band supported us, and the crowd was pretty decent. The Boonies went down just slightly better than a lead balloon; I recall the band sounding great and I enjoyed it. Later, the boys did a Tex Fillet Five set in the Art Centre bar. They were a lot better received than the Boonierats! Needless to say, we all got drunk again as the next day we would be on the long road home! I got invited to another party and I ended up losing the guys and getting lost in Norwich. Imagine this drunk Scottish guy trying to find a white van parked outside a pub late at night! Not pretty. I was going about asking people directions to the White Lion pub. Forgetting we parked outside the Red Lion. I did eventually find the van and my bed and had another uncomfortable night's sleep! The journey home was long and boring!

We continued to try and do as many gigs as we could, but they were few and far between. We played at The Venue in Edinburgh and my girlfriend Beth who was an excellent amateur photographer came and took some brilliant photos that she developed by her own hand. Pre Photoshop effects were added, which made the boys all look a bit weird and distorted. We used these for promotional material and we also planned to go back into Pier House to record some 'non war' songs!

The most depressing Boonierats' gig happened at a music festival in Fife. Live Earth Day/Fife Aid was to be a big event with the proceeds going towards environmental causes. TV's David Bellamy was there as a special guest. The main stage looked on to a big green field. There was a smaller stage inside a big tent for us local bands. They had booked some big names for the main stage, but the only one I remember was Fish from Marillion, who had now gone solo. As we collected the rental van the Edinburgh skies were dark, and an icy wind blew up from the Forth. Before we got to cross over to Fife, the rain lashed it down. Across in Fife it had been raining all night and the weather was hellish. The festival grounds were a muddy mess when we arrived. It did not bode well. They gave all the bands area access ID and lucky for me I snagged an 'access all area's' badge. As the band were to play inside a big tent, at least we would be dry.

There were loads of wee tents everywhere selling stuff and a big beer tent. The main stage was huge and the field in front was totally waterlogged. Throughout the day many bands played on the wee stage in the tent. They booked our 30-minute set for late afternoon. There was nothing to do but visit the beer tent. Everyone was miserably wet, muddy and cold, so getting drunk seemed like a good idea. Periodically I would wander backstage at the main stage just to see what was happening. Muddied and soaked the security always stopped me, but as soon as I flashed my ID, they allowed me through. By the time of the Boonies set we were all steaming drunk. It was the only way to get through the day. At least the band had a crowd to play to as most people were inside sheltering from the rain. The sound from the PA was as muddy as the onlookers. It was not an impressive set. Once over we had to get all the gear off stage and back into our once white, now brown van ASAP. We hung around for a while, but we were cold and hungry. I made one more visit to the main stage, hoping to see Fish. I was a huge Marillion fan, so meeting him would be cool. Luckily, he was there at the back waiting to go on. He looked as happy as I felt. I wanted to speak to him, to say how much Marillion's first three albums meant to me, but he didn't look in the mood. I wished him good luck and he said thanks. I watched half his set before the rain got even worse and I went to find the boys to call it a very wet day. In the of the van we sat in steamy silence all the way back to a now dry Edinburgh.

One of the last gigs that I can remember took us to a freezing Inverness were the boys played at the Ice Rink as the Boonies and the Tex Fillet Five. The gig was more memorable for the after-gig party, which took us to the fancier part of the town and a nice big warm house. On our way back to our digs Les passed a garden that had some lovely big daffodils growing and he plucked a big handful, stuck them under his baseball cap and ran around like a madman with this big yellow quiff! I nearly died laughing!

The Boonies shared so much with the Tex Fillet that it's sometimes difficult to remember whose gigs were who. The Tex Fillet made more money than the Boonies, they helped finance travel and recording! The Tex Fillet was also more fun to be

around and as time moved on more and more of my energies
went into this ramshackle busking band!

The Tex Fillet Five

The first time I saw the Tex Fillet Five was in the Edinburgh
pub: Oddfellows. This eclectic bunch played a mixture of
Country and Western, 60s pop and a wee bit of rockabilly. As
the name suggests they were a five-piece band. George on the
drum which he carried at his side hanging from a shoulder
strap. Clive on lead guitar. Davie on rhythm guitar, Glen
singing and Les on double bass. Clive dressed in a 'cowboy' suit
topped with black wide-brimmed hat. The rest of the band
dressed like rejected extras from the movie 'Deliverance'. It was
the late 80s and in Edinburgh they stood out. Particularly
George, who liked to wear a big furry 'Davy Crockett' hat. I
think it was fake fur.

They in no way, shape or form took what they were doing
seriously. In the pub they played an 'acoustic' set which meant
that only Clive and Davie's guitars got plugged into a mini amp.
They had no vocal PA! I thought it sounded total crap, but the
band were having a good laugh and the punters enjoyed it. At
this time, I was still getting to know the band and began
hanging out with them more and more.

From 1988 onwards, I began arranging gigs for them. Being
'acoustic' in theory meant less gear, but for me they did not
sound great, especially the vocals. It was almost impossible to
hear Glen's fake American accent! Initially they busked on
Princes Street. We moved back and forth from the top of
Waverley Market to the East End of Princes Street, opposite the
Waverley Hotel. I preferred the Waverley space as it allowed for
bigger crowds, and folk could sit around on the walls if the
weather was good. Often, we got chased away by the market

security guards! We would get sizeable crowds gathering round during the summer months with many people throwing their loose change onto Clive's guitar case. If I was not working, I would hang out with them. Regularly I would remove Clive's cowboy hat and go round the punters encouraging them to dig deep into their pockets. They would also play on the mound at the side of the art gallery, and on a good day we attracted a fair number of onlookers. The TF5 made a decent amount of money from busking. Clive was the only member who was not involved with the Boonierats and once he was paid the rest of the money went towards funding the Boonies' musical endeavours. The band trusted me with their money, and we opened a band account with Bank of Scotland.

Busking could be fun, but only if the Scottish weather was your friend. I concentrated on getting them pub gigs. Compared to before I found getting them gigs far easier. People liked the TF5, the band loved to laugh, drink and carry on, so what was not to like? With the use of Ali Aitken's PA, we began playing regularly in Edinburgh pubs. This was great for the Boonierats because all the money they made went towards funding new recordings.

One of the first gigs I was involved with was a busking gig, but this time it was a competition at London's Covent Garden. This had the potential for a laugh. It would be my first time proper to go to London and I was a wee bit nervous. I'm not sure why. Later on in life, London would become my home.

The journey in the back of a rental van was not luxurious. We would also sleep in that van. This being a competition, there were loads of street acts. Most of whom were better than us. All we really went for was the day out. They allocated us a pitch and a timeslot, and the boys did their thing. We won nothing, but at least it did not rain. I got to see this unusual-looking guy in a paisley patterned jacket doing some type of comedy routine. He would later become a big star and one of my favourite comedians. Mr Eddie Izzard!

That night we went to the Electric Ballroom in Camden and got blind drunk. I got lucky with the accommodation as friends of the band let me stay in their spare room. Unfortunately, it was in Catford and I had to scramble my way back to Covent Garden in the morning to get on the van before it left for home!

The Phoenix bar in Inverness had been a place where I had booked D.C.

Desouza before and was lucky to get a booking for the 'TF5'. Lucky because the following day I had booked the band to play the Broadford Gala Day on the Isle of Skye. I really liked the Phoenix. It was friendly and they not only paid you but let you stay in an upstairs apartment close to the bar. It would be a stretch to call it a luxury flat. Hell, it was not even a furnished flat. Just a couple of rooms with mattresses on the floor. Apart from George, we all got totally steaming drunk. Most of us went to a party, but Clive had retired early. When we got back to the flat Clive was unconscious on the floor. Still fully suited, and he had removed the flat's curtains and was using them as a blanket! Poor guy!

The next day we were all hungover in the back of the van on our way to Skye. I had booked the gig through Karl Ross in Broadford and we would crash on his floor. What I had kept secret from the boys was that before the actual gig I had arranged for them to 'busk' on a float being driven through the village. Once we arrived and I spoke with Karl and asked him not to mention anything about the band being on a float. Not yet anyway. He bought a case of beer, which I took over to the boys, and I broke the float news! They were ok with it ultimately and the beer helped seal the deal. They played on the back of a lorry and I could not stop laughing at them. I wish I had taken some photos. The evening gig was in a tent in a field and my only memories of it were that it was muddy and there were plenty of people dancing! The rest is a total blur. Sorry!

Back in Edinburgh I got the band two residency bookings, which meant two gigs a week guaranteed. This was not an easy thing to do, but for the TF5 we got lucky. Sunday nights we would play at the Trading Post at The Shore in Leith. This pub/restaurant had recently opened up and hoped to capitalize on the fact that the area was becoming more fashionable. There obviously had been a lot of money spent on the place. It was a 'Western' themed bar. I'm not sure who thought this would work in Edinburgh, but they were dead wrong.

The great thing for us was that they fed us, and they gave us free beer. It was one of the first bars to have Budweiser on tap! The bad thing was that a Sunday night was bereft of pub goers. We had a bunch of regular 'fans' who would come to see the band, but that was about it. We got paid, and we got drunk, so it was fine by me.

On a Tuesday night we played at Negociant's – this was a better gig. Sometimes we played twice a week there. Downstairs in this late-night bar, it was always totally packed. For over a year, probably longer, we played every week.

The band played in Glasgow and my old man came to see them. I booked them into the Spiegel Tent, which was in George Square at the time. Big Gerry had a blast and being a bass player himself, he really loved Les and his double bass.

One of the funniest gigs the band played was at a private party at Pollock Halls, a student hall of residence on the Southside. The students had seen the band many times in Negociant's and asked them to play. When we got there, we saw that there were three plastic bins filled with a homemade punch. From then on, we knew the night was going to be messy. The boys set up in the lounge. We had been given a couple of cases of beer, so the band was well oiled before they started! The night descended into surreal chaos. The band, apart from George, were totally wasted. I was too, and was sitting drunkenly on a comfy lounge chair. The students went mental, even more so when the female contingent arrived. Les was on top form, winding them all up. They loved it. Poor Clive was unfortunately taking a large swig of beer when Les insulted one dancer. Clive laughed so much that the beer sprayed out of his nose like a fountain. At one point a bunch of students asked the band to play a 'metal' song and true to form, they made one up on the spot. The two guitarists started riffing, George started beating the drum like a maniac and Les sang a made up on-the-spot song called 'The Skies Have Eyes'. If only we had camera phones back in the day!

Promotional material for the band was all done courtesy of Clive, who is an excellent artist with a twisted sense of humour. He created many very cool posters, flyers and cover for the 'live' cassette which we sold at gigs. Clive worked with every band I managed. When it came to artwork, he was a total monster.

With these residency gigs and playing Oddfellows and The Pelican bar in the Grassmarket regularly, things were looking up! Gigs were easier to book as the band were well known on the Edinburgh pub scene. One afternoon Glen informed us he was going on holiday for a month! We had a lot of gigs booked WTF were we going to do? George and Les came up with a solution? I would step in and be the singer! I had experience, and I was an ok pub singer, so it made sense. The problem was I had one day of rehearsal to learn all the effin' songs!

Luckily, I had been to loads of their gigs and I pretty much knew their set off by heart, but it's different when you were sitting in the comfort of the crowd as opposed to being up there in front of everyone.

The first gig was at Negociant's and I would be lying if I said that I was not nervous. I totally was! Once we set up, it was time to get some Stella Artois down my neck. Usually, we did the first set at around 9.30 and the seating area was full, but the pub was not too busy. It got packed after 11 o'clock when the other pubs had called last orders! Suitably imbibed with Dutch (Belgian) courage, I got up and did the set. It went down really well, as did the second set. After a week, I was performing like a Las Vegas pro!

Over that month I played many gigs, and we even added a couple of new songs. When Glen returned from holiday, we decided that I would remain singing with the band. I don't think it bothered him too much to have a vocal partner on stage.

Many times, I would be working a late shift in the Renal Isolation Unit of the Royal Infirmary. I would finish at 10 and rush over the road to Negociant's to start our first set. I really enjoyed most nights there. The bar staff were friendly and would slip me free beer. I got to sing the new songs, and we had such an effin' laugh. Well, I did! It really was a period of wine (beer), women and song!

Not all the gigs were great, though. I did not like playing in Oddfellows; it had absolutely no atmosphere. The same with

The Pelican. We booked a gig in a social club outside Edinburgh and we only completed the first set. They would not let us finish as we were not what they expected. They thought we were a serious 'Country and Western' band and realised immediately that we were anything but. We also got booked to play a 'freshers' gig at the Grindlay Street Student Union. I was looking forward to this as we would sing through a professional PA. I don't think the new students 'got' the band, and as they gave us free booze, we all got totally wrecked. Les was not drinking that night. Later, when I went to get paid, the guy who booked us was very annoyed because of how drunk the double bass player was! Strange, he was sober all night!

One of the last times we played at the Trading Post was on a Saturday. At least we had a crowd compared to playing on a Sunday, but it was obvious that the bar would not survive. That night we had planned to do a version of 'Stand by your Man'. The guitar and drums began and as Les came in on his double bass, the wooden bridge that is held under the tension of strings bounced out and onto the dance floor. Just as I was about to sing! The night went downhill fast. I blame the draught Bud.

We did a 'barn dance' somewhere on the Ayrshire coast, twice. Duncan Macdonald my Portee High pal joined us on bass as Les was unavailable. We sang on top of a trailer! It was a good night, and the pay was generous. They booked us again the following year.

All good things come to an end and that happened to the Tex Fillet Five. We continued our gigs in Negociants with the help of Roy on drums, George had other commitments. My good pal Steve also sat in on drums once or twice. Everyone was busy doing their own things so getting the boys together became a real chore. We went out with a whimper rather than a bang.

I want to finish my TF5 memories with a gig we did during the Edinburgh festival of 1990. We were booked to play at Potterow Students' Union. We did not think too much about it until we arrived, and it turned out that we were to play to attendees of the Science festival. Not students or drunken festival goers. No, we were booked to entertain academics from across the globe. The Lord Provost of Edinburgh and a group from her office were also in attendance. Surely there must have been some communication breakdown with the entertainment booker? Potterow is large venue, and they have a nice stage. There was a lot of beer available for us, and Les had been drinking before the gig. We got on and did our thing. The looks from the crowd were of confusion. They did not know whether to laugh or cry or leave ASAP. There were people there with suits and women with ball gowns! It was turning into a wee bit of a nightmare.

The first set did not go down well. Not because we played badly. The audience did not know what to make of us! I think a jazz dance band would have been more suited for this crowd. Things changed as the evening progressed. It was a free bar, and the audience took advantage of it, as did we! By the start of our second set, the band and the punters were seriously pished! Right from the get go, the atmosphere changed from stuffy indifference to wild excitement. Remember these were not students, they were scientists and their spouses from many countries!

As I sang our way through the set, every song was met with a cheer, a dance and an ovation afterwards. It was amazing. We got drunker, but the audience were well ahead of us in the downing of alcohol. The funniest and most embarrassing (for me at least) moment was during our version of Kenny Rogers 'Ruby'. I had noticed a chair to the side of the stage. I thought about dragging it into the middle and finishing the song sitting down. In my inebriated state, I thought it would be cool. That's how drunk I was. I dragged the chair whilst sing 'Oh Ruby, don't take your love to town'. I sat down and both the back legs of the chair broke and I landed flat on my back. Still singing 'Ruby'. The audience thought it was part of the act! They loved it! Later, Clive thought he could lean back on the wall behind the stage. It was just a curtain, no wall, and he fell backwards off the stage. Drunk as a skunk! The crowd cheered!

Our last song of the night was a song we had never sung before. 'Auld Lang Syne'. The audience had requested it. We agreed! I didn't even know the words to the effin' thing apart from the chorus. There, in front of the stage stood the audience, hands interlocked. Each one singing at the top of their voices! As the song ended, we sped it up into a rocker so that the drunken scientists could have one more dance. And dance they did! They did not want the night to end! Now that was an effin' gig! Recently I had to call Les and ask him about this gig to see if he remembered anything about it. I don't remember if Glen was there that night or was I singing on my own? His memories were similar to mine: he had drunk a lot before the gig and was getting more and more outrageous as the night progressed. Something I forgot was that there was a big celebration cake on one table and as we finally ended our set, the Lord Provost approached Les and said to him, 'You have single-handedly ruined this evening.' He just looked at her drunkenly and asked, 'Is there any chance of getting a bit of that cake?' She walked off, miffed. I'm not sure why she was so annoyed?

Was it only with him or with the whole band? Was the gig that bad? He remembers it being a great night and that ultimately, once they were steaming, the audience had a brilliant time! Perhaps we should ask the Lord Provost?

Barking Mad

It was a Saturday afternoon and the TF5 were busking at the East end of Princes Street. During a break two guys approached us and we talked about the band and busking in Edinburgh. The two of them were filmmakers, and they wanted to make a short documentary about the Tex Fillet Five for Public Access TV and for the Edinburgh Film Festival. We agreed immediately, and soon enough it was time for the cameras to roll. The documentary can be seen on YouTube called 'Barking at the Moon'.

They filmed it around early 1989 and it began with me being interviewed in my Bruntsfield kitchen. Strangely, I take up a lot of the half-hour documentary. Our kitchen colour scheme was hardly an ideal background and me spouting rubbish is amusing, if ever so slightly cringe worthy to watch now. The documentary centred around the premise that the busking band financed the Boonierats. Everyone was interviewed individually, and they filmed us collectively sitting chatting in Oddfellows pub.

Les was interviewed in my living room holding his double bass and at that time our walls were decorated with very dark wallpaper. The lighting does not do the place any justice. They also included interviews with some other people, one being a local councillor who talked about the legality of busking in Edinburgh. In the first part of my interview, I had talked about how we had been moved by the police several times at the East End, ostensibly for causing an obstruction of the walkway. Not us, but the people who had circled round to watch the band obstructed people from walking past.

They included footage of the band playing on top of the Waverley Centre and interviewing members of the public. For me, the worst interview was in a very busy café on the Bridges. They set the camera up on the seat opposite me, and amidst the buzz of café I was to talk. They counted down and as soon as I spoke the café became graveyard silent. All ears were on me. I had to tell a boring story about taking loads of money bags full of coins to change for notes in the bank. At the end I took a sip of my coffee, looked straight into the café and said, 'That's rock-and-roll!'

The filmmakers were also interested to make a promo video for the new Boonierats demo, and we had gathered at a venue on the Southside. We had rented a bunch of fancy dress hats and hoped that we could include them in the filming. The day did not go very well, as the director's vision did not fit very well with what the band wanted. We ended up abandoning the shoot after a very long day. Check out the documentary if you're really bored!

Mind Bomb

Released in 1989, this piece of vinyl was introduced to Bruntsfield Place by Mr Jimmy McLeod, our old drummer pal. With lots of smoke blowing in the flat and the haunting opening of 'Good Morning Beautiful', I was mesmerized and hypnotized. I was at a crossroads in my relationship with Beth, and I got involved with a girl who made me believe in love at first sight. 'Mind Bomb' spoke to me, a musical commentary on what was going on around the world. Another track, 'Armageddon Days' is a sing-along song for the apocalypse. The duet with Sinead O'Connor may well have been written about how I felt, sadly. The new decade was coming, and changes were afoot with my life. This record helped me make it through the remaining months of 1989.

The End/New Beginnings

I often say to myself (not out loud) the purpose of documenting my life is to remember the people who played significant parts in it and for me to reflect on things that I could or should have done better. Case in point was the end of the relationship with Beth. No matter how you try to end it, the process is painful, especially when the parting is not mutual (and it rarely is). I had a special four-year relationship with her, and she was a very important part of my 1980s life. We laughed a lot, and we loved a lot and for that I'm forever grateful.

By the middle of 1989 I was unhappy with our relationship, but I didn't have the courage to finish it. The end came when I had what one could call a Festival fling. It was more than that really, but it did only last the length of the Edinburgh Festival.

It was one of those rare warm summer Edinburgh evenings. I was singing with the Tex Fillet Five in Negociant's. It was busy but not totally jammed. During the break, I noticed a girl sitting at the corner table just by the door. I believed we shared an 'eye' moment. She was with a female friend, and I did not feel brave enough to barge in and say hello. Anyway, the second set was beginning. I only hoped that she would stay till the end. Luckily after the band said goodnight she was still there sitting. I took a deep breath and made my move.

Her name was Celia, she was American, and she was appearing in a Fringe play. She had long blonde curly hair and a quite beautiful face. She wore a nose ring which looked really cool. We got on like the proverbial house on fire. Both of us were upfront about being in relationships. Beth was at her folks' on Skye. Celia lived with her boyfriend in London. She was staying in a flat across the Meadows in Marchmont and as I was close in Bruntsfield, I offered to walk her home (what a gentleman). That night was t-shirt-wearing weather, that's how warm it was. We walked and talked all the way down middle Meadow walk and crossed over the road in front of the Whalebones. It was around 3 am and we sat on a wooden bench. We spent a good couple of hours there chatting and smoking. The sun was showing its face when we said goodbye. We arranged to meet up and I got a wee kiss goodnight.

I felt good. I was the king of the world and everything in Edinburgh was beautiful on that early morning walk home across the green of Bruntsfield links. I did my best to fight the guilt that I was feeling and fell asleep with love hearts on my brain.

Over the next three weeks, we did our best to try and see each other as often as we could. Celia was still in her teens when we met, but she had an old soul and beautiful eyes. I could not stop thinking about her. Day and night. We did a lot of walking and talking. We spent afternoons in Lilligs on Victoria Street, drinking tea and occasionally eating their yummy asparagus toast. I went to see her in her play. They named it after the author James Thurber. I enjoyed it but I ignored everyone on stage apart from her. It really was pretty innocent over those weeks and the one weekend her boyfriend came up from London, I did not to see her.

All too soon the Festival was coming to an end and she would leave. It was inevitable and sad. We spent the last two nights together going out drinking at the Pelican in the Grassmarket and eating Chinese food on the Royal Mile. She spent two nights with me in Bruntsfield and on the Sunday, early morning I waved goodbye as she walked down my stairs. She travelled back to London. It was over.

We kept in touch for a while, but as she had a boyfriend and I was getting out of a long-term relationship, the hopes that we might have had to see each other faded. I met up with her briefly in Islington. It was only for a couple of drinks and then I had to watch her leave to be with her boyfriend.

Coincidentally, I bumped into her on Princes Street during the following Festival. She was with her boyfriend. We exchanged a few pleasantries, and I said my farewell. I had another girl on my mind that day.

I often wondered what had become of her, and I'm very happy to report that we reconnected via the ubiquitous Facebook. It's great to know that she is doing very well as a respected vegetarian Chef and author. Well done you!

September in Edinburgh can be pretty miserable. My misery was double as I thought about Celia and what I had to do about Beth. It ended badly. I regret how I did it. My only excuse being I was an immature idiot.

I've also reconnected with Beth on Facebook and I'm very happy to report that she is well and working in the world of ceramics which she loves.

Waking Hours

1989 was a great musical year for me. I discovered several albums that eased my soul as my personal life was in a real slump. The new decade was coming, and I was unsure of what it would bring. I was also a wee bit lovesick. Del Amitri's second album was a great comforter to me. With 'Kiss this thing Goodbye' leading into a bunch of songs that all appeared to relate to how I was feeling. 'When I Want You' and 'This Side of the Morning' got played almost daily. 'Nothing Ever Happens' is just a beautiful piece of art. 'You're Gone' was exactly how I felt that Edinburgh Festive period. 'Move Away Jimmy Blue' is another top song to sing-along to.

Infected

It took a while. Almost three years. For me to understand and appreciate The The's second album. I was given a tape copy by the Tex Fillet Five's stand in drummer, Roy. Right from the get-go 'Sweet Bird of Truth' grabs you and sucks you into this record. Every single song is a killer. All lyrics remain relevant today. 'Heartland's chorus is completely relevant to the UK over that last few years. The coming winters are going to be challenging for everyone, young and old until the COVID-19 pandemic is over. I totally related to 'Out of the Blue (Into the Fire)'. The lyrics touched me deeply and I have to admit that at times that song could have been written for me and my misbehaviour. How many times had I been in a situation like that? A classic 1980s album that should be in the collection of any discerning music fan. Buy it.

Green

REM's 1988 album never reached me till late 1989, but when it did, it kick started a love affair between me and the band that remains strong till this day. Loaded with brilliant tunes, this release caught me during my personal love life transition and songs like 'You are the Everything' made me think of my Festival love, Celia, I loved that song so much along with loving her. 'World Leader Pretend' and 'Turn You Inside Out' are classics. 'Hairshirt' can bring a tear to my oft jaded eye. Pop Song 89 should have been number one around the world, and I still sing it now.

Madrid

For the New Year of 1989 going into 1990 Les, Glen and I planned to travel to Madrid. Paul and Sonia were friends of the boys and they arranged accommodation for us. Paul is Scottish and his girlfriend Sonia is Spanish. I nearly did not make it as my passport had expired and I did not notice (I had hardly used it over the past five years). Luckily, through the Post Office I got a temporary one that allowed you to travel throughout the EU.

This holiday would be the very first time I was to board a plane and I was really excited. We flew from Glasgow and I remember the exhilaration of the plane speeding up immediately before take-off. Loved it as we soared into the air. It was night when we arrived in the city and as we made our way to the flat, I asked Les to teach me the Spanish for a pack of cigarettes, please. He taught me the please, but he made me ask for a pack of elephants please!

Our accommodation was really cool. It belonged to a couple that Les and Glen knew, who were spending their New Year elsewhere. It had only one bedroom and I don't know how I managed it, but I got the bedroom. Les and Glen kipped on the living room sofas.

Now I will not talk at length about our week's vacation, as most of it was a blur of alcohol and smoke. We hung around with a great group of Spanish people and we were out partying every night. We slept till 5 p.m. Got up and went out on the ran dan, returning at 7 a.m. We would always start our beer fest at a wee bar called Nairobi. There we ate tapas, smoked and got totally wasted before heading off to somewhere late for a night of debauchery.

New Year was interesting. On New Year's Eve we had all gathered at Paul and Sonia's. We were well on our way before midnight. Fortuna and beers going down well. Then, before the clock was to strike in 1990, champagne and grapes were brought to the living room table. I was told that it was a tradition that on each strike of the midnight bell you had to eat one grape and take one slug of champers! Sounded easy to me! I was ready as the bell tolled. It was not as easy as it sounded. Especially when you were doing your best not to laugh. We got to around 7 grapes when I burst out laughing, half choking with champagne running from my nose! This set the boys off and it was a real struggle to finish, but finish we did! What a great way to see in the new decade!

On another memorable night we ended up in this weird basement club. Full of strange creatures of the night. Beer and smoke had taken its toll on Les, who was convinced that the place was full of terrorists looking to cause some aggro. We just ignored him in our quest for more beer. I remember being chatted up by this Spanish girl. Her only English spoken to me was, 'I like you'. I replied the same and thought my luck was in when this drunken English guy came out of the toilet and grabbed her away saying, 'Get the eff away from my girlfriend'. We left that strange place around eight in the morning and went for doughnuts and hot chocolate. These I ate ravenously but by the time I got back to the flat the late-night drinking had taken its toll on my body and I was violently sick. We were supposed to go to Seville that day, but I could not get out of my bed I was so ill.

The day of our departure I was the most organised and tried to get the guys together and get on our way to the airport. It was an evening flight and we ended up smoking and drinking in the afternoon. I kept telling Les and Glen that we had to go, but they insisted that there was plenty of time. There was not. Especially when we got lost on the subway and got off at the wrong station. In a panic, we ran to the nearest big road and flagged down a taxi. We just made it by the skin of our teeth. When we were on the plane, the week caught up with my two buddies who looked pretty green all the way to Glasgow, but I felt good, so much so that I ate both their evening meals! Smoking makes you hungry!

༄

Semi Summer Love

Coming out of a long-term relationship and having a Festival affair took its toll on my heartstrings as winter 1990 rolled into spring. I was not looking to get involved with anyone, and that was that. I was pretty much working full-time agency nursing in the Renal Isolation Unit (RIU) at the Royal Infirmary of Edinburgh. We had a third-year student nurse working with us and one afternoon she brought a friend to the unit. Jane was a first-year student nurse. She was young, around 18 or 19 from Dingwall in the Highlands. She looked nervous to be in the unit, so I did my best to be friendly, that's the kind of guy I am. It helped that there was something about her that I really liked. She was slim, with long dark brown hair and beautiful warm blue eyes. I really wanted to ask her out but felt it was a bit much as I had only just met her.

It wasn't long after we met that there was a night out and I knew she would be there. This was my chance. In the pub I sat beside her and we got on really well. She laughed at my jokes, so that was a good sign. I accidentally knocked a pint of beer over her skirt and she still laughed at my jokes. I asked her out and she agreed.

We spent the next couple of months together and it was just what my soul needed. I might even go as far to say that I fell in love with her, but it was obvious that it would never last. I wasn't sure that she was happy with nursing, with me or with living in Edinburgh. Before the 1990 Festival began, our relationship ended, and I found it hard. I missed her for months. I later heard that she had left nursing and was pregnant and living in her home town. Wherever she is now, I hope she is fine and dandy.

Edinburgh Acting

During late 1989 and up till the end of 1991, I had joined an acting class at Edinburgh Acting School. It was something that I had wanted to do for a long while but never got round to. I always enjoyed being in school plays and as part of the Tex Fillet Five I was acting the part of a singer most nights. They held the class in the main theatre at the Pleasance. The teacher, Anna was not only an outstanding teacher, but she was also a real good down-to-earth person who I am still in touch with via Facebook.

My old mucker Alan Shedlock joined me for the class, and I was lucky that my classmates were funny and talented folk from various walks of life. We had one gregarious American lady who at first seemed slightly standoffish with me (but that's another story).

Most of the first semester was taken up with a lot of exercises, trust situations, and improvisation. As the Edinburgh Festival of 1991 grew closer, the school hired a hall and put on several shows. We had all been preparing for parts or to be involved in the technical aspect of putting on a Fringe show.

The venue we had was a Church close to York Place, just behind the St James Centre. It was a decent hall, and we had a wee bar and restaurant. The show I had a part in was a musical revue called 'Back to the 60s'. We would do short skits and songs from each year of the 60s. It wasn't great, but it was great fun. I was not working, and I spent a most of time helping with other shows. I did the sound for the kids show 'The Sound of Music'. Every single night my head was full of 'the hills are alive'. It was good fun. Some of those young kids were real effin' divas.

Our show was a late-night revue starting after 10 p.m. We had an under-rehearsed live band and some truly awful stage costumes. The show was on at the weekends and I think it was full each night. I was not a disciplined cast member. We had a lovely choreographer come to teach us some moves, and I could not learn the most basic dance routine. It's just not in my DNA. I'm sure I annoyed some cast members who now believed they were 'serious' performers. As it was a late-night show, I was always drinking in the bar and trying my best to hide it from Anna.

The review was funny in parts that were meant to be serious, sometimes more so than in the parts that were meant to be funny. We had some fantastic singers and some not so good. My star turn would come around the middle of the show when I would grab the microphone and start rocking into 'the Hippy Hippy Shake'. The cast behind me had their own dance routine, and I just lumbered about the stage trying to get the crowd going! Most of the time it worked! One night Les and the boys came, and I could hear them piss themselves laughing as we performed.

The last song of the evening was me again singing 'My Generation'. This would go on for ages as the cast would dance their way offstage and into the crowd. Getting the audience off their seat and pulling them down to the front to dance. It was pretty funny. More so because I did not know all the lyrics to the effin' song. After each show was a total beer fest. I really enjoyed it myself. I achieved my goal of being in a Festival Fringe show and making a fool of myself.

This ended my short-lived acting career.

Fear of a Black Planet

Ever since I heard The Sugarhill Gang's 'Rapper's Delight' in Linicro. I was a fan of rap. It wasn't a genre I was overly familiar with other than the pop rap stuff that made it on to Top of the Pops. Hanging out with Les meant I got more exposure to the world of rap and hip hop. I liked it. A lot. NWA's 'Straight Outta Compton' was always getting played by me and although it's a classic it did not hit me like Public Enemy's decade-defining 'Fear of a Black Planet'. 'Welcome to the Terrordome' is one of the greatest songs ever. 'Fight the Power' used to brilliant effect at the beginning of Spike Lee's joint 'Do the Right Thing' is another classic. For me, this is a rap concept album. Controversial and totally in your face, this watershed album remains a firm favourite and many times I walk home to 'Terrordome' blasting too loud in my Airpods.

Helen

This is difficult to put into words. Rather than start off about how we met, I have to begin this piece by saying that my good pal Helen died a couple of years ago. Her passing happened a year after her beautiful daughter Skye died tragically young. I suffer from terrible guilt as I did not call her when Skye passed. We were communicating via messenger and email and through her son Stephen. Many times, I attempted to lift the phone but was not brave enough to dial the number because I was a coward and did not know what to say to her. Helen lived for her two kids. She loved that girl, and I didn't have the guts to phone her during her grieving, which I know she never got over. It's something that sits with me and that I will carry forever. Life can be all too short.

We first met at the Edinburgh Acting School. At first, I thought she was a wee bit standoffish and a typical American. She was neither. When we got to know each other, she told me the reason she looked at me funny was that I was the spitting image of one of her New York actor friends and it freaked her out. She lived in the West End with her husband Donald and her son Stephen. Poor Don was always working, and I never met him when they lived in Edinburgh.

Stephen was a cute, very polite, blue-eyed blonde boy. He and his mother did everything together. I hung out at her place a lot. She loved to cook. She was a superb cook, actually. I was always sent home with loads of extra food after eating at her place. She loved to talk. She thought I was hilarious, and we just got on well together like a bizarre brother and big sister. When Twin Peaks had its UK television premier, we watched it together and loved it. At the Acting School Helen, Alan and I did a wee show to an invited audience. My only memory of it was being dressed up like a nun. Safe to say Helen liked to go over the top!

At Stephen's school, we organised a pal of mine to film the school play. This we packaged up and sold to the parents! By the end of 1992 Donald, who worked for Exxon, was transferred back to the US and they set up home in Houston. We kept in touch. She was funny. She would send me photographs of their new house and draw wee stickman and write things like. 'Raymond sitting by the pool'. 'Raymond lying in the lounge watching TV'. She was desperate for me to come visit. By 1993 she had another child, a baby girl they named Skye. Named after my island home. I was told that is where she was conceived! Her phone calls and letters inviting me to Houston would finally convince me to visit.

Coco and the Bean

The Tex Fillet Five succumbed to natural causes around late 1990/91. The band had run its course along with its sibling Boonierats. It was time for a change.

Les had been germinating an idea for a new musical project. This venture really was exciting and a wee bit different. This time around we enlisted the technical guru, our pal Taf. He was a musician. He was a sound man. He was an engineer, and luckily, he was also a good guy.

Les was living in a flat in Lothian House on Lothian Road. This building was a commercial property converted into luxury flats. He shared it with our friend, the late Gus Bell. Gus was a Merchant Seaman and could be at sea for long spells, so for the most part Les had the flat to himself. We had many a good laugh there over the years … and some tears.

We had a small studio set up in Les's bedroom and as we discussed the new musical project, we decided to buy a sampler. These were not cheap, but somehow I found the money to buy an Akai S100. I was working agency shifts almost exclusively in the Renal Unit of the Royal. It was like a full-time job. I think we paid over a grand for that one piece of equipment.

This new musical project was going to be very different from what we had done before. Les had written loads of songs. That were very catchy and hip hop dancey. With Taf on-board, we got to work on what we thought would be the first demo.

'Money' was (and still is) a funky rap song. Layered with samples, it really blew me away when I heard rough takes. Les did the guide rapping and even with that I thought it sounded brilliant. I was still in touch with my mate Simon in London and when he heard the demos, he too got excited. We decided that we could put it out as a 12 inch 'white label' single.

Simon and I formed a record label and after a few duff suggestions from me he came up with this cool name. Our label would be known as 'Baghdad Radio Records'.

Money was now ready for recording the vocals. We chose a local rapper that Les knew with the moniker of 'Dravidian'. For the female backing we enlisted the help of our pal Avril Jameson. Avril was well known in the local music scene and she was a member of Edinburgh musical hopefuls The Indian Givers.

Once the track and several remixes were ready, we sent it off for pressing. A limited edition 'white label' with only 1,000 copies made. Luckily, I had the cash to finance it and I was very happy to do so. I thought the song was totally effin' brilliant. It was an exciting time!

I could not wait for the singles to arrive at Bruntsfield Place. I was like a child impatiently waiting for my Christmas presents. Below my flat was an office supply shop, and I had ordered two rubber stamps. One said, 'Baghdad Radio Records' the other said 'Money'. When at last the boxes came, I individually stamped each record. It was not the most exciting job in the world, but I enjoyed it.

Out of all the bands I worked with, Coco and the Bean was the only one that I truly felt I was a member of the band. And though I still continued my daily nursing job, the grind of work was made so much easier by knowing that I was doing it for a good cause. I believed in the music so much. To this day I consider Les one of my favourite songwriters and he and Taf made music worthy of being heard by millions.

The single was a promotional tool and not for sale. We sent it out to many people in the industry and it was very well received with excellent reviews all round. The first time I heard it being played at an Edinburgh club, I felt proud as hell. 'Money' and the remixes on the B-side still sounds effin' brilliant today.

With me doing all the mailing and promotion doing my best to get people interested in Coco and the Bean. Les and Taf began working on what would be the next single. The plan was that we would release three records on Baghdad Radio and then we would look to get signed by a major record company or at the very least a major independent record label. The plan almost worked!

'Talking with a No 6' differed from 'Money'. This time we had Mike, an American student, rapping. With several weird and wonderful remixes, we pressed this single, not as a white label but as a mail order release and promotional tool. I really loved the label artwork by our mate Clive. It has the Coco and the Bean and Baghdad Radio Records logo on either side. I thought it looked very cool. Again, we got busy sending it out for review and to radio stations. We sent to anyone we thought could help get our music heard by as many ears as possible. Production wise, this was a unique record. I think some people who had loved the first single found it difficult to understand. It got excellent reviews and increased the band's profile.

We began work on what would be Coco and the Bean's third and final release on Baghdad Radio Records. An EP called 'Burn the Flags'. If people were confused with 'Talking with a Number 6' their minds were going to be blown by this record. The main track was to be a song 'Give it Up' sung by Jackie, the lead singer from Edinburgh combo Mouth Music. The rest of the EP would include several remixes of 'Give it Up' and some beautifully weird and wonderful musical interludes that had a strong political message about the state of the union and the British class system. It was going to be a cracker. Or so I thought.

We had loads of ideas for this EP, and we got to work on the artwork. Luckily for us, Clive was working for a local newspaper in Wester Hailes and we had access to their computers at night. What a laugh we had there working, smoking and playing Lemmings. It was a great time. I could not stop playing 'Burn the Flags' this musical magic kept me very positive about the band's future. Even today I love it.

Edinburgh contemporary Sugar Bullet did a remix of 'Give it Up' and at the beginning everything appeared to be going well. Les and Taf were working long hours on the music in Lothian House. If I was not working, I would be there, and we would literally spend hours and hours smoking and listening. Perhaps we smoked too much?

The EP could not get finished and the work on it seemed never ending. Ultimately, I think we were so intense about what we were trying to accomplish that we lost perspective. The main track 'Give it Up' which lyrically was very strong just jarred my ears somehow. Not being a musician, I could not explain it. I wanted to really love it, but I couldn't. I was more interested in blasting 'Burn the Flags' late into the smoking night.

It looked like we would never finish. We kept adding more musical pieces with a lot of weirdness and we prematurely thought about doing an album. 'Tales from the Mouse House'. At night in Wester Hailes we began working on the cover art for an album and we were still enjoying ourselves. The EP was no nearer completion, though. Sometimes I would go to the studio and Taf would be working on a drum loop and I would leave and then come back hours later and he would still be working on the same drum loop! How long this went on for I don't recall. We were all kind of lost in a fug.

Matters were taken out of our hands ultimately when Les got sick and that's his story to tell. He was unable to work for a good while. The stress of it all was got to everyone, and we had disagreements and arguments. It's not worth talking about the details because it was just stupid stuff.

With me working full-time, my closest friend becoming ill, not finishing the effin' EP and us arguing all the time it was inevitable something had to give.

I left Coco and the Bean. It was incredibly difficult, but it had to be done. I needed to detach myself from Les and Taf for quite some time. I did not want a repeat of what happened to Ali and me after I left D.C. Desouza. I couldn't lose them as friends. For around two months I did not see either of them, and it was hard. I missed my pals. I just worked and worked in the Renal Unit and felt sorry for myself. I was fortunate to have as a friend Andy, ex guitarist of the Boonierats. A talented guy. He had been through similar stuff, so he understood how I felt.

Thank God Les got better. We all remained friends. Coco and the Bean signed to a major independent label and released 'Tales from the Mouse House'. It was nothing like we originally envisioned but is a very good first album with some brilliant songs. They toured and did videos, and I was happy to be a fan and still be friends. I still wish we had finished the 'Burn the Flags' EP though!

Screamadelica

I really wanted to hate 'Loaded'. I saw Primal Scream on Top of the Pops and I just gave in to them. Not knowing what to expect I purchased this tape and with the aid of smoking and wine I realised I was listening to something that was era defining. I was getting too old for the 'rave' scene, but it did not stop me from wanting to shake my booty. 'Don't fight It, Feel It', 'Higher than the Sun' and 'Inner Flight' transported me somewhere nice and soft. 'Come Together' played forever and when blasted in Bruntsfield I loved everyone.

Singleton

The 1990s for me began with a couple of short but intense relationships. I was happy enough to be a single guy out on the streets of Edinburgh. From 1993 for almost a year, I was not single, although to the outside world, it would appear that I was.

From a friendship blossomed a secret romance and as I'm writing this, I fully planned to tell her name and now I find myself reticent to do so. I fear that she might not want me to, even after all the years that have passed. She probably won't even get to read this, but since it was a secret, then perhaps that's the way it should remain.

For the time that we spent together, I was very happy. I think she was too. She spent a lot of time at my place in Bruntsfield, and we went on a few holidays together. Once to Skye, the other to visit her friends in Amsterdam.

For the Skye visit, we spent a long weekend in my Aunt Annie's caravan in Linicro. We had hired a car and both of us took turns driving. She was a better driver than me. Margaret was still alive then, and we even cooked her dinner, and she ate with us in the comfort of the caravan.

We had a splendid night with my old Skye pal Duncan Macinnes and his lovely wife Fiona Anne. We drank and talked. Well, I think I did most of the talking. During the evening I needed the bog, so I went for a pee. Their two boys were around 7 or 8? Like their father, they were big highland laddies. One of them held onto the toilet door and would not let me out. I did not have the strength to push open the door because this one 7-year-old was stronger than me! Don't tell anyone that please.

Magic mushroom tea ruined the last night in Linicro. I'm not sure why I drank it because my previous experience with these mushrooms of magic was not that positive. I collapsed onto the bed and was out of action for a terrible couple of hours. It was not pleasant. Luckily for her, my partner didn't feel as bad as me.

On returning to Edinburgh, it was dark, and I was too lazy to look for an unrestricted parking spot. I parked on Bruntsfield place and planned to wake early and return the car to the Tollcross Arnold Clark. I effin' slept in and when I finally got up the car was nowhere to be seen.

At first, I thought someone had stolen it, but I soon realised that the council had towed it. I had to get down to Leith Walk sharpish like and pay the rather big fine to free my hired car. At least I managed to return it to the hire office without being charged a late penalty fee!

The secret relationship ended. I missed her, but it felt right and natural that we no longer were together. In my heart, she remains.

Other Baghdad Bands

After Coco and the Bean, I continued to work with bands, although my enthusiasm was on the wane. As Baghdad Radio Records, we released our first and only CD by rockers: The Sons of the Shaking Earth. I loved that band and really rated them as musicians. One afternoon I received what I thought was a prank call. The guy on the other end of the phone said that he was Tommy Vance (a well-known rock radio DJ in the UK)! It turned out not to be a prank. It was actually him calling to say he really liked the release! We pressed a thousand CDs and easily secured a distributor.

I organised a CD release night at the Venue in Edinburgh, and I promised a free CD to the first 10 people through the door! Unfortunately, there was a delay in the CDs being shipped from down south, so they were still in transit on the night! It was a brilliant night though and the first 10 who turned up at the door eventually got their freebie!

During a 'Sons' gig in Falkirk, we had a young local band called Tarmac as support. I really liked them and when they changed their name to Cage, I put out a white label 45 single for them. One Festival Friday I brought them all through to Edinburgh and said I would take them to a nightclub. They were all under 18, so I told them just to be careful. There was a 'rock' night at the Venue on Carlton Road, I thought it would be ideal place to show the guys what nightlife the big city offered. As we neared the front door, I again warned them to be careful if they got asked their age. We walked in and they all paid and went through, but as I went through suddenly two bouncers grabbed me! They said something about drug dealing and I protested my innocence, but they would not let me in! The band all had to get a refund, and we ended up going somewhere else. It was mistaken ID in case you wondered!

Another band I worked with for a wee while was Sam Harlot. They really were excellent. Kind of folky rock stuff with an excellent Irish singer who was one of Ireland's famed Fureys' sons. The band ultimately moved to Ireland.

My last project was to assist our old pal Andy get some of his musical ideas demoed. It did not work out with his Heaven Hill project. A real shame because his demos were absolutely effin' excellent.

Around 1996, I formally retired from the music scene. It was time. I had done enough, and I had lost my passion for it. The rot set in after the Coco and the Bean situation. I was ready for something new. I know that throughout the 80s and 90s friends and family thought I had wasted my time and money on these musical projects, but I don't see it like that. It's not like I spent millions and for the most part I was really happy with what I achieved. I feel pride as I type this now. And 'Burn the Flags' is still an effin' good track.

The Royal Infirmary of Edinburgh

The main reason I worked at the RIE was that it was only five minutes' walk away from my flat. Remember, I'm very lazy. I was an agency RN, and the routine was that the agency would call and book me for a shift at the Royal. I would make my way to the Nursing Office in the main building and there a Nursing Officer assigned me to a ward or unit. I worked all over the hospital for a while, then one day they asked if I would like to work in the Renal Unit. I said I didn't mind, but that I had no experience in that specialty. They said no experience necessary. My first ever Renal Unit shift began. Initially they sent me to the 'chronic' outpatient dialysis unit, which was a porta-cabin on two levels. The windows looked on to middle Meadow walk. Having never set my blue eyes on a dialysis machine, I found it interesting. The staff were nice enough, and it was simple work.

Most of the time was spent checking people's vitals and making beds. We could smoke in the staff room and we did! Often, I was looking out the window to check out any females walking up the Meadows!

Having gone to the Renal Unit several times it was apparent no other agency nurses were keen to work there. My name was always booked for that particular assignment. The Renal Unit had four areas. The 'chronic' area where I mostly worked. They had a ward, a home dialysis training unit and the RIU, standing for Renal Isolation Unit. This was a four-bedded Renal High Dependency Unit that was hidden behind dark wooden doors opposite the Renal ward. On one shift I was booked to go there, it was not my area of choice. I preferred the outpatients which, by now, I was used to. I did not enjoy the shift, not because of the work but because of the staff at the time. They could be a wee bit challenging to work with. This might have been the reason that the RIU found it hard to book agency staff. After that first shift, they kept booking me to work. I ended up preferring the RIU to any other area and so began my long unplanned career as a Renal High Dependency Nurse.

Out of Time

The opening bars of 'Radio Song' always remind me of walking along the Meadows in the sunshine and thinking about Jane from the year before. What could have been, and what didn't happen. Not that I was unhappy, but I missed her, and this album always turned my mind towards our short but intense summer relationship. This album made REM superstars and I love every effin' song. Stand out tracks are 'Low', Country Feedback' and 'Me in Honey'. It may have made me think of losing Jane, but it did not make me feel miserable. The opposite, actually. It gave me hope.

First Full Time

From mid-1989 till early 1992 I worked pretty much full-time agency shifts in the Renal HDU and over the years the staff, Manager and Nursing Officer encouraged me to apply for full-time posts. I capitulated after holding out for a good while. The interview with the Nursing Officer was a fleeting affair. She knew me well; she knew that I knew the job well and the only thing of note she said was that I had to improve my handwriting! Which I didn't do (even till this day).

So began my first 'real' nursing job since I qualified almost five years before. I was lucky enough to start off as an 'E' Grade Staff Nurse, and my take home salary was around £1,100–£1,300 a month. I was still in Bruntsfield and although there had been a rent increase, I was only paying £125 per month, which was incredibly cheap for the size of the room and the area.

The principal reason I took the job, to be honest, was that it seemed crazy to be working there full time with the agency and getting no benefits. I also enjoyed it and got on well with most of the nurses and Physicians. It was a fantastic team back then. Although it was High Dependency, there were only four rooms and the nurse-to-patient ratio was always 1-1. I enjoyed the machinery and became a bit of an expert.

The RIU moved to a bigger unit in another building of the Royal and our bed capacity went up to five inpatient beds and two beds we used for dialysing patients who were in the Renal ward below us. Ward 42 replaced the RIU and was a great place for me to work. The only downside was the night duty, which was not my favourite shift. The Unit Manager Kirsten Sutherland and I became good buddies and there was a hard core few who'd go out drinking together.

We had Willie Hastie from the Renal Ward who was a good guy. Tall, red-cheeked and who liked to party. I called him the human centrifuge as when he was drunk, he liked to pick folk up and spin them around. There was also Alasdair Lawrie or 'big Al' or as I called him 'big Al serial killer'. He had that look. He had a great sense of humour once you got past his serial killer face. He and Kirsten got together and eventually they got married.

Ian Dymock was an Agency Nurse who, like me, only ever seemed to work in the Renal Unit and we four became very close friends. Ian was a young-minded slightly more mature gay guy who used to wear a male nurse's shirt that had 1970s winged collars, from beneath which a hairy chest always threatened to burst! Originally from Glasgow, he had worked many places and had spent a lot of time in Saudi Arabia during the 1980s. Ian liked to spray his cologne liberally, and I would joke that you knew he was working the minute you entered the hospital main building as you could smell his Kouros wafting through the ancient corridors.

I'm happy to report by then I was more mature and had no fear of gay guys. Ian was a totally brilliant, kind and generous person who had an eye for younger men! What a bunch we made when after a late shift we would head out for some late-night debauchery! With him I ended up going to many gay clubs and pubs and always found myself having a laugh and occasionally scoring with a lady or two.

Once, in the old RIU I had come on to a late shift after having been out to the wee hours with him. He was on the early. I asked where he was, and someone pointed to a drawn curtained room. I went to check on how he was feeling, as I was feeling rough. When I opened the door. The patient was sitting on the commode and Ian was hanging over the sink retching.

The poor patient looked very sad and apologised for the smell. I took over from my hungover pal.

Around 1996 we had a couple of fresh, newly qualified Staff Nurses who joined our team. Wendy and Gillian fitted in well. Both in their early twenties, I would make fun of them and do my best to laugh through our shifts. I was always worried about Wendy, though. I wondered if she didn't like me as sometimes, I got that feeling. I needn't have been so concerned though, as evidenced by our first 'big' night out.

The Renal Unit always made an effort with Christmas nights out, and we always had a drunken laugh. Any excuse for a piss up and we would drink until we couldn't. This Christmas outing Wendy was wearing an oriental style dress. She looked totally gorgeous. As the night progressed to the early hours, it was obvious that there was something going on between us. I will say here and now that I was a gentleman and behaved myself. She had a boyfriend at the time. Being a new Staff Nurse, she had to rotate to the 'chronic' dialysis unit for several months and I missed her. One day I bumped into her outside the hospital's cafeteria, and I invited her to visit my new apartment. Over the next several months we had a secret affair. We tried our best to keep it quiet from the rest of the Unit. It was difficult, and soon everybody knew we had become an 'item'.

I worked in the Renal High Dependency Unit until September 1997. It's difficult to explain why I left. There was something inside, telling me to move on. I was in a relationship with someone I loved. I had my own flat and I enjoyed living in Edinburgh. Still, that feeling was in my chest again. I very nearly stayed, and that was because of Wendy.

We reconnected on Facebook and for that I'm happy. Both of us have beautiful kids and busy lives.

Automatic for the People

Who didn't like this album? Man, I'm still in love with it. From 'Drive' to 'The Sidewinder Sleeps Tonight'. Every song is a perfectly crafted musical surprise. 'Night Swimming' would remind me of my dear friend Helen. I was not hurting at the time of 'Everybody Hurts' and 'Man on the Moon' is just plain good. A perfect album for an imperfect world.

Random Access (Renal) Memories

Here are just a few wee snippets of experiences I had over the years working in Renal High Dependency. The first being a lady whose big ear-to-ear smile remains crystal clear in its clarity to this day. I was at Tollcross in Edinburgh, withdrawing money from the Royal Bank of Scotland's ATM. I was entering my PIN and like most people, I twisted my neck to check if there was anyone close to me with robbing on their mind. The coast was clear, but out of the corner of my eye I saw her. She was short, slightly rounded and had an enormous smile on her face, which appeared to be directed at me. With no recognition registering, I turned back to the cash-giving machine. As I grabbed my money, I looked again, and this female was almost upon me, her grin increasing. I turned to see if she was looking at anybody beside me, but no, the look was directed at my personage. She stood in front of me and said 'Hi'. I replied the same. She said, 'You don't remember me, do you? I was one of your patients in the Renal Unit'. I said, 'Oh…sorry but we see many patients and my memory is bad.' 'I remember you very well,' was her friendly reply. 'I had been taken into the Renal

Isolation Unit in the middle of the night with acute renal failure.' 'Oh, I see,' was all I could muster. 'You were on night duty,' she said. 'I pressed the call bell, and you came. I will never forget it.' She continued smiling from ear to ear. 'I had slipped down the bed and I asked you to lift me up and I have never forgotten your reply.' Uh oh, I thought. 'You said to me, 'Who do you think I am? Arnold Schwarzenegger?' We both burst out laughing, and then my memory tripped.

Having stumbled into a career in Renal Nursing in 1989, I spent the next eight years working in Edinburgh's Royal Infirmary Renal High Dependency Unit. The great thing about being a Staff Nurse there was that patients came in with life-threatening kidney failure, some very near to death. Our team would then get to work and with the correct renal replacement therapy aka dialysis, many of them left with their kidneys in good working order. Very rewarding. One symptom of acute kidney failure is uraemia, which is the build-up of toxins in the blood. This could lead to very acute confusion and bizarre behaviour. This often led to several amusing situations.

To survive in nursing, it is a necessity to own a good sense of humour. You have to be able to laugh, it's your sword and shield, protecting you in often very depressing circumstances. I have these random memories that pop into my mind, make me laugh and then they are offloaded back to the hard drive that is my brain. Here are a few for your amusement.

One duty night I returned to my unit in the wee hours having completed dialysis on a patient in the ICU. Normally in Ward 43 it was very quiet, but something was afoot? My colleagues appeared to be trying to pull open the patients' bathroom door. As I neared, I noticed that one nurse's white uniform was covered in what I thought was blood! WTF? On closer inspection, I realized it was betadine (iodine for cleaning skin). 'What's going on?' I asked, thinking the worst. It was explained to me that one of our female patients had jumped out of bed screaming something about aliens! As my colleague went to her aid the patient grabbed a bottle of betadine, opened it and threw it at her and then ran into the toilet! Taken by surprise, the nurse dabbed herself with a nearby towel, then followed the patient. As she tried to pull open the toilet door, the lady on the other side developed superhuman strength! She was holding the door closed and two nurses could not get enough purchase to wrestle the door open. That's where I came in and proceeded to grab at the door. That wee woman on the other side was strong, but with one giant heave we opened the white wooden door. Inside, the patient had opened all the taps on the hand washing sinks and made a beeline for a cubicle. We caught her before she entered and tried to escort her back to bed. She became even wilder and was shouting at us to let her go. By this time the on-call doctor had come and had (quickly) prescribed a sedating injection which was drawn up at speed. We bum-rushed her onto her bed and tried gently to hold her squirming body as the needle approached. 'Nooooooo!' she screeched like a banshee, kicking my colleagues away! I ended up trying to hold her like a WWE wrestler does to win the bout, whilst my colleague re-grabbed her kicking legs! The injection was eventually administered, but it took a good while to have any effect. Slowly, and with us trying our best to verbally calm her, she stopped her struggle. We could then sit on the bed and hold her hand, offering words of night-time comfort. Luckily nobody was hurt, and my colleague changed her iodine-soaked uniform. Poor Wendy!

A few nights later this patient was lucid and apologetic. She remembered everything and explained that she believed that the unit was being invaded by aliens and running water was her only defence against them!

After an afternoon handover, they assigned me a patient who was reported to be very confused. I went about my late shift business. I entered the patient's room and introduced myself to the elderly but fit looking man sitting up in bed. As I went about charting and so on, we made small talk about the weather and the area of Edinburgh that he lived in. As I sat on the bed about to take his blood pressure, he appeared to be orientated to time and place ... we always ask them 'Do you know where you are? Do you know what date it is?' Funny, I thought, he does not seem confused at all. He then asked me about the room's décor. Strange. This was a high dependency bed with lots of equipment in the room. Again, he asked about the décor. I did not understand what he meant. He then said, with a totally serious face, 'Is this room Jacobean?' I burst out laughing. He remained straight faced, awaiting my decor answer! The report of his confusion was correct!

I looked after this really nice, soft-spoken guy who had a very loving and supportive family. He was unwell but lucid, and we got on famously. We eventually had to put him on a slow continuous dialysis. He also had several IV lines attached to a central venous catheter attached opposite his dialysis catheter. He appeared to be tolerating the treatment well. I had just gone to the nearby nurses' station to get some medicine when he suddenly shouted, 'Get me the F out of here.' Shocked, I turned to look at him and he was out of bed pulling at all his lines. He continued shouting and swearing like a trooper! I noticed he tugged on the dialysis catheter, which was inserted in a major blood vessel. I sprinted over to him, shouting for help from my colleagues. I grabbed his hand, and he tried to head butt me. Luckily, his forehead only hit my shoulder. He was strong, and I lost my balance and fell onto him with both of us landing in his bed! 'Get this effing B away from me,' he screamed as alarms went off from every machine he was attached to. I struggled like mad to stop him pulling at that catheter, and he nearly beat me. The air was blue with his language and eventually with the help of some of my strong female staff co-workers we pinned him on the bed until we could introduce a mind relaxer. Unlike the movies, sedation takes a while to work, but slowly he stopped fighting. A few days later he was back to normal and apologising profusely to me. He remembered everything, and he explained that he suddenly thought I was Freddy Krueger, and I was out to get him with my knives for fingers! He said it was so real, and he knew he had to escape! We both killed ourselves laughing especially when we explained it to his family!

Mr A was one of our regular chronic dialysis patients who would get sick occasionally. When I first met him, I was not his primary nurse but as it was a small unit, we all pitched in and got to know each other's charges. He was in his 70s and his stock answer when you asked him how he was, was 'It's my back passage, nurse.' Always the same!

One night duty I was covering his primary nurse's break when he called me and asked me to telephone his mother. Assuming he was confused, I replied that it was very late and that she would be asleep, knowing full well that his mother was probably long dead. He persisted to ask about his mother and, exasperated, I said that we could not contact the dead. 'What do you mean?' he said. I made my excuses and his primary nurse returned. I reported that his confusion was getting worse, and that he was asking for his dead mother. His nurse replied that his mother was not dead and that she was 101 years old and had been recently admitted to Female Medical!

Later, I went to apologise, and he said, 'That's all right nurse'. As I left, I asked how he was and he replied, 'It's my back passage nurse'!

The funniest one liner piece of confusion that I ever heard and still makes me chuckle today is when I casually asked one patient how he was feeling and he replied, 'I'm as sick as a pelican'! The Edinburgh Royal's old Nursing School badge has a pelican as its logo!

Finally, we had one very sweet elderly gentleman who had been very sick for weeks and was totally out of it when one day, as if by magic, his lucidity reappeared. I was looking over him when he 'woke up' and from that moment on he was convinced that I had saved his life!

Every Christmas until I left the Royal in 1997, he would come to the unit with two bottles of wine and thank me for saving him. Sweet! I explained that it was a team effort, but he was convinced that I was the one that had brought him back!

⌒⌒

August and Everything After

I had never heard of Counting Crows until one day Sue Kirk, one of the Renal Unit managers, gave me a loan of her CD. All I want to say is thanks, Sue. This debut album is just one brilliantly beautiful song after another. Over the years, this album has been my constant companion. 'Round Here' could have been written for me on the Isle of Skye. 'Omaha' is a folksy country classic. I literally have been in those 'Perfect Blue Buildings' and 'Anna Begins' is succour for the lost. I shared 'Raining in Baltimore' and 'A Murder of One' with a special lady and I know she remembers me when she listens to them,

༄

New York

Helen's insistence paid off. I bought a plane ticket for my first ever visit to the good old US of A. My plan was to spend the month of September with her and her family. Helen being Helen wanted my first US vacation to be memorable, so she made a plan.

From Glasgow to New York via Heathrow, I landed at JFK, making my way into Manhattan to the Days Inn. I will admit to being a wee bit nervous about going to the Big Apple. I had watched too many 1980s crime movies, I'm afraid. From the airport I took a bus which dropped me off not too far from my destination. With my rucksack secured, I went for my first walk in NYC. The nerves fell away, and I fell in love with the place! Making it to the hotel, I found that typical of Helen; she had invited some friends. She had booked only one room with two double beds! After greeting her, she uncapped a cold bottle of Bud and told me of her plans for all of us over the next couple of days.

There would be six adults in the room. Three of whom I had never met before. I was introduced to Debbie, who was Helen's closest friend from school. She was cool. Helen's friend Michael I had met in Edinburgh when he was on vacation there and was a total over the top camp hoot. Friendly and hilarious. Michael's current boyfriend and his ex-boyfriend were the other two guys in this eclectic group. I believe Chip was the name of the ex. The current's name is lost to history. The next few days were going to be very interesting.

The first place visited was Central Park, near the Dakota building and the John Lennon memorial. It was a grey warm day, and I don't think I laughed as much with strangers as I did that day and over the next couple of days. Helen wanted to make sure that I saw some tourist sites rather than just the inside of bars and clubs!

Places of note were Canal Street. The Empire State Building and the garish Trump Tower. I wanted to go to the Twin Towers but was not sober enough for that long. We only had a couple of nights there, so we just drank and wandered about Manhattan.

Chip had been successfully living with HIV and had brought a massive bottle of THC capsules. THC is the active ingredient of marijuana. These were prescribed to patients to stimulate their appetite. Basically, it gave them the 'munchies'. We all took more than a few. Thankfully, the effect was very positive, and I really thought that I would die of laughing. I don't think we slept the last night. We all giggled into the morning. The three boys in one double bed. The ladies and me in the other!

৩

Pennsylvania

We left the city to visit Pennsylvania, Helen and Debbie's home state. We would stay with Debbie and her husband Willie, who have this absolutely stunning house in the Pocono Mountains near Lehigh Valley. Debbie had arranged that we would 'tube' down the Delaware River. It was a beautiful day and the river, though cold, was not freezing like its Scottish cousins. I loved it. We seemed to float for hours. Meandering through the countryside. I had one of those disposable cameras and snapped a few cracking photos.

From the river we drove to Debbie's and had a wonderful evening eating and drinking. We sat out on the porch and the noise from the crickets was loud and wonderful. Our laughter could be heard in Allentown. The boys would leave the next day and I was sad to see my buddies go, but I would see Michael again on another of my stateside vacations.

Debbie took me to the Lehigh Valley Mall, and we ended up going to Chilis for margarita time. I was merry as hell after sinking two. I thought Debbie had gone to the bathroom. As I waited for her return, a bunch of Chilis employees gathered round me and sang me a happy birthday song! Debbie thought that that would be funny! I sat there with a fake grin on my half-drunk face. Thanking them afterward and also thanking other patrons who wished me well. We staggered about the mall for a couple of hours.

I loved staying at Debbie and Willie's place. It's secluded and beautiful. It also helps that they have a very nice Jacuzzi bath. Soon, though, it was time to be travelling, and Helen and I jumped on a plane to Houston.

Houston

I had never travelled to anywhere 'hot' before, so when I walked out of the plane, heat that I had never experienced before blasted me. It was effin' hot! Helen and Donald stayed around the Clear Lake area of greater Houston in a cul-de-sac of what I thought looked like the housing estate in the movie Poltergeist. I loved their house. It had two upstairs bedrooms for the kids and downstairs master bedroom with the biggest double bed my Scottish eyes had ever seen. A really nice lounge with patio doors opening out to their swimming pool. For me, it was a total luxury. They billeted me in the bedroom of their 2-year-old daughter Skye, who I was meeting for the first time.

She was the cutest thing I ever saw. Blonde curly hair and deep blue eyes. She was smart and spoke English better than me!

My days in Houston were relaxed, and Helen and Donald treated me like a Scottish King. It was here that I got to know them both better and to me they were the original 'odd couple' and I mean that with love. Don was this very serious PhD scientist, quiet and thoughtful, whilst Helen was this gregarious ex dance teacher who liked to talk. A lot. It worked though, and they loved their two beautiful kids to bits.

For the first time in my life, I got a tan from sitting out at the pool and just hanging. Half the time Helen, Skye and I were in the car driving that wee blonde bundle of fun to photo shoots. She did a lot of modelling jobs and was getting into acting. She appeared to love it. Stephen, her brother, was doing modelling and acting jobs too, but most of the work then was for Skye.

Skye was funny with me. I don't think she knew what to make of me. I had absolutely no experience with young kids, so I spoke to her like she was a small adult. She would not come too close to me during the day, always wary and keeping her distance, but at night before her bed she would come close and ask me questions and look at my face. Too cute. Also, as I was sleeping in her room, nearly every morning she would come in and check on me sleeping. Perhaps she could not understand why a grown man was sleeping in her very girlie bed?

Doug and Dana were Helen's next-door neighbours. She was a teacher and really liked to chat with me. Doug was this typical Texan guy who I thought that I would not like or relate to, but it turned out that beneath that tough exterior he was a very decent and kind human being. They had a lake house a few hours outside of Houston and we all packed up to go there for the weekend. I drove with Doug, who sat with a loaded gun underneath his seat.

The lake that their house was on was man made. To one end there was a large concrete dam, and on a far shore there was a big power station. It might not seem that it was beautiful, but it was and strangely at night with the lights from the power station I thought that it looked industrially magical. We had barely unpacked when Doug wanted to take me out on his motorboat. With a drink in my hand, I said yes! We went buzzing around the whole of the lake right up to the dam wall and then we sat for a while enjoying our alcoholic beverage.

The lake water was warm and ideal for swimming, and I can never forget the late-night boating trips and going night swimming. It was so cool. The water like a tepid bath was refreshing and underneath just tickling your toes was a cool current. The last night we went out there was a full moon. I had had a few beers and went skinny dipping. There is a great photo of me jumping off the boat with the camera flash bouncing its light of my lily-white Scottish bum. That night there were two full moons.

My last adventure before I returned to Edinburgh was a weekend in Galveston. I only hoped to walk the sandy beach and to sing Glen Campbell's hit song. Here was the first time that I ever swam in warm sea water. It was amazing. Not like the cold Minch off Skye. This water was almost hot. Whilst standing with my back to the gentle waves and each time one rolled up behind me, I felt these wee fish bounce off my back.

Before too long the holiday was over and I was on a plane back home. It would not be my last visit to Houston and the Bartusiak family.

The Bends

I fully admit that I wrote off Radiohead. Their debut had some excellent songs and 'Creep' is a modern-day classic, but I really did not hold out much hope for them. I was wrong. Their second album was an absolute beauty. Right from the start, with 'Planet Telex' and 'Fake Plastic Trees'. The title track and 'High and Dry' along with 'Street Spirit (Fade Out) proved without a doubt that this band was worthy of my serious attention. The Bends is an album you keep going back to it. Now it's never that far away from me.

Something's Wrong

At the beginning of 1996, I was feeling not quite right. I could not put my finger on it, but that feeling in my chest was back, and it was getting stronger. Les and I took a trip to Paris and although I enjoyed it, there was an anxiety hanging about at the back of my head. We flew from Edinburgh to Paris De Gaulle via the East Midlands Airport. Through friends of Les they had arranged that we stay with this incredibly friendly girl called Sonia. She had a very nice apartment in a modern building, and we bunked down in her graphic studio floor.

My anxiety which seemed to come from nowhere was under control. Just. I did my utmost to enjoy my time in one of my favourite cities. We hung out with a brilliant bunch of French guys and gals who were friends of friends and whose names are too many to remember. They showed us kindness and gener-osity, and luckily most could speak some English. French was Les's subject at university, so he spoke fluently.

We spent a good deal of time at this wee bar called Nordines. Totally local and to us very friendly. Our budget was not what one could call massive, so we had to be careful. Close to the bar was a small family-run Chinese restaurant and most nights we afforded ourselves a bite there, usually eating their cheapest dishes. The owner was very friendly and would pour us copious amounts of rice wine, free of charge. We always laughed because the small rice wine cups had a glass bottom with a small erotic photo and when you poured in the clear wine, it magnified the photo! Our last night eating there, he gave one to Les and me as a memento. I might still have it in a box in Glasgow.

This trip I promised myself that I would make it to the top of the Eiffel Tower. It being wintertime, there were far fewer tourists, and we easily got into the elevator with no queuing. The elevator ride was a total nightmare. For some reason my anxiety ramped up to over 100 and as we elevated to the top in this mostly glass contraption, I was totally shitting myself. I put on a brave face so that Les wouldn't notice, but it was nearly a full-blown panic attack! It was precipitated no doubt by the height and the confined space. I had noticed a crack in one window and although it was not huge, my mind focused on this crack as if the whole car would blow out all its glass. Heart pumping like a madman, we finally made it to the top! Once outside I felt immediately better, and we spent an enjoyable hour checking out the 360 view of the city. The journey back down was anxiety free.

Being in Paris, we took the chance to visit Disneyland with one of our French buddies. We hopped on the train to the magic kingdom to find that it was practically empty. Granted, it did snow lightly when we were there, so it was not exactly high season. There were no queues to speak of and the latest attraction 'Space Mountain' we rode about 10 times! There was a 'Raiders of the Lost Ark' roller coaster which had one of those cameras that took photos of the riders which you then could buy. Once we discovered the location of the camera, we three wanted to get flashed flipping the bird! Not very adult, I know, but we thought it would be funny. Each ride we would try. Get off and check the photo, then get back on to get a perfect shot. We managed it after about four rides. We paid for the A4-sized photos of three grown men giving the finger at Disney! That photo was given pride of place on the wall in Nordines bar, and who knows it might still be there now. On our way back on the train to Paris we did not get asked to buy a ticket, so we thought we had lucked out. On arrival at the station, we soon discovered that you could not get out without a valid ticket. Recently there had been several bombings in Paris and the armed police were out in force. We looked around and saw the only way to get out without paying was to walk directly behind a paying customer as they exited the gate. We had to get up close and personal or you would get caught in the swinging doors. We managed without too much incident, but I would have rather paid the money and not had the stress!

We got invited to a Friday night party in this cool flat near the river. It was our last couple of days in the city, so we made a night of it. Suitably steaming drunk, we headed out to the party. They played a lot of techno and The Prodigy in particular. Les and I were bouncing around like idiots for hours. I'm sure the other guests thought we were on speed, but we were just happy! All that dancing and head banging took away those anxiety feelings in my chest. We danced a lot to the Prodigy song, 'Poison/Remedy'. The next afternoon we surfaced, and not only did we have a mother of all hangovers, both our necks were so stiff from head banging. The first thing Les said was 'I've had the poison and now I need the remedy!' I laughed all day about that!

Nothing could have prepared me for what was in store after we said cheerio to Paris. We got to the airport with no issues. Got on the plane and all was fine. I vividly remember picking up a newspaper to read during take-off. As we got near to cruising height, I had an effin' full blown panic attack! Nothing caused it. The flight was smooth, and the plane was half full. I did not know what to do. I was dying in my seat. I was too embarrassed to tell Les who was happy looking out of the window saying that he could see the channel and both country coasts. My only thought was, I want to get off. I had these visions of running up and down the plane being chased by the flight crew. I thought I might try to speak to the pilot and ask him to land anywhere. None of that happened except in my mind, which was running ten to the dozen. I gripped the chair arms and tried to breathe. It was worse when I closed my eyes. I was praying to touch down quickly in the East Midlands, and I planned how I would get to Edinburgh by land. After what seemed like days, we descended and landed safely. I exhaled an enormous sigh of total relief. How was I going to get on to the next plane to Edinburgh? I nearly blurted it out to Les that I couldn't get on the plane. The changeover happened swiftly. We did not go to the terminal. Rather, we walked across the tarmac from one plane to another. We ran towards the stairs and both of us were waving to non-existent fans and laughing but inside I was scared. Strangely, the second flight was fine, and I was back to normal. I even ate something. Still, I was glad when we landed in Edinburgh.

Hale-Bopp

The anxiety remained with me but appeared to be manageable. Or so I thought. With my work pals Kirsten and Alasdair, we hired a car and went to the Isle of Skye for a long weekend during the Hale-Bopp comets passing of earth. With the clear skies and no streetlights, we figured Linicro would be a great place to do some comet watching.

On the Saturday night my Totescore friend Archie Macinnes, his wife and sister and us three, hired a minibus for a night out in the Flodigarry Hotel. The alcohol calmed my feelings somewhat, but they were still there underneath. I did my best to have a good night and with the drinks flowing the live music playing I just about managed it. Slightly ruined by one of my old drunken school mates coming over and being very aggressive towards me! I must have pissed him off on the school bus way back when and he was getting his revenge. Nothing happened, and the night carried on till the wee hours.

After our return to the caravan, Kirsten and Al went to bed. I could not sleep. My brain would not turn off. I sat outside for a while staring at the comet, which was high above those black Harris hills in the sea distance. I tried to lay my head down, and I had this weird sensation that something burst inside my head like a pipe. It felt that my brain was being covered in something cool, but it was not calming.

After saying our farewell to my Aunt Margaret, we travelled over to Waternish on our way back to Edinburgh. For all the years I lived on Skye and the many times I visited, not once did I go to the place that could be seen from Linicro across the Minch and passed the Ascrib Isles. From Waternish I wanted to see how Linicro looked. I wish I had taken a photo.

Three Months of Hell

We have all heard about people having a 'nervous breakdown' but that phrase means nothing. Most of us, whether we would like to admit it or not, have had times when our mental health was challenged and somehow, we muddled through. I was not sure what was going on with me, but during the three months of April, May and June I was having an invisible 'nervous breakdown'. I say invisible because to the normal eye looking at my surface, everything seemed calm and as it should be. If they had scratched away the thinnest of veneer, they would have seen the emotional maelstrom I was going through.

It had been coming all year. I was not feeling great on and off. There had been no big emotional upsets in my life. No breakups. No depressing life changes, family bereavements. Nothing. Everything was just moving along fine. The only thing was that I did not feel fine.

I was having genuine problems sleeping. My mind would not rest. My eyes were open to all hours, which impacted my working day. I felt highly anxious at work. Sometimes I broke into a physical sweat for no reason. Most of the time if I suspected I looked not normal, I would turn on the old me and start trying to be funny. Work was far from making things worse. To be honest with you, it was work that saved me. If I had been left to suffer in my Bruntsfield bedroom God knows if I would have recovered.

I dreaded going to bed. It was almost like a fear. I was scared to go to bed. There were more than a few times I slept on the living room sofa just so that I could see the streetlights and hear normal night life going past my grimy window. At one point I thought that maybe I had mad cow disease as I seemed to have developed some symptoms! There was no smoking during this time, it just made me worse. I did like to have a bottle of wine at night as this gave me some respite from the lump in my stomach and the throbbing in my chest.

My bedroom really depressed me, so I organised for it to be repainted and bought new curtains and a rug. Anything to make it less crappy looking. I think that helped. I slowly began to feel better. The only thing I obsessed about was my next flight on a plane. After my Paris panic attack, each time I thought of sitting on a plane made me sweat with fear. There was no way I could not get on a flight. The thought of it was a nightmare. Today I fly quite a lot but not without the aid of some calming medication from the doctor. Why should I put myself through that mental anguish? That and a couple of beers makes me positively enjoy the flight.

Things improved, and I got on a plane to the US of A for another Houston holiday. I came back feeling good. I tried to think what would have caused the hell that I had just been through? I have no answer really. Perhaps it was a build of many stresses over the previous five years until it finally exploded like a firework in my head. I'm not saying it didn't happen again, it did but it was not as acute and did not last the same amount of time.

Leaving Bruntsfield

After a decade of ups and downs, my life in Bruntsfield was ending. My landlady had decided to sell up and gave me a reasonable amount of notice to move out. I had been so used to staying there with such a cheap rent that trying to fund a similar situation in the same area would be impossible. My only choice would be to buy my own place. My landlady had called and said she was prepared to sell to me for a discount, but my salary would not cover the cost of even a discounted Bruntsfield price.

My problem was my incredible laziness. It was December when I had secured a mortgage and I was looking through the properties for sale that fitted my budget and were within walking distance of my job at the Royal. I was not in a hurry and my landlady was not pushing me, so I left the decision till after the New Year.

I had spotted a small flat for sale in the property listings in a place called East Fountainbridge. A cold January Sunday afternoon found me walking towards the Grassmarket. I was not familiar with the street, but as I rounded the corner at the Point Hotel, I found it. The building was just opposite the hotel. It was a two-storey tenement which looked like it had seen better days. To one side of it there was the DHSS and as you looked along the other side it led you to the area known locally as the 'pubic triangle'. Named so because of the 'Go Go' bars nearby.

Opposite the building was a sex shop, close to a 'massage' parlour, a euphemism in Edinburgh for a 'knocking shop' which is another euphemism for a brothel. I decided that it was the perfect area for me! Literally five minutes from work. The flat I would view was on the first floor above a barbershop.

I rang the buzzer and went up the stairs. I walked into a very cosy and extremely warm apartment. I made my mind up. It was on the market for thirty-six thousand and I put an offer in the very next day for thirty-eight and they accepted it. For the first time in my life, I was a property owner.

⌒

East Fountainbridge

It was at the beginning of March that I packed my stuff and said cheerio to Bruntsfield Place. I really was not too sad about leaving. It seemed the right thing to do. Luckily my two work mates Kirsten and Ali came to help with the shift. We hired a van and managed the flit in two loads. We tried to take the sofa and one chair from Bruntsfield; the reason being that this was the sofa we had in Galloway Street. It was still in good nick for its age and very comfortable. It was big though, and we could not get it round the very tight angle from my new front door into the living room. We gave up pushing and took it to a dump outside of the city. I was sadder to see that sofa go than I was about leaving Bruntsfield. We kept one chair, so that was better than nothing.

My new pad was compact but had a decent-sized living room and a decent-sized bedroom with fitted wardrobes. There was a small but perfectly sized kitchen in between living and bedroom, and the bathroom was off the world's smallest hall just before my front door. There were two windows in the living room which were supposed to be double-glazed but they were not particularly soundproof. The entire building contained six flats which had been renovated in the mid-1980s. My view out of these windows was the corner of the Point Hotel, which I did not mind as it's a truly beautiful building. The road at East Fountainbridge is busy with traffic, but really not any louder than Bruntsfield Place. The funny thing was that if a double-decker bus passed, those punters on the top deck could see directly into the living room. They were so close you could almost touch them!

The flat was so handy for work, though. It only took a couple of minutes of walking to be in Ward 42. At the time I only had a single bed in the bedroom which had two mattresses so anytime my special friend Wendy would stay over we would lay the two mattresses on the floor to fashion a double bed. My happiest memories of that flat were of our time there together. One thing we used to giggle at was the fact that my road was where lots of drunken Grassmarketeers would walk past eating their late-night snacks on their way home. They would throw their empty containers and papers on the ground. We would regularly hear that wee Council road sweeper outside. It would do a number of rounds, but no matter how many it would do when we got up the next day, the place was pure manky with 'chippy' litter strewn everywhere. We wondered what the actual eff that road sweeper swept.

My lovely pal Ian had donated a three-seat sofa so at least I had somewhere to stretch out in the living room and I loved to stare out the windows once I cleaned them and look over to the Point. The guests in those corner rooms could see me there, smoking and dreaming.

Directly beneath the flat was an old-style barbershop, which I thought was cool. What wasn't cool was that the owners had an effin' karaoke machine and in the mornings when there were no customers they would be 'geeing it laldy' singing hits from the 60s and 70s! The soundproofing in my place was zero! Very annoying if I was on a late shift or on nights. It soon changed hands and became a tattoo shop. Now every time I came home that shop was full of young lassies wanting to get a tattoo. At least there was no karaoke!

Leaving Edinburgh

By the summer of 1997, my life was pretty settled. I had a good job that was five minutes from my flat. I had my own place. I was seeing a beautiful girl. What more could anyone ask for? Unfortunately, there was something inside me whispering it's time for a change! What that change was meant to be, I didn't know. I couldn't shake it. I was annoyed by myself. I was 34 years old, and it was time to settle down. Nope. It was not the time I suppose. But what to do?

I looked at jobs in the Middle East. My pal Ian had worked in Saudi for a long time, and he had a great time, so I looked at finding a job in a Renal Unit in Saudi Arabia. In the Nursing Times, a company called Arabian Solutions advertised for locum Renal Nurses. You could go for three months and if you liked it, you could convert to permanent. It seemed good to me. Try before you buy.

My application sent, it did not take them too long to call me and an interview was arranged in London. The appointment was early afternoon, but as I was going on the train and coming back on the same day; they were flexible with me. I arrived late morning. My return train was at five o'clock. From Kings Cross I jumped in a taxi to Soho where the company offices were. The interview was conducted by one lady in a big office, and it literally was over in five minutes. They were desperate for nurses and the fact that I was willing and breathing secured the job.

It took around a month to do all the paperwork and eventually they sent me details of where and when I was going. My destination was North West Armed Forces Hospital in Tabuk. I would go just before Christmas on the 23rd. My friend Kirsten had by now left our unit and was working in Kirkcaldy. Our new manager Andy was very good to me. He had worked in the Renal Unit of the Saudi Hospital that I was going to, so I really had a good amount of information before I was to arrive there.

Ward 42 had a wee night out for me in the bar of the Bruntsfield Hotel. I hate those kinds of things, so I wanted it low key. I think Wendy did most of the organising. They gave me a cracking Swatch watch, which I had for years until someone stole it here in the Hospital that I currently work in! Swine! They also gave me a Renal textbook co-written by one of our physician colleagues, Liam.

I'm not saying I was not sad to be leaving, I was. I was sad to leave my job. To leave Wendy. To leave Edinburgh, but I felt inside that I had no choice. It had to be done. I also was nervous about going to a strange country and working abroad for the first time. All these mixed-up feelings made it difficult, but not so difficult that I would change my mind.

Saudi Arabia

Time for Tabuk

It was a cold and dark December morning when I began my trip to Tabuk. I flew to Heathrow then Jeddah and from there I finally arrived at Tabuk airport. It was the wee hours when Shawkat from the hospital meet-and-greet team picked me up. Tired and disorientated, he took me to where I would stay for the duration of my trip. In a daze I decanted from the minibus and made my way to this prefabricated 'villa'. There I was introduced to a Canadian guy called Dale. After some small talk he directed me to my room, and I fell on to the bed and slept.

Waking in the morning, I did not know where the hell I was. It took a minute or two to realize that I had done it. I was in a foreign country about to start work. Actually, I had the weekend (Thursday, Friday) to recover and then I was to start work on the Saturday. I lifted my head up and looked outside of the window and I thought WTF have I done?

Having arrived in the dark, I did not see my surroundings, and I was more than a little disappointed when I did. From my window I could see a burned-out villa, some leafless trees and a lot of dirt. The place looked like a 'shanty town'. It was not a modern, beautifully kept expatriate compound, that's for sure. Dale was on nights that evening, so we had time to get to know each other and he gave me the rundown on where the hell I was!

The area where my non-luxury accommodation was situated was known as 'Briga'. Originally this area of desert was where they housed the workers who had built the hospital. It was now greener and was home to married couples and single guys. Single ladies stayed in apartments inside the hospital grounds. Briga was approximately 20 minutes' drive from my work.

Dale worked on Medical/Surgical and had been there for a few years. Our villa was a three-bedroomed affair with kitchen, bathroom and a nice sizeable living room. I was bunked in the smallest room, which was fine by me. By the evening he was off to work in his SUV and I was left in on my own for my first Saudi night. It wasn't so bad. Dale had a satellite TV system set up, so at least I could watch something. It was around eight or nine when someone knocked on the door. I went to answer and was greeted by a fellow Briga resident inviting me to a party. I really was not in the mood but went anyway. I hopped in his Land Rover and we drove to another villa. Unlike ours, high wooden fences surrounded this one. No prying eye could see what went on behind these wooden curtains.

It was Christmas, so there was a Christmas party going on. I was introduced to a myriad of people whose names I would never remember and was handed a drink. This party had everything that was prohibited in the Kingdom and there I was barely 24 hours there and I was drinking, smoking and eating bacon! I latched on to a beautiful couple Christine and Eamon who, like me, were relatively new to Tabuk. They were from Perth in Australia. He worked as a technician in the Cardiac lab, and she worked in Administration. Along with Dale, they were the only people I was interested in getting to know. Both were extremely nice and friendly. I still keep in contact with Christine via Facebook.

I left the party in the early hours of the morning, a wee bit worse for wear. It was still dark with only dim yellow street-lights to guide me. I had arrived by car, so I had no effin' idea where I was or where my villa was. The place had loads of villas that all looked the same. I remembered about the neighbouring burned down villa and the Jodrell Bank sized satellite dish of Dale's in our garden. I wandered about for half an hour, eventually finding my house. I crashed out and slept like a baby.

Saudi Renal Unit

Normally when you come to work in a new hospital in the Middle East, you go through an orientation programme for around two weeks. You are then on three months' probation. You need to be assessed and signed off as competent to carry on working after the probationary period. As a locum Staff Nurse, you don't get any orientation you are sent straight to the unit and expected to work on the same day!

That first Saturday morning I awoke from a broken sleep. I was anxious. I had to walk to the main gate of Briga to join the crowd waiting for the bus to the hospital. It was winter and in North West Saudi Arabia it was effin' freezing. The bus that arrived was one of those 'coaster' type and there was a mad scramble to get on. It was clear that some folk would have to wait till the next one. I got on and it was packed. As we drove towards the hospital, I was struck by the lack of pristine sand dunes. As far as my eyes could see there were no beautiful cinematic dunes, just a lot of dirty looking sand!

The Iqama is the Saudi residency permit that every expat has. This you need to carry with you at all times. Being a locum, they gave me a temporary Iqama, which was basically a piece of A4 paper with Arabic writing and a stapled-on passport photo. Our hospital was a military facility, so you had to get through security, and they would come on the bus asking to see ID. They always spent ages checking mine, which was a real pain in the butt. Maybe they had never seen a temporary Iqama before?

The Renal Unit was in the main hospital building, although they were completing a standalone unit outside in the hospital grounds whilst I was there. Through a big double door, I walked into the place where I would work for the next three months. There was just one row of about nine machines in this room. There was an isolation cubicle for dialysing patients with infectious diseases. Separating the machines and the nurses was a long nurses' station. It was an odd design and when you sat behind it you had no view of the patients whatsoever.

The nursing team was a mixture of South African, Filipino and English. There was a girl there who had worked in the Outpatient Dialysis unit of the Royal in Edinburgh for a short time, although I had never met her. Her name was Joss. Thank God for her as she was very kind and patient with me. The Unit Acting Manager was a very chatty lady from one of the Caribbean Islands. She managed the ICU and was covering the Renal Unit until they found a permanent manager. The only good thing about the place on that first day was that it was all the same Gambro dialysis machines that I had used in Edinburgh.

They quickly showed me where to find emergency equipment and what numbers to dial in case of a cardiac arrest. They allocated me three patients. My first day was male patients. Female patients would come in the following day. None of the guys wanted the new nurse sticking needles in them. Saudi, it seems, did not differ from Scotland. My nerves were showing. I had no Arabic language other than a wee phrasebook given to me by Joan from the renal ward in Edinburgh. I thought all these old patients looked mean. My first two were fine but the last one was this really scary looking baba with a long beard and dark piercing Arabian eyes. He had a 'Gore-Tex' graft dialysis shunt on his inner thigh, and with these, you had to use a little more strength to pierce them with the needle. For him, I used too much strength and my needle punctured the graft. It's a common mistake and what you have to do is to wait and apply pressure before attempting another cannulation. He looked as mad as hell and was saying stuff, but as I did not understand I just smiled and nodded! That first day was a nightmare. It got easier though, and after a while both the men and the women were asking me to be their dialysis nurse for the day. With the support of the staff, I learned some Arabic too.

To say Tabuk was a culture shock is an understatement. I thought I was prepared and knowing someone who had worked there before helped me with that preparation, but nothing can really prepare you. Every expat goes through it and most survive! You just have to muddle through as best you can. Obviously, I must enjoy living in Saudi I'm still here after all these years.

It's a Backache

Every nurse in this land and beyond, faces the ever-present danger of hurting their back, seriously. Especially, if like me, you trained in the early 80s or before. These were the days when unsafe practices like the 'Australian lift' were a daily occurrence. Here's the thing about lifting bone bags. Unlike inanimate objects, people are unpredictable. Especially if that patient is confused and is as slippery as a slippery eel.

My unfortunate back incident happened way back, as a student in my first ward. D1 Surgical at Edinburgh's Western General. As a novice Australian lifter, I paired with a petite Staff Nurse in an effort to move a patient from being horizontal to semi vertical. When performing such a movement it is preferable that your weightlifting partner be of similar height to yourself. I was a skinny 5ft 11 and my particular partner did not breach 5ft. The aforementioned patient was (to say the least) oot ae it! And as we performed the manoeuvre, the patient squirmed with most of their weight bearing on me. Ouch! I felt something 'go' but it did not appear to be a serious injury. A day or two later I was incapacitated with a hell of a back muscle spasm! It had me writhing on the floor, trying to breathe and not blubbering like the big(ish) baby that I am. It took a good three days for me to recover and since then I have had intermittent 'back attacks'!

A week or two into my locum, I felt a nagging pain in the lower left flank of my peely wally back. The spasm was not there, but it was definitely on its way. This morning they assigned me to the isolation room where we dialysed patients with infectious diseases. To make matters worse, my patient was very (and I mean *very*) confused. As I gowned and masked up in my sweat-producing personal protection equipment, the patient was shouting God knows what in Arabic. After prepping the patient's arm, I picked up the dialysis needle and bent down to insert it. It was at this precise moment I experienced a serious back spasm that pulled me to my knees. I was on the floor quivering like a large jelly in total agony. The poor patient reacted by shouting even louder, and I was completely unable to move. After what seemed like hours (minutes in actuality) one of my co-workers saw me and rushed to my aid. I could barely speak as the pain gripped me spasm after spasm either side of my spine. They eventually got me out of my gown and on to a wheelchair. In a panic, the nursing assistant who was tasked with transporting my writhing self to the ER bumped me into every single door leading to the Emergency Room. Double ouch!

After a pain and muscle-relaxing injection, they arranged for a driver to take me back to the housing compound. I hobbled outside to find that rather than a car they had arranged an ambulance to take me back. The Saudi driver wanted me to lie on the stretcher in the ambulance's rear, but I insisted to sit up the front with him. After a twisty, bumpy 20 minutes' drive, we neared my Briga home. In front of our door stood a tree and God bless the driver he tried to get me as close to the door as possible but as the tree neared, I realized he had misjudged his positioning. He hit the effin' tree! Luckily, we were only moving at a snail's pace, but still there was a painful back jolt.

Eventually I got inside and attempted to remove my scrubs. As my trousers dropped to my ankles, my back took another major spasm! Triple ouch! I was rolling on the floor in agony and could not pull up my breeks. My housemate Dale was at work. Luckily, an Angel appeared in the form of my Canadian Paramedic neighbour who had heard of my back troubles. He immediately sprang into action, drawing up some much-needed Valium and spiking my bare bum. He was killing himself, laughing as he helped me off the floor. He pulled up my trousers and positioned me on our lumpy sofa! Three sick days later, I was fit enough to return to work. My back was still painful and the only pain killers they gave me was Diclofenac and they were upsetting my stomach. Whilst in the Unit I found some patient medication that had expired, including a tray of Tramadol. I was not that familiar with it, but I knew it was for moderate-to-severe pain. I took two. After an hour there was no action. I took another two. I waited another hour, and I felt some relief, but not much. Thinking the efficacy was less because the capsules were past their expiry date, I took the last couple on the tray as I was leaving to catch the bus home. It was only as I boarded the bus that the full effect of all the tablets kicked in! I was as high as a kite. It was the best 20-minute bus journey I had ever been on. I walked home feeling no pain and with a smile on my high face. Everything was just dreamy. Only negative thing was that I could not sleep. I must have been too high to sleep. It was an interesting experience, but I never took that much Tramadol again.

Work

I'm not saying it was easy, but I eventually settled into a work routine. I had learned to speak more Arabic, and I now felt more confidence with the patients. We had a lovely Saudi nurse Aziza who really helped me every shift and one of the patients, Ali, was a teacher and he taught me how to count in Arabic. Dialysis becomes a routine as you see the same patients three times a week, every week, and you inevitably get to know them well. It can be a challenge, and it does not matter if it's Scotland or Saudi. Patients with chronic illness can be difficult. You just have to take a deep breath sometimes and do what they tell you. Even down to the smallest thing, like how they want the tape that holds the needles in their arms during treatment placed. As a nurse you realise that they are only trying to gain some control of their lives which, mostly, is controlled by an artificial kidney machine. I'm not a saint. I sometimes lost my cool with them.

I preferred the female dialysis days, although at the beginning these were a bit of a nightmare. Not one of them wanted me to look after them. It took a wee while for me to build up trust. Half of them were in their twenties and as Tabuk is so remote I was probably the first Western guy they ever saw up close. Slowly it got easier. All the ladies covered their faces with a black veil. Only a few of our old 'Mamas' showed their faces.

The only time I would see a face was when there was some emergency and we had to resuscitate them. During mealtimes, after I had served their food, I would go sit behind the large nurses' station. From there I could observe them directly and they couldn't see me. They would unveil to eat. Occasionally for a laugh I would stand up quickly and show my face. Immediately there was a flap of black as each patient all along the unit scrambled to cover their faces like a Mexican veil wave.

Briga Days and Nights

When not at work I mostly chilled in the villa watching videos. If Dale was not working, we would hang out. At weekends I would attend some local parties hoping I might meet a lady, but in Briga it was near to impossible to meet someone who was not married or did not have a boyfriend or was carrying more emotional baggage than me! At weekends in Briga they would smuggle single women in the boot of cars so that they could spend their days off with their boyfriends.

On a Sunday we would go to what was the old community café besides a waterless swimming pool. This place was probably nice once, but its glory days were long gone. The only reason to go was that bacon was served for brunch! There was a local store for food shopping, and they had a phone that you could use for calling home. You told the guy what country you were phoning, and he would time you and then charge a fee based on some rate that they probably just made up. It took me a while to enjoy the food in Tabuk, and I lost a fair bit of weight.

Occasionally Eamon and Christine would take me into town for an enjoyable meal and a wander around the shops. Tabuk was very conservative and Christine, whose family is Mauritian, had light brown skin. With her black abaya and headscarf, she could easily have passed for a Saudi lady. The 'Mattawa' or religious police were constantly driving about in Toyota Land Cruisers, making sure that people were not 'sinning'! It was OK for me to be with a married couple but not OK if there was a single female. If so, they would demand to see a marriage licence or shout at us to separate. One night Eamon and I wanted to go to the local 'music' shop to pick up some tapes. There they sold all these brilliant bootleg cassette collections, of which I bought many. They allowed no females in this shop. Outside on the pavement is where they had to stand and there was a kiosk-like window where they could be served. This night I had left Eamon waiting to pay for his purchases and I joined Chris out on the street. From out of nowhere a bunch of short thobe-wearing, bearded guys came rushing towards us demanding to see our marriage certificate. Initially, they thought she was Saudi! We pointed to Eamon in the shop, and he came out immediately to show his legal documents. I was told to move away from the lady!

Dale, my roomie was not one for going out and partying, but one evening we persuaded him to take us to a night out at the nearby British Aerospace compound. It would be my first and only time there, and when we arrived, I saw that they lived in a beautiful place compared to our Briga shanty town. Pleasant villas and manicured lawns. They also had a 'function' hall and to my surprise had a fully stocked bar. There was a live band playing too. And they served tasty food. You could dance with whoever you wanted! It was a real eye opener for me. We all got pretty trashed that night and I was lucky not to have been arrested as on the way home I was hanging out the back window of Dale's truck shouting 'I love you' to all passing Saudi cars! I never learn!

Many people thought that Dale and I were brothers because we looked alike. He was a slightly older version of me! Unlike me, he liked to keep himself to himself in Briga. There were a fair few Canadians there and I got on well with most of them, although we had an issue with our neighbour 'Brad' who was in charge of Briga maintenance. It was not a problem with him as a person, it was that we had a major issue with the toilet in our villa. It was prone to overflowing, and it was nearly impossible to take a #2 unless you wanted to clean it off the floor after flushing. Not nice. Seemingly it was the roots of all the Briga trees invading all the drainage the pipes and blocking them. We had taken to sitting on the toilet with a plastic bag to catch our waste! We then had to tie it up and throw it in the bin! Effin' nightmare! I was so fed up with the poor service we got from the maintenance crew that I took it to higher management. I received a very irate call from Brad saying that I should have come to him and not gone over his head. Now it made him look bad. This was not my purpose, but I was equally annoyed telling him that I was so fed up with shitting into plastic bags and something had to be done. He sent a crew over and they fixed it, but for the rest of my time there Brad was less friendly towards me! I didn't mind.

Another incredibly annoying thing about Briga life was the amount of effin' cats there were on the compound. Half feral and always hungry. I like cats, but there were literally 100s of them wandering around. Dale was a big softie, and he liked to feed the cat gang regularly. Every morning as I was leaving to go to work, when you opened the front door loads of effin' cats invaded our porch area – all wanting to get into the villa. Every single morning for three months I would have to fend off this marauding gang of purring perps.

I also got stoned once more in Tabuk, but it's not what you think. I needed to find a bank to cash my salary cheque and I couldn't be arsed going into town. I was given directions to a bank in the Hospital compound. This compound was ginormous. It being a beautifully sunny day and not too hot, I walked. First thing that happened was that a car followed me. There was a young guy in a beat up old American Chevy who drove past me and double backed a couple of time. I was a wee bit worried. Eventually he pulled up next to me and said in his best English, 'I would like to offer you a ride.' I thanked him but said I preferred to walk. This he didn't understand, so I had to show my preference physically to him and I think he got the idea. Not long after he disappeared, I was walking past a primary school that was just letting out its pupils. I doubt any of them had seen a white guy up close and personal. Once they spotted me, they all shouted and laughed. I thought it was cute. The next thing was that two of them picked up some pebbles and lobbed them at me! Then many of their pals joined them until there was a flurry of wee stones coming through the air in my direction. Not wanting to embarrass myself and run, I quickened my step to get as far away from the wee stone throwers as quickly as possible. I could still hear their laughter in the distance.

Before I left Tabuk, we went on a day trip to the Red Sea. I was desperate to see a coral reef and some colourful fish. Christine and Eamon, Dale and I set out on what was a long drive. It was worth it, though. The scenery was totally breath-taking in its stark sandy ruggedness. We could have been on Mars. There were jagged peaks, and lonely stretches of nothing. It was March, and the weather was perfect for me. Akin to a good Scottish summer! We finally arrived and set up our wee camp for the day. My work mate Joss had told me to be careful about 'fire coral'. If it scratched your legs, it was very painful. All day I was totally paranoid about this. I had borrowed a boiler suit from someone as I thought it would protect me from this underwater fire stuff! I looked like a total madman walking into the Red Sea with a black boiler suit on! My three mates were killing themselves, laughing as I put on my mask and snorkel. The water was not Skye cold, but it was not warm. Also, we had to walk for ages over dead coral to finally find the actual live stuff. My head was freezing as I tried my best to paddle around in my boiler suit using my snorkel. My pals were still laughing at me, but I saw some beautifully coloured fish and the beautiful reef before the cold drove me back to shore. We had lunch and a laugh and eventually packed up and made our long way home.

$$\mathcal{O}$$

Leaving Tabuk

I survived my three-month locum. I survived my first time working abroad, but my Tabuk time was ending. The Consultant in charge of the Renal Unit and the acting Manager tried to persuade me to stay. My co-workers were happy with me and it appeared I was a hit with the patients. The Renal Unit would soon move into their new building and I could get a senior position. I was tempted, but there were other things on my mind and my future was not to be in Tabuk.

There was to be one more meaningful experience that occurred not long before I was about to fly home to Scotland. It turned out to be one of the most beautiful and touching experiences I would have as a professional nurse.

Amna was one patient who dialysed in our unit. She was a young mother who had her face covered when I attached her to the machine. After having me care for her during her sessions, she removed the veil to reveal a pretty and kind face. Her eyes were always full of mischief. She spoke as much English as I did Arabic, we just communicated visually as best we could. Many times, as I was about to put the dialysis needle in her arms, she would move it away yelling 'Ouch', then breaking into hysterics! She thought this hilarious. Other times, as I would pass, she would throw pieces of flat bread at me and pretend to be sleeping. It was all innocent fun just to help her pass away the dialysis hours. It was Ramadan when I first arrived in Tabuk and there was a show on the Saudi channel called 'Tash Ma Tash'. It was a comedy show that poked gentle fun at Saudi culture and the people loved it. I learned the theme song and would sing it to all the ladies who would all laugh at this skinny white guy trying to amuse them.

This female dialysis day Amna arrived very excited and was really trying to tell me something. I enlisted the help of Aziza to translate, and it turned out that Amna was going to get a kidney transplant. Wow! One of her relatives had been matched and would donate one of their precious organs to her. I was over the moon for her and through Aziza told her this. She asked that I come visit her after her surgery. I said I would. Post-surgery in the evening, I grabbed Aziza and went to the ICU to check on Amna. When we arrived, we were told by her nurse that when she awoke the first person she asked for was me. I truly was touched. Entering the room, she was so excited to see me. She looked so happy. I had to tell her that I would leave the country soon and that I would not see her again. She cried. Aziza went to comfort her. Amna struggled to get something out of her locker. She found the small toiletry bag given free by the hospital and she wanted me to have it as a leaving gift. She then took my hand and squeezed and told Aziza to tell me thanks for talking care of her over the last few months. It was a touching moment, and I had a wee tear come from my eye when I said goodbye. I have never forgotten that moment and how it made me feel.

A few days later I was back on an aeroplane flying home. Reflecting on what I had just been through and what I was now going to do on my return to Edinburgh. I had rented my flat out, but I was so lucky that my good pal Ian let me stay in his beautiful flat just off Bruntsfield Road and from there I was to plan the next step of my life.

∽

A Murder of One

This gets a wee bit complicated and slightly convoluted but is typical of me and my life. Or should I say my love life? I need to take you back to around 1992 (ish). Whilst working in the Renal Isolation Unit. I was not the only agency nurse as there were a couple of us who were regulars, one of them being my pal, Stuart. Working life was easy then, and we would do our best to have a laugh. It was a time when a group of us would regularly go out and get drunk. It was around this time that Connie came to work with us. She was originally from Scotland, but her adopted parents had moved to Australia. She was travelling with her boyfriend and had based herself in Edinburgh. They lived in Morningside. She was one of those rare people who was beautiful both inside and out. I have been lucky in my life to have met a few girls with this quality. The last being my wife, Janya.

Connie immediately fitted into our crowd and was always up for going out on the town and enjoying herself. She didn't drink much, and she seemed happy to be sober and partying. Over the months that we worked together and got to know each other I had a wee fancy for her which I kept to myself. I believe it was reciprocated as we got closer and closer with nothing actually happening. I carried on living my single guy life and it was fine. Our bunch from work continued to party on. Close to the time that she and her boyfriend were about to move on several of us were at a 1970s club held in Moray House Student Union. Anyone who has ever been to this venue knows a club night there is hot and sticky. As the night was ending, Connie and I were holding each other very close. I felt the desire to make a lip move, but I did not want to spoil the moment. Two hot sweating bodies holding each other close. I felt it and so did she. We walked home together. Passing my Bruntsfield door, I told her I would walk her home. She agreed for me to walk her halfway back. Compromise made, we strolled and talked all the way to the beginning of Morningside Road. This is where we agreed to part. As we hugged goodnight, inevitably, we kissed. Let's just say that it was not a friendly peck on the cheek. We said goodnight and goodbye.

Time ticked by as time is wont to do and my agency job turned into a full-time employment. By 1996 I had that feeling in my chest and I was getting edgy about my life and what I should do. Something was off and I was unsure how to get it back on. I received a call one winter night and a familiar voice that I had not heard for a number of years was on the other end of the line. 'Do you know who this is?' She asked. I knew immediately. It was Connie, back in Scotland. She was staying just outside Edinburgh and she wanted to meet up, so we arranged for a drink the following evening. I met her off the train and as she would get the last train back, I suggested we go to the pub on the Mound formerly known as Misty's. There we sat and drank a few and caught up with each other's lives over the last four odd years. She was more beautiful than I remembered, and I felt a heart-string tug. I was conscious of the ticking time and the fact that she needed to get to the station for her train. In my mind, I had planned to see her on the train. Get up the road and watch a movie. My plan did not go to plan!

Expecting my good-looking friend to say it's getting late, and she better be making a move. She took me by surprise by asking, 'Do you remember our last night together?' I said something like 'How could I forget!' She then hit me with a sucker punch and said that she would like to carry on from where we had left off the last time. Surprised, I asked what about her train and her reply was that she could get one first thing in the morning! We kissed. It was totally unexpected, and I was totally excited. We moved on to Negociant's for a drink where our hugging and kissing continued. Like teenagers, we laughed and drank and made our way to Bruntsfield Place. It was worth the four year wait to have her with me for those night hours. True to her word, she left early.

The next day I was on night shift when a call came through to the nurses' station. It was Connie. She just wanted to hear my voice. She wished she had stayed longer with me in Bruntsfield. I agreed as we voiced our goodbyes. She would soon be back on a plane to the other side of the world, and I would be all on my own.

Over the next year we kept in touch. Sometimes stealing a phone call as she lived with her boyfriend. I wrote her letters of love and sent cassette compilations for her to listen to in the hope that the songs would remind her of me. I think we both felt the same. It was easier for me to express my feelings as she was so far away, and I thought I would probably never see her again. Very typical of me. It was a fantasy. Connie was breaking up with her long-term boyfriend, and the last thing she would do was jump into another serious relationship with me. She also had some deeply personal issues surfacing, and again getting into something with me was not her plan.

It was fine. I moved on. Wendy worked with me in Renal High Dependency, and we got together in a secret relationship that soon turned into a *not* secret relationship. It was great. Honestly, it was better than great. It really was … until that feeling in my chest returned and made me leave my job and fly to Saudi Arabia!

During my last month in Tabuk I came up with a plan to do something I thought I would never do, and that was to work in

London. I would join a London-based nursing agency and see how things went until I decided what my next move was.

A week or so before my flight I got a letter from Connie saying that she was flying to the UK and would be based in London. I did not know what to think or what to do. If I told her that I was planning to go to London, she might have thought that I was only going because of her and I didn't want her to think that.

Back in Edinburgh staying alone in Ian's flat I worked on my plan and was waiting for an agency to contact me regarding work at the Renal Unit of University College Hospital. I needed cash so went back to my old unit in the Royal for a couple of months. I really shouldn't have as it was like taking a big step back, but I was too lazy to work anywhere else. Whilst in Saudi I really missed Edinburgh and Wendy, but when I got back there, I was not happy. I felt guilty about Wendy, and I – being me – explained nothing to her, which I totally regret. She deserved better. I was in contact with Connie, and we spent a few days together in Edinburgh. The time we spent was special, and I tried to ignore that chest feeling and the heart-strings tugging. I just wanted to enjoy the closeness with Connie before she returned to London and mostly I did. Before she left, I told her of my plan, and I tried to make it clear it was not to chase her. I wanted to chase her, but I knew what the outcome would be. She was dealing with her own stuff. This I knew.

I made the move to the *big*, big city. By this time my Edinburgh pal Ian worked in St Thomas's Hospital and had a studio flat nearby. He let me bunk with him till I could find my own place. Once I had settled in London and was working, I tried not to call her. I tried not to see her. I really did, but it was difficult. I loved her and knew that she did not love me. Those first months in London were surreal.

We met a couple of times and spent one last day together in Ian's wee flat. I tried to breathe that day and enjoy as we caressed on his veranda in the muggy London afternoon. We spent one more night together, and that was the last time I saw her. It was better for me and my heart.

London

I joined the Hibernian Nursing Agency in North London. I liked their name! They promised me E Grade shifts in the Renal Unit of the Middlesex Hospital on Mortimer Street. This hospital was part of the University College of London group. The Manager had called me in Edinburgh and said they were desperately in need of good staff. I could work as much or as little as I wanted.

The only problem I had was not having anywhere to stay. Luckily for me I had an angel called Ian who worked as a night Nursing Officer at St Thomas's Hospital, and he offered to let me stay with him. I had just spent the last few months living in his Edinburgh apartment rent free! My plan was to work solid for six weeks. Save as much as possible and then I'd fly over to the US for a two-month vacation.

Both the agency and the Middlesex knew of my travel plans, and both said I could work as much as I wanted before and after my holiday. Ian was kind enough to let me stay until I got back from America. Then I would have to find a room of my own. America was not where I wanted to be, but I thought that it would take my mind off my pulled heartstrings. It did, and it didn't.

This was not the first time I had stayed at Ian's small but perfectly formed London flat. Kirsten and I had visited him for a long weekend of drinking a couple of years back, so it was not totally strange to me. On my arrival at Kings Cross, I afforded myself the luxury of a taxi to Ian's. I was too lazy to lug my rucksack about in the underground.

His apartment was in a block way behind the old GLC building opposite the Houses of Parliament. Close to his work. His flat was close to Waterloo station where the Euro-Express train was based before they moved it. I got intimately familiar with Waterloo as the noise from the trains and the lines became my lullaby to sleep. I knew every set of points' sound as it changed.

From an aesthetic point of view, the apartment complex was a concrete carbuncle, but I really liked the look of it. Very 1960s. Ian's pad was a studio with a wee kitchen and toilet with an inordinately deep bath. A living/bedroom and a sizeable veranda. Ian had excellent taste and he had it very nicely decorated. The veranda contained a large number of potted plants. The single bed doubled as a sofa, and if I remember right, he also had a futon. He would come home to crash just as I was leaving. It worked out fine because we never saw too much of each other. If we had he probably would have bounced me very quickly.

Getting to work did not take too long, as the hospital was not that far from Ian's. I would get the Waterloo Underground to Goodge Street and then walk along Mortimer Street to the hospital. The unit looked decent, and the staff were friendly to me. The worst thing about the place was the heat. It was summer in the city, and the Middlesex had no AC that I could see. We just opened all the windows. The building was old, but the ward layout was practical, with enough space to work. They even had one Scottish lady working there who at the time I thought enjoyed having me as a colleague, but it turned out that I was wrong. She fed the manager a lot of nonsense about me whilst trying her best to get my shifts cancelled. What I did to deserve it, I don't know. Colleagues can be strange sometimes. The work was what I enjoyed; we had pleasant patients and not too many acute cases. They had one guy who was a Kurdish refugee and whose kidneys failed because he had been tortured in Turkey. I can never forget the look in his eyes. The eyes of someone who had suffered real pain.

This was the summer of 1998, and it was World Cup time. It was the last World Cup finals that Scotland qualified for and it was they who would play Brazil in the opening match in Paris. I spent that day watching the game in a pub off Tottenham Court Road. All on my ownsome. I was no doubt depressed and with a certain degree of anxiety, but I got through it. I knew things ultimately would get better I just didn't know when! Scotland got beat, by the way.

Those weeks just disappeared in a daze for me, and it was getting close to my trip to America. This vacation I would visit the East and the West Coast on what would be my last time stateside.

༄

Raining in Baltimore

It's amazing how different you feel when flying from Heathrow to JFK without first having to fly down from Glasgow. The journey seemed incredibly quick. Helen picked me up and drove me all the way to Debbie's house in the Poconos of Pennsylvania. There we picked up her cute daughter, Skye. This trip there would be no Houston. Helen had been living in this nice country cabin near Harrisburg. It was rural and about an hour's drive from Wilkes-Barre. If my mood had been less grey, I would have said that the countryside was exquisite. Which it was, I was just not in the mood to appreciate it. Helen knew I had been on a downward trajectory, and she did her level best to help me. Some days were better than others. Most of the first couple of weeks went past in a fugue of depression and feeling sorry for myself.

Whilst there I had decided to go to Canada and visit my old Saudi roomie, Dale. He lived in Regina, Saskatchewan, and the only way I could get there on a budget was by bus. I spent my last night in Pennsylvania at the Wilkes-Barre Holiday Inn, as Helen had arranged for her friend Billy to take me to the bus station early the next day. Boredom led me to the hotel bar. It was early evening and empty. I got talking to the barman, who was glad of some company. There was a band setting up, so I thought I would stay, and the barman informed me that tonight was 'singles' night. Maybe I would get lucky! I didn't. The band was excellent, a real professional club act. I was downing the Buds pretty swiftly, and at one point the singer came over to me and encouraged me to sing the line of a Meatloaf song. I sang 'I want you,' she sang 'I need you' and then carried on with 'don't be sad coz two out of three aint bad.' After the bar closed, I ended up outside with the barman and a few of his friends in his 1970s corvette smoking and talking crap in the hotel parking lot for a couple of hours. It was a laugh. I had to wake up very early and had a rotten hangover when Billy came to pick me up. He was a good guy. Before dropping me off, he had loaded his pipe and told me to take as many puffs as possible before he stopped. The effect took hours to wear off, and it was Toronto before I knew what was happening!

I was to be on a bus for three and a half effin' days! Surprisingly, it was not that bad. The last six hours were the worst!

I wouldn't recommend that journey back then, but now with the amount of tech to keep me amused, I would do it. Back in 98, I only had my Walkman blasting out Counting Crows who were helping me through this bad time. As we drove close to the Great Lakes, I understood why they got their name. They were never ending.

I made it to Dale's in one piece and after a shower and some food I was feeling relatively human. He had a nice one-bedroom apartment, and I slept on the sofa. He was working a lot, so most of the time I just chilled. I enjoyed Regina and I could have easily stayed there and lived in the place. Dale's family were super nice, and we ended up having a few drunken nights. One night Dale, his brother and I lay in the outside Jacuzzi drinking beer and smoking, staring into the Saskatchewan sky. It was cool.

After a short week, it was time for me to move again. Dale dropped me at the airport, and I made my way to San Jose via San Francisco. My Aunt Anne who is my Dad's sister has lived there for years and this was my first visit to stay with her and her family. My mood was lightening up, and I did not want to show them I was in any way, shape or form depressed! This would be the first time to meet my Police Officer Uncle Maury. My Dad had led me to believe that he was a quiet guy because he did not speak too much to my Dad when he visited. I found the opposite to be true. He chatted with me all the time. He was a really cool guy. I might not have agreed with some of his views, but I found him to be a genuinely friendly guy who treated me very well. I soon realised that the reason my Dad thought that he was quiet was that Maury found it difficult to understand his Glasgow accent, so he kept conversations short so as not to embarrass himself or my old man! One of the first things he told me was how easy it was to understand me when I spoke! Uncle Maury has passed, but I will never forget him and especially his visits to Glasgow.

My Auntie Anne is my Godmother, so perhaps she has always had a soft spot for me. I love her dearly, although like her husband I don't always agree with her point of view. As this was my first West Coast visit, she really pulled out all the stops for me. In my short time there, we did a lot. They lived on Penitencia Creek Road, which was shadowed by some beautiful rolling green hills. It was a sedate neighbourhood. They treated me like a king, and I had some time to get to know my younger cousins Kyle, Heather and Ryan. Very cool kids. Now the boys are men with their own families. I'm Facebook friends with them, and I hope they don't mistake my dislike for their country's (and mine's) government and their foreign policies as a dislike of America. Nothing could be further from the truth. You just have to look at my favourite bands, movies and TV shows to see how much I love America and the positive effect these artists have had on me.

Our first adventure was to San Francisco, by train. God bless my auntie because she booked us into the Fairmont Hotel, which was used in the TV series of Arthur Hailey's book Hotel starring James Brolin. I loved that show. I loved Rod Taylor and Karl Malden in the 1960s movie version too. My Aunt Anne likes her wine, and I would say that she is a wee bit of a connoisseur. She is a big red wine fan who would spend a fortune on a bottle from a vineyard that she liked. Me, I'm colour blind, I like red and white. We went to the hotel bar for a drink, and I just enjoyed sipping beer in such a cool place.

We did all the tourist things which was great. It really took my mind off my personal struggles and I felt less and less sorry about my situation. We ate at a fancy Chinese restaurant in

Chinatown. We wandered the streets and checked out the shops. We rode a tram car all the way down to the terminus where you got off and helped turn the car around. Loved that. We got on a boat and went to Alcatraz Island and walked the floors of the prison. What an effin' nightmare it must have been to have found yourself locked up on that hellish Island. There is a camera spool somewhere with a photo of me in one cell. It was creepy, but I really enjoyed every minute of it.

San Francisco is one of the cities that I felt straight at home in just like Paris, London, New York and Kuala Lumpur. Perhaps I lived there in a past life? The next day my aunt planned a champagne breakfast in the Fairmont, which involved riding a lift to the top of a modern tower and finding the restaurant with panoramic views across the city. Very fancy. I kind of felt out of place. That night, which was to be our last, she took me to another fancy restaurant whose name has gone from my mind. I just remember the walls being covered in a dark red velvet wallpaper and lots of heavy drapes. I had one of the best steaks that I have ever eaten in my entire life. We tried not to drink too much as the next day we were being picked up early to go to the Napa Valley.

Slightly hung over the next morning, a maroon stretch-limousine that she had hired to take us to Napa greeted our hung-over bodies. It was very cool. The inside had luxurious red seats and after we got out of the city; I put my head down for a pre-Napa nap. We were booked into a boutique type hotel and we rested up because the next morning we would be up early.

Where we were going was to be a surprise, but it was a very early rise. The same limo driver met us and took us off into the countryside. When we stopped, I saw what my aunt had planned for us this early Napa morning. She had booked us on a hot-air balloon with a champagne breakfast! I would be lying if I said I wasn't nervous. This fear of flying had also turned into a bit of fear of heights, too. There were many people milling around and around five balloons being prepared for take-off. Once fully inflated we all got loaded into the basket. Perhaps around twelve people. Most were young couples apart from me and my old(ish) aunt! The noise of the gas-powered flame thing above our heads was deafening. I was really crapping it for a while. We rose, and we rose. I tried not to look over the edge and I also tried not to look scared! Difficult. By the time we got to our cruising height, my nerves had finally eased, and I could enjoy the beautiful view of the valley and of all the other balloons floating in the early morning air. There was a morning mist stretching along the green rolling hills and vineyards. If only I had a camera! Napa is beautiful from the air. We had to land, and it was not as bumpy as some other balloons. On the ground they welcomed us with our champagne breakie. Brilliant!

The limo driver was local to the area, and I asked him if there was any place for us 'young folk' to hang out at night as I fancied ditching my aunt for the evening. He suggested a pub, and he said he would come and pick me up and take me there free of charge! My aunt had probably given him a very good tip before. True to his word, he turned up in the evening with his stretch limo and took me to this live music bar. Funny thing was that it had rather large front windows, so many punters saw the limo pull up and this pale skinny guy get out and walk into the bar. Maybe they thought I was someone famous. I had a nice but uneventful night and returned to our hotel safely relatively sober.

The rest of the Napa trip is a bit of a blur because of the amount of grape juice imbibed. We visited numerous wineries and sampled a lot of their wines. Most of the time I was steamboats drunk. My aunt had hired this nice convertible for touring the wineries. If you have ever seen the movie 'Sideways' imagine it was a middle-aged woman and her nephew. That's what we were like. One day we were both under the wine influence. My aunt had purchased a rather expensive case of wine and I staggered with it to the car boot. We ended up forgetting about it and only remembered she had bought it when we travelled back to San Jose. Our last adventure was on a wine train. I thought it was cool, but my memory of it is clouded in wine mist. We travelled in a silver carriage. We ate lunch and I remember somebody talking about wines and us passengers getting to sample them. I sampled too much.

On our return to San Jose, I just tried to chill. It was getting close to going back to London. I spent the day at a local festival of arts and music in an enormous park, and one evening when Anne and I were out I stayed out to see what the San Jose nightlife was like. She was worried. I don't think she wanted me to be on my own, but I told her I was a big boy and would be fine! I ended up stocious, doing a bar crawl, finishing in this upmarket night club. Plenty of pretty ladies. Not one of them looked in my direction. I jumped a taxi home, and the driver was this really cool Sikh guy who told me to call him anytime I needed a cab. He delivered me safely back to the house of my aunt.

All too soon, my longish vacation was over. My mood was better leaving the States than it was arriving. I was so grateful to my aunt and her family for making my trip memorable. With a call to London, I had arranged to stay a night with Ian and then go to my new accommodation, organised by my nursing agency. I called the Middlesex and booked some shifts. Early morning and I was all packed to go. Anne delivered me to a minibus that drove me to San Francisco airport. Anyone who has travelled from this airport knows that because of the unpredictable weather there are numerous flight delays. This happened to me and my first flight was late taking off and I missed my connecting flight to London. I don't remember what airport it was, but I could not find one person to help. I called my aunt and told her I was stuck she just told me to get back on a flight to San Francisco and call her from there. Walking about in a daze, I decided to go downstairs where I found numerous desks. Luckily, the first desk lady solved all my problems. She booked me on a flight leaving ASAP and got me to the gate just in time. I was out of breath as I took my 747 seat. I did not have enough time to fear flying.

Back at Heathrow my luggage had been lost, and I was told to call them later as I did not know my new address. Arriving back in London and walking across Westminster Bridge I felt some degree of positivity.

Recovering the Satellites

If any album can describe me and my emotional self it has to be Counting Crow's second recording. It's funny, I loved their debut album, but I did not buy their second record for the longest time. I was worried that I would be disappointed. I now realise that it was fate that made me wait. It was not till I was on vacation in the US that I eventually bought the tape from a music shop in Scranton. The minute I played it in my friend Helen's car, it was love baby. I was in an emotional tornado, and each and every song on this album was like a musical medicine. From the opening chords of 'Catapult' to the end song 'Long December', I knew in my soul that this record had been written for me and my ears only. From lonely American days to lonely London nights, I carried this constantly. The title track was exactly how I felt at the time. 'Mercury' was how I felt about Connie. 'I'm not Sleeping Anymore' described me to my core. 'Millers Angels' and 'Goodnight Elizabeth' were lullabies for my adult heart. If you were to pin me down and force me to choose my most favourite album ever, I think I would have to choose this. Thank you, Counting Crows.

Tottenham

With a name like Hibernian, it was obvious that my nursing agency had Irish connections. Having returned from the US, they informed me that they had found me a room in a terraced house in Rosebery Avenue, Tottenham. I knew very little about the area and only had negative feelings about Tottenham because it's where Broadwater Farm estate is, which was notorious in the 1980s. I was told to meet the landlady at Tottenham Hale Underground, and she would show me to the house. The landlady was Irish. She picked me up as arranged and drove a few minutes to a narrow road lined with red bricked terrace houses either side. I was told that there were three Irish girls in the house sharing. She showed me to my room, which was what one would call the front parlour or living room. The house had a small lounge with a TV and a kitchen and bathroom built into a back extension. It was nice and clean. My room had a double bed and a wardrobe, along with a chair and a fireplace. It was a good size, and it would do me fine. The landlady handed me the rent book and told me that she would collect the rent every month. I paid one month's rent as a deposit. She left me to unpack.

Later on, I would meet my new housemates and find out that one of them had their boyfriend in permanent residence. They were all in their early twenties and as far as I could see they were always out on the lash. Very friendly, though. They treated me like the old man of the house. That first night they took me to an Irish pub just off the High Road and they all got slaughtered. I didn't as I was working the next day.

I had booked shifts at the Middlesex to honour but found that working there was no longer fun and so asked the agency to find me other work. I said my bye byes to the staff who I liked, and I never returned to the Renal Unit, although I still worked in other wards in the Hospital. One shift I did on an oncology ward. One of my charges was an older Irish guy who was in the last stages of lung cancer. He had a very young-looking wife, and I would make a joke or two about that with him. I felt very sorry for him. Actually, that unit was so short staffed I felt sorry for all the patients. My Irish patient had been lying in soiled linen when I came on, and he was obviously embarrassed about it. The first thing I did was clean him up and change his bed sheets. Later in the hospital lobby, his wife caught up with me and thanked me for being so good to her husband. I never returned to that ward, but I can still see that guy's face and he was probably about the same age as I am now.

Moorfields

Mobile phones were becoming more common in 1998, but they were too expensive for my pocket. In our Tottenham house the landlady had installed a small coin-operated phone and that's what rang one day with my agency on the other end. They asked me if I would like to do some shifts at Moorfields Eye Hospital. I had never heard of it, and I had never worked in ophthalmology before. This I told my agency, and they said no problem. I said yes.

Getting to the hospital was not like the old days in Edinburgh's Royal when I could just walk. No, this journey required some planning and took an effin' long time! I would have to get the train from Tottenham Hale Underground, change at Kings Cross, and get to Old Street. Then walk along City Road till I came to the hospital doors. It took a good hour to get there. They booked me to work on the ward and I was slightly nervous as this was the first time I had stepped into an eye hospital. Ever. I was greeted by the Sister and shown around to get my bearings. My shift began. Two things were noticeable after a wee while of work. The first being that it was like travelling back in time regarding the nurses. By that I mean their uniforms with pinafores and fancy hats. On my break I did not see one male nurse, it was all females. The nursing officers had fancy headwear, again harking back to an earlier age. There was definitely an old school vibe, but it was not unpleasant. My other thought was how the hell did I not know about this kind of nursing before? Most of the patients were ambulatory, and they only had issues with their eyes, so it was pretty light work for my old back. After the shift ended, the ward sister asked me to work more shifts. I said yes without hesitation. It was only a few shifts that I did in the ward, then I was asked if I would work in the Emergency Room. Yes, was my answer.

That 'yes' led me to pretty much working full time between the A&E and the Outpatient clinics for more than a year. The clinics were always busy, but the day went past quickly. There was a great bunch of staff working there, which included administration and technicians. I really enjoyed it. My job was to test the patients' Visual Acuity and to put dilating drops into their eyes. Very simple. I worked with patients from all over London and educated myself about various eye conditions.

Working in the A&E was great because we saw nothing but eye emergencies and as I was not permanent staff, some duties I could not do. This suited my lazy bones down to the ground. The Nursing Officer in Charge was also very kind to me, and it was fun as everybody was so proper. There were few if any male nurses. I even considered doing the Moorfields Ophthalmology Nursing course. Moorfields is a world-renowned ophthalmology hospital, and the course would really help my career. If only that chest feeling was not present. It was. But it was dull. I missed Connie too, but I was working and travelling back and forwards from Tottenham I didn't have much time for anything else.

‿✦‿

Take the High Road

Although I worked most of the time, I had free time to spend with myself, mostly. My house mates were cool and all that, but I didn't really want to hang out with them that much. This meant I was on my own, a lot. I enjoyed living in Tottenham. My fears about it were unwarranted, and I found myself at home there. I liked the High Road, which was just a walk away. At that time in the late 90s it had seen better days but still had a few shops worth visiting. Sometimes if I was on a late shift, I would walk the road till I got to Seven Sisters Underground, then I would jump the train to work. Similarly, on the way home from an early shift, I would get off at Seven Sisters and walk. Weather permitting, of course. I found myself a local pub in The Plough, which was not too far from my house. There I was quite happy to be on my own and drink a few pints and watch the world go by. My best pal Les came to visit me and I took him to my local. Even he enjoyed just sitting, watching life go by. Sometimes for a scenery I would cross the road to another pub, but it was always too busy. Usually, I would have no more than three pints. It was Kronenbourg 1664 or Carling Black Label that I would sup. Three pints would get me merry and that was fine by me.

In an effort to get fit, I joined the gym at the nearby Tottenham Sports Centre. I would go there up to five times a week. Between light work outs and swimming, I would use the tanning bed too, just to remove some of my peely wallyness. For months I got into a routine with work and then the gym, rewarding myself with a few Plough pints. It took my mind off Connie and made me feel good. I reckon it was the fittest I have ever been when I lived in Tottenham.

It was during these gym sessions that I noticed this very attractive girl who, like me, seemed to regularly 'get physical'. Being a guy and single at the time I would often try to steal a glance without being caught. I didn't want to come across as a pervert or get thrown out of the gym! Over the coming days and weeks I had convinced myself that this super attractive lady was giving me the 'eye'. I was *so* 100% sure of her hidden optical affections that I planned to talk to her. At the water fountain is where I made my move. I just said hello. Nothing else. A few more weeks passed, and we got to saying 'Hi' to each other and I was sure I was still receiving her amorous eye as we worked out. The gym was not that big, so who else could she have been looking at?

Eventually I caught a break, and we ended up leaving the Sports Centre at the same time. As we walked towards the High Road, I realized that it was now or never! Palpitating and sweaty palmed, I forced the words out. 'Wanna go out for a drink?' fell from my mouth in expectant hope. For what seemed like a lifetime, the air between us hung as silent as a room where a pin drop could be heard. Her eventual answer? 'No!' As knock backs go, it was not the first (or last) and I took it like a man. I still saw her often working out, and I was still sure she was giving me the eye!

Because of the alcohol adventures of my housemates and the fact that they never paid their rent on time (I always did) we were asked to vacate the premises in Tottenham. Working more than full time at Moorfields, I knew that many of the female nurses that I worked with stayed in the nurses' accommodation which was just off City Road close to the hospital. They suggested I ask if I could move in there. I thought that being an agency nurse it would be impossible, but I had not considered the amount of goodwill credit I had because of my willingness to work any shift at brief notice. The A&E Nursing Officer put in a kind word for me to the Nursing Officer in Charge and they allowed me to rent a room. Unheard of at the time for a non-Moorfields nurse to be staying in the accommodation. At least now my journey to work was short!

One morning I was working in one of the busy clinics. The routine would be that we would call the patients first, check their visual acuity, and then instil dilating drops in each eye. They would then return to their seat until the drops worked. It would normally take around twenty minutes. We would then call them to be seen by the doctor. I grabbed the first file on the pile and called out the patient's name. Out of the crowded waiting area came this gorgeous girl. It was the girl from the gym! God's honest! I greeted her with a warm smile and as she neared, a smile of recognition lit up her face. Hellos done, I sat her down to check her vision. Because of her eye condition, she had very poor distant vision and was a Moorfields regular. As I dropped the stinging eye drops the realisation that all of those times in the gym, she was not giving me the 'eye' – she could hardly see six feet in front of her. Her head was facing my direction, but those beautiful eyes of hers did not see far enough to notice my skinny white frame. I laughed to myself as I waved cheerio to her after her appointment. Never to see her again.

Moorfields Nurses' Home

Look, I was sad to leave Tottenham, but I was happy to be back living somewhere that it only took me a few minutes to get to work. My only bag packed, I moved into the Cayton Street accommodation. It was a rather large building, probably erected when they built the hospital. At one time it could have all been apartments, but now was split into single rooms. I had a key with a room number, and I opened the front door and went on the hunt for my new accommodation.

My memory tells me the rent was 70 quid a week, which was very decent for London. No bills. My room was on the lower floor at the back. I think they placed me far away from any females. It was a barebones room. A bed. A cupboard and a chair. One sink and the window was a tiny affair that opened out to the back of the hospital laundry. Not much sunlight came in. I didn't mind – it was home to me. I shared a kitchen and bathroom with the other nurse on my floor. From an electronics shop near Old Street, I had bought one of those 10-inch mini portable black-and-white TVs. My room had an aerial socket, so at least my picture was clear. I used to enjoy watching Match of the Day after a Saturday late shift. Now I have a 65-inch UHD TV.

Life was fine for a time. There was a pub close to the accommodation that I liked to sit and have my drinks in. Work was going well and on my days off I would walk all the way to Upper Street in Islington and wander about. Here was where the Monopoly-famous Angel Islington was. I would often sit in the Kings Head pub and have a few merry making beers and then happily stroll back to my room listening to music on my Walkman.

It was around about this time that I met Jasmine. She was a senior nurse at the hospital, and I liked her. She was very proper but had a good sense of humour and we got on well. She lived around the corner from me in other hospital accommodation. For the rest of my time in London, we were together.

Next Move

As 1999 rolled on I was feeling pretty good. The job was fine. I was enjoying London living. I had a great girlfriend, so on paper everything was copacetic. Then why that feeling in my chest again? I considered my next move. For a short time, I thought about New York. I joined an agency who sent me all the forms to fill out but ultimately, I could not be bothered having to do extra work like the NCLEX exam. Since I had dipped my toes in the Middle East, it made sense to concentrate there. Another agency I joined sent me out a package with all the vacant positions. One job piqued my interest, and that was working in Apheresis. This was collecting blood plasma and platelets from blood donation. It was similar to dialysis in that we hooked up patients to a machine, so I told the agency to send my CV to the hospital. With all of this planning to leave London, I did feel guilty about leaving Jasmine. It was not fair on her. That feeling in my chest just kept getting stronger though.

By around March the agency contacted me about the position, which was a Senior Staff Nurse job at Tawam Hospital, Al Ain in Abu Dhabi. They arranged for someone from the IV Team to call the nurses' home and interview me over the phone. When they called, it was not really an interview. I spoke to Norma, the only other nurse in the IV Team and she said they would welcome me there. I agreed and told the agency to start moving on all the paperwork.

My date for travel came through and as the beginning of August got closer, I prepared for leaving. The A&E staff gave me a wee night out which was so sweet of them and I knew I would miss them. My last shift ended in a blur of goodbyes and I moved out of the nurses' accommodation and in with Jasmine for my last few days. She had to fly Brussels for a course, and I was left in her place for a day or two and when she returned, we had one more night together. Saying goodbye is never easy, but that's what I did, and she had arranged for a car to take me to Heathrow. This made my onward trip easier. It would be a wee while before I would see her again.

Tawam Hospital

Stepping out of Dubai airport in the blast furnace of the late night, I was totally zonked. I was sobering up from having a few beers on the plane. This white guy came over to me with a clipboard and he said in a Fife accent, 'Are you for Tawam Hospital?' Taken aback slightly, I semi slurred 'yep.' Thinking he was one of the welcoming party, I asked where we were to go, and he said, 'I dinnae know I've just landed here myself.' We joined forces and finally found a guy beside a minibus holding a sign saying Tawam. We introduced ourselves, he took our bags, and we boarded the bus. There were three blondes sitting inside already. One was a Canadian guy, the other was a wee Scottish woman, and beside her a Swedish lassie. We took off into the night. We all introduced ourselves, and the only name I don't remember is of the Scottish blonde. Louise was the Swede, the other was the handsome devil, Andrew West. My Scottish non-blonde buddy was Mr Vincent Farquhar. Andrew, Vince and I would become fast friends and are still connected via the wonders of Facebook.

The drive from Dubai to Al Ain after you have been on a long flight seemed to take days. Reality was probably a couple of hours and in the very wee hours we were in the hospital compound and being dropped off to what would be our temporary accommodation. This was a small prefab villa split in two. Not much to look at, but once inside it was fine, and it was clean. They even left us a nice wee welcome package of some food. I just fell into bed, AC blasting above my head.

Waking in the morning, I had no clue where I was. It took my brain sometime to clear and tell me I was back in the Middle East. I showered, then went outside to have a look around. I was in a row of prefabs. In front of me looked like a swimming pool and in the near distance I could see what was clearly the hospital. Not far to walk! Great for my lazy self!

My bus buddies and I found each other and as it was the weekend before we were to start work, we all went into Al Ain to see what night life it had to offer. After an alfresco meal, we headed for the Hilton Hotel bar. I don't remember the name of the nightclub; we ended up in, but it became a regular weekend destination for us. It was packed and there were a lot of ladies, so for me things were looking good. That night I staggered home in company and did not sleep in an empty bed. That was the beginning of a year of drink and debauchery!

IV Team

After a week of orientation classes, I began work as a Senior Staff Nurse in the IV Team. The team being me and my colleague Norma. She had been at Tawam for a number of years, and I could not have asked for a better work mate. She was Jamaican and was warm and friendly. She was excellent at her job too. Our 'Unit' was a tiny area off the Oncology Ward, comprising only two rooms. When you entered the main door, there was a room that had two patient chairs. This is where we did the apheresis treatment. Inside was the office, which was big enough to fit a table, two chairs, a desk and filing cabinet. We recorded all our work on paper, not one computer in sight.

Most of our work was collecting platelets and plasma donations for the Hospital. We also received calls from the other Units if they had difficulty getting an IV needle into a patient. Luckily Norma was a total expert at cannulation as I was the opposite. We agreed that she would take the calls and I would connect the patients to the machines to harvest their blood products. They paid each patient 500 Dirhams approximately 100 GBP for a donation, so we had no shortage of clients! If it was a quiet day either Norma or me would get hooked up to the machine and donate. My platelets were few, so I only gave plasma. They allowed patients to return every two months, so we got to know our regulars really well.

As the procedure took around two hours, to entertain our donors, we had a TV and video player and a vast collection of donated movies on tape. Once I hooked them up to the machine, I would put on a movie and usually sit and watch it with them. I must have seen our movie collection around a hundred times. I knew the dialogue off by heart! Many of the hospital staff would come to donate blood products. Especially near the end of the month when they were broke!

Work was good, actually work was great. I didn't have to work shifts; we were never that busy and Norma was so easy to get along with. It was one of those easy workdays when I had finished cleaning up after a patient and as I was putting some video tapes back onto the shelves, I had this weird feeling in my back. It was not the usual type of back pain it was something worse! An effin' kidney stone!

The pain moved down my flank, and it floored me. Luckily it subsided long enough for me to get to the ER where I was given some pain relief and told to drink copious amounts of fluids. On the X-Ray I was told that the stone had passed from my ureter into my bladder so eventually I would pee it out. There were still stones in my kidney, and they booked me for litho-tripsy. This is where they use shock waves to break up stones into tiny pieces that you eventually pass painlessly. The next day I had drunk loads of water and I rushed to the toilet dying for a wiz. As I tried to turn on the pee tap nothing came out! WTF? It was like something was blocking the urine. Then, like a geyser whoosh out, all the water came along with a rather large stone. Thank God. I still had to endure the lithotripsy, which they told me would not be painful. They lied. It felt like someone was kicking my kidney with a steel toe capped boot. My back went into spasm and I was in agony! I managed one more treatment and then I was done. But not done with the stones!

Badi Boys

We stayed in the temporary accommodation for around a month and whilst I liked it I was glad to move. Vince, Andrew, and I were moved into town to a new apartment building. This shiny new block was called the Badi Building. Andrew was opposite me and Vince was just upstairs. This was a brand spanking new apartment. It was very nice. With a good-sized living room, two and half bathrooms and a kitchen. It had central AC and a wee balcony. Rent and bill free! The only downside was that we had to walk to a nearby square to catch a Coaster minibus to work each day. This meant getting up earlier. Sometimes to snatch a few minutes' extra sleep I would just jump in a taxi to work. Not always, but quite often.

It was great having Vince and Andrew so close; we got on well with each other. I love them like brothers, and I know I'm not the easiest person to get along with sometimes. Both of them treated me like family, and the bond we had was very special. Vince, who was an ER Nurse bought a nice red Cherokee SUV, so we were mobile. Andrew was a Respiratory Therapist who would later do his Doctorate. Very proud of Dr West, who is now an in-demand expert. Some stories I could tell at one of his seminars!

Al Ain shared a border with Oman and close to the official customs border you could take a taxi to Buraimi, which technically was in Oman. There I found a wee shop that sold bootleg movies on video. This was before DVD. I usually went there a couple of times a month for new and old movies. Food shopping was easy as we had a large Choithrams supermarket within five minutes of our building. All in all, it was a fantastic time in my life, and I was determined to enjoy myself before the chest feeling returned.

Post Orgasmic Chill

What an effin' album to see me into the new millennium. The
voice of singer Skin is all at once rocking hard and lovingly
sweet. This album I blasted for months in my Badi building
apartment. 'Charlie Big Potato' is indescribable. What the hell?
What an effin' riff. What an effin' voice. With 'Secretly' I was
moved. I mean really moved. 'Lately' is another topper. This
entire album hit me when things were changing inside of me. I
was slowly tiring of the single man out partying and was being
attracted to the idea of settling down.

Nightlife

We spent many of our weekend nights at the local hotel disco. It
was not too bad, but some weekends it could be quiet. We
would normally start off in a bar, then meander down to the
Filipino nightclub, which always had a live band. Usually we
got pretty wrecked there, then staggered to the disco. From the
get-go, I knew Andrew was gay. He did not hide it, but we both
got a surprise when Mr Farquhar came out to us. Vince was
hiding his true self in Scotland and even to us. Andrew, I think
knew, but I didn't. It made sense though because I kept pushing
him towards women and he kept resisting. I thought it was
because he was shy. I was not shocked when he told me, and I
was glad he at last felt free enough to be true to himself. He
could not do this in Scotland. My thought was that now there is
more ladies for me!

The hospital recreation department and one of the local hotels
had regular pool parties where there was a bar and disco. The
nights were hot, but it was great fun. The three of us were
always out on the hunt for some night action. Sometimes we

were lucky. Often, we were not. One pool party at the hotel Vince was walking past Andrew and me and we just grabbed him and threw him into the cool water! Soaked. He never got angry, but he was annoyed about his phone getting water damaged! Some weekends they would be working either day or night shifts and I would go out on my own. By this time, I was pretty well known and had more than a few people to talk to at the club. It's lucky Vince and Andrew were not with me as I tended to get up to nonsense and found myself more than a few times sneaking out of a girls' apartment in town and staggering home hungover and dehydrated. Al Ain is not that big and neither is the expat community. Soon I had a reputation for being a love you and leave you kind of guy!

There was one post club night, I was riding in a taxi with this Finnish girl who worked in the hospital. She stayed in the female compound on the hospital grounds. They allowed no guys through the gates at night. What you had to do was pretend to drop her off, and then you took the taxi toward our old accommodation. From there you would pay the driver and get out to make your way across the sand to the female accommodation's surrounding wall. You then had to climb it and meet up with your female friend. That wall was pretty high. When you are steaming drunk, it's even higher. It took me a good half hour to climb over. One time I was so under the influence I fell off it and gave myself a severe knee injury and had to go to our ER the following day. If you scaled the wall and got into an apartment for the night, the next day you could walk out the main gate. They commonly called this 'the walk of shame'.

Once a month or more we would go to either Abu Dhabi City or Dubai for the weekend. If you worked for the Ministry of Health, you got pretty good discounts in a lot of fancy hotels. There was a group of us who regularly went. Including two of our Canadian female friends Joanne and Heather. We would always have a brilliant laugh.

The only thing I didn't enjoy about Dubai nightlife is that no matter where you went, upmarket or down-market clubs were always full of hookers. Some club's female contingent was

probably all ladies of the night. It truly was not my scene. Abu
Dhabi had a lot fewer noticeably pay-to-play women. Now I
know what you're thinking. 'Was he ever tempted?' Of course, I
was. There were many beautiful girls, but the fun of the chase
was not there, so for me it was pointless. That's the honest
truth, Ruth. Most times in Dubai we would go to a well-known
gay bar and had a much better time there. Always hungover the
next day we would try to spend some time on the beach and
then get ready to go out on the lash again!

Holidays

One of the prime motivators for nurses working in the Middle
East, apart from tax free salary, is that you are in the perfect
region for travelling East or West. Most people I have known
over the years have travelled to many countries across the
globe because working tax-free leaves you with a sizeable
chunk of disposable income.

My problem with vacations is that I'm so effin' lazy. Andrew,
Vince and the girls were highly motivated travellers, not only
were younger than me but they were also not as lazy. Add to the
mix my fear of flying and it does not bode well for being a globe
trotter extraordinaire. Still, I had to try. The first vacation for
me was easy as I visited my pal from Baghdad Radio Records,
Simon who was living and working in Singapore.

Flying from Dubai I had to have a few stiff ones in the bar. After
that the flight was smooth and easy! Simon met me at Changi,
and we went straight to the apartment he was renting. I loved
that apartment. He shared with a guy who was away working
whilst I visited, so I got a lovely air-conned room for my
two-week stay. It was my first time to visit, and I will tell you
right here and right now: it is one of my favourite places in the
world. OK, it might be a wee bit hot and humid and incredibly

expensive, but everything else is totally brilliant. Safe, clean (but not as clean as people think) and plenty to do. Simon was working a lot whilst I was there, so most days I just relaxed. That was fine by me. We did some touristy things like have a cocktail at Raffles, but most of the time we just hung out. Eating cheaply and drinking expensively was the order of the day. Things got a wee bit more interesting when we decided to go to Kuala Lumpur for the weekend!

We took the train from Singapore across to Malaysia and up to KL. I recommend anyone who visits Singapore to do the same. It's a very pleasant scenic journey which ends in the city's heart. I really loved KL. It's hot and sweaty and in some places dirty, but I felt at home there each time I visited. This first visit we were doing on a budget, so we booked into this hotel in China Town. To say it was basic is stretching the use of the word basic. What I know and we only realised later was that it was to all intents and purposes a 'knocking shop'. Still, we did not plan to be in our room too much!

Our first stop was KL's Hard Rock Cafe and from there we ended up at the nightclub 'Beach Club', the place was jumping, and we got in tow with a bunch of people who took us to another club which played Techno music super-loud. Finally, we all ended up in this bar that served food and by about six am we retired.

Hung-over we endeavoured to do some sightseeing but ended up trying the hair of the dog, which luckily worked. That night was a repeat of the previous, except no Techno.

By the next day we caught the train and sat hungover till Singapore. That night we went to bed early. I would return to KL to visit a girl that I met called Lily Wong, and we had a good time wandering about the shops, restaurants, pubs and clubs for a week. The relationship did not go anywhere though.

My next holiday would be in the company of Vince and for some reason we chose to spend a week in Amsterdam, then fly to Lebanon and spend a week there. He had arranged for one of his pals to fly from Scotland and meet us. We landed the day before and booked into a cheap hotel. Sharing a double bed. Once we dumped our stuff of course we hit a coffee shop. Both of us were totally spaced the rest of the day. That night I encouraged Vince to put his glad rags on and go to a nearby gay bar. He was not too keen, but eventually he got himself out and had a bit of an Amsterdam adventure that night, but that's his story. I stayed in the hotel watching MTV, totally wasted.

The next day we packed our bags and went to meet his pal. We then rented a flat for the rest of the time there. It was in a typical Dutch house near a canal and had enormous windows with a ledge that you could just sit for hours watching Amsterdam life go by in a fug of smoke. We became coffee house connoisseurs. Amsterdam is such a beautiful place just to walk around in a daze and enjoy the scenery. We ate out every night and the weirdest place we ended up in (wasted) was this German-type place with very dark and oppressive décor, but it was well known for selling wild boar. Which we ordered. It was delicious. Soon it was time to fly again.

My fear of flying meant that when we landed at Beirut Airport, both of us were steaming. The first thing we asked the driver was to take us to our hotel. Ominously called Hotel Mace. We then asked him about the best night club. He waited whilst we checked in and then took us straight to this very busy club with loads of beautiful people. Nobody looked at us, though.

I really loved Beirut, it's such a beautiful place, but you did not have to walk far to see reminders of the civil war. There were plenty of bombed-out buildings still standing. There were many bullet-hole-ridden buildings standing alongside newly built buildings. The biggest reminder of the war was the fact that the Syrian Army still had a heavy presence on the street. Their uniforms were so raggedy that I got to calling them tramps with guns. They were all very friendly and happy to talk to tourists. Especially those who had a wee bit of Arabic.

We spent most days walking along the corniche and chilling out. The worst thing about the city was the effin' taxi drivers, who would crawl beside you beeping their horn. They would never give up. Effin' horns beeped all night in Beirut.

As we were drinking less, we made an effort to do some tourist things. My favourite was a visit to the Roman ruins in the

Beqaa Valley. This trip I loved. Before we arrived there, the tour let us visit a vineyard and sample their wines. Very nice. Beqaa is a stronghold of Hezbollah supporters and there were flags everywhere, but the atmosphere was great. I would recommend Beqaa to anyone travelling to the Middle East. On our way back to Beirut we stopped for food and it was here that I first tried hummus! I don't know why I never fancied it before, but the restaurant served it with flat bread and virgin olive oil. Yum. I eat the stuff all the time now.

Our last adventure was to ride the Telepherique. This is a famous cable car ride just outside of the city. My mind told me it was going to be something big but not too high. I was wrong. The cars were only for a two people. We sat opposite each other in a very confined space. I did not have a good feeling about being stuck in this wee red container. Vince made it worse by rocking it back and forth. We took off and almost immediately we were transported high above a very busy highway. I was peeing myself, but not literally. We passed so close to some tall apartment buildings that you could almost see in the windows, then we headed up this steep hill towards 'Our Lady of Lebanon' statue on the hilltop. I was so glad to get out. We slunk about for a short time and I had to psyche myself up to get back in that wee red swing thing. Going down was not much better than climbing up.

Soon enough it was time to return to the Emirates. Our plan was to fly into Dubai meet up with Andrew and the girls and have a night out before going back to Al Ain. The taxi taking us to the airport was funny. It was an old Mercedes. Completely battered up. When we got in the back, we saw that the seat was just a plank of wood! Not too comfy, as you can imagine. Everything at the airport went relatively smoothly, and we boarded the Emirates flight. We were in the smoking section. It was once we hit cruising height that I had a panic attack similar to the one I had in Paris all those years before. It was an effin' nightmare. I didn't want to reveal my fear to Vince, who continued to talk about something I couldn't hear. My heart was pounding heart-hammer like. All I could think about was 'Where is the effin' drinks trolley?' The crew eventually reached us and when the lady asked, 'Would you like a drink?' I said,

'Wine please.' 'Red or white?' I asked for 'both'. She gave me them and I downed both in a oner; it took around ten minutes for the alcohol to take effect, but soon I began to hear Vince's voice again and the fear slipped away. I drank a couple more wines and enjoyed the rest of the flight to Dubai.

For my last trip of that contract year, I fancied to go somewhere a wee bit different. Zanzibar was the destination. Andrew would be my travel mate and of course we would set off from Dubai. Our plan was to fly to Nairobi and spend a day and night there then get a plane to Zanzibar.

We sat in TGI Fridays in Dubai Airport having some food and for me some beer to calm my pre-flight nerves. I drank too much of course and not long into the flight I totally zonked out for hours. They awoke me about an hour before we had to land. It was early morning when we got to our Nairobi hotel. Andrew had stayed there before, and it was cheap, safe and clean. We both crashed out. Later we would go for a wander around the streets, but I felt hung-over and needed a hair of the dog. Little did I know that the drink would lead us on a Nairobi night adventure?

For our dog hair we stepped into the bar at the Nairobi Hilton and had a beer or two. It worked and we ordered something to eat. After eating and a few more beers, I was back to normal. Beside our table was a group of girls who talked to us, and we joined them. We were having a blast, and they invited us to a nightclub. I have searched my brain and Google to find out the name of the nightclub, but it's gone. I remember it being on a couple of floors and halfway through the night the music stopped. A bunch of guys came out and mopped the floor, and then out popped these dancers. It was surreal. I was drinking Safari beer, and the night was going down well. I got close to one girl; Annabelle was her name. She was pretty if a little young. By the end of the night, we were all totally stocious. Bizarrely on our way back to the hotel, we jumped in a British Hackney cab. Annabelle and her friend were with us, and we had to sneak them past the hotel security. We had to be up in a few hours for our flight to Zanzibar, so by the time we woke up and said our goodbyes (after getting email and contact details) we were back on the hung-over road to the airport.

The flight was uneventful, but it was a small plane, and I was nervous the whole way to the island. Zanzibar airport was not what one could call of 'international'. Most of it was shacks, and often you were standing out in the open. We jumped in a taxi to Stone Town and to the Stone Town Inn – both of us, the worse for wear because of our late night. We chose the Stone Town Inn because it had excellent reviews. It looked the part from outside. The lady checked us in and went to show us our room. She walked ahead of us and as she opened the door, she took a deep breath and quickly closed it. WTF? She said we would have to wait until someone would come to clean the floor. We were so tired we told her it's ok. We just wanted to crash out. We opened the door, and I had never seen so many large cockroaches in my life scurrying about the floor. We did our best to kill a few, but I just jumped on my bed and pulled down the mosquito net and went bye byes. Andrew continued to cockroach kill for another ten minutes before he crashed. The room was pleasant enough and cool. Apart from the insect guests, it was OK. We moved to another room the next day that was less roach infested.

It was the summer of 2000 and Euro 2000 football tournament was on TVs everywhere, so we spent a lot of time in wee bars watching the games, drinking Safari. We did some touristy things like going on a 'spice' trip and visiting some local sights, but mostly we strolled around Stone Town. I liked it. The people were friendly enough without being overly in your face. Everyone said 'Jambo' to you, and I really liked the Omani influence on a lot of the old buildings. We wandered the beaches and sat around. It was nice and laid back. One disturbing thing happened on the beach. This young girl approached us. Perhaps around twelve. We thought she would just say 'Jambo' and walk on but no she was there to offer us some sexual services. I felt terrible to see such a thing, and we both left the area quickly.

After a couple of days in the Stone Town Inn, we got fed up with the bugs. We moved across the road to this fancier hotel, which was clean, had AC and more importantly had a TV. There we enjoyed the rest of the football. The only downside of this hotel was that it was Muslim owned, which meant no beer. We had to go out and sneak in our own supply.

Our return to Dubai was not bad, but only because at Nairobi Airport we had our last couple of Safari beers before boarding. The trip had been interesting, but I was glad to be back in my nice wee Al Ain flat.

Serial Killer

In the new year of the new millennium, it was rumoured that a killer was on the loose in Al Ain, specifically attacking taxi drivers. Like most Gulf countries, the UAE is heavily censored and there are secret police everywhere. There was no official news of deaths, but the rumour mill went into overdrive and they reported that the killer sprayed acid in the driver's faces! I'm not making this up. Honest! People lived in fear and taxi drivers became as nervous as a very nervous person.

I had unexpectedly gone out drinking on a school night. Ending up with an hour or two's sleep. Awake, late for work, and hung-over. I only had time to splash water on my face and brush my teeth before I ran out to find a taxi ASAP (ish). Dazed and desiccated, I found a shop selling sports drinks. I bought comforting cold lemon and lime Gatorade. The one with the twisty nozzle that you insert in yer gub as if playing a woodwind instrument. There I was on the highway, looking like death (extremely) warmed up and feeling worse as the morning desert sun beat down on my receding hairline.

Something was wrong? Every effin' taxi I waved at passed me by. No matter how animated my wave was, it appeared that I had suddenly become invisible. I stumbled on in the general direction of the hospital. Sucking on the Gatorade bottle.

Eventually a taxi stopped. Thank God, I thought as I positioned my frame in the front seat and targeted the AC outlets to my sweaty red face. I placed the half full Gatorade at my feet. Enjoying the cool breeze, it suddenly became apparent that all was not well. The car was not moving fast, and driver had a panicked look on his face, and he refused to meet my gaze. His eyes kept looking at the bottle of anti-dehydration fluid at my feet. Fear apparent and fidgeting like mad. WTF? It dawned on my slowed by alcohol brain that he thought I was the taxi driver killer!

His English poor, I did my best to allay his fears to no avail. In fact, it made him ever more skittish. I realised that the greeny yellow drink was what he was scared about. Could it be acid? As I went to grab the plastic bottle (planning to take a calming taxi driver swig) he braked hard and, in a millisecond, he was out of the car. God's honest truth! I gathered my thoughts and my hung-over self and got out the other side. My plan was to show him he was in no danger by taking a gigantic gulp of my tasty liquid. This would surely appease him, and we could get back on the road again.

I overly exaggerated my drinking motion just to be crystal clear with him that he was in no danger and as I did this, he jumped back in his car and took off at speed. With the passenger door still open. And my bag inside! Dear God. Up the road a bit he stopped. Threw my bag out and disappeared into the Al Ain traffic. Nightmare!

Doubly hot and dehydrated, I found my bag, finished my drink and eventually got on a bus to work! I arrived looking like a Dawn of the Dead extra and feeling like hot hell. Thank the lord that we did not have many patients booked that day! Later that year they captured the Taxi Driver Killer, but they never reported the number of victims. Or that he used acid as his modus operandi.

Time to Go

My contract year was ending at Tawam, and it was time to decide about my future. I really liked it there. The job was fine, and I had great pals and a sweet apartment. I was even seeing a girl on a semi-regular basis. The feeling in my chest though told me I had to make a move. But to where?

Having visited Singapore, I had looked at the possibilities of working there as a nurse. It would not be easy like the Middle East. The salary would be less and the benefits not as good, but I said to myself to give it a chance. I applied to the National Kidney Foundation of Singapore as they advertised for dialysis nurses. In the meantime, it was time to pack and fly back to Scotland.

Leaving the boys and my flat was hard, but I had decided and whilst I waited for word from Singapore, I would probably do agency work in Scotland. I had rented my apartment in Edinburgh out, but I got lucky because my friend Anna from the Edinburgh Acting School offered me to house-sit her flat in Trinity. I jumped at the chance. It was summer, coming on to the Festival and her place was lovely. I even invited my old mate Andy to come and stay with me for a wee holiday!

September in Edinburgh is worth escaping from, so I contacted my London nursing agent and got them to arrange work and accommodation. I hopped on a train and was back in London in under five hours. My old Guinness-drinking mate from Moorfields, Mo McGeorge, would let me stay with her for a day or two until the agency sorted out a room for me. It was great catching up with her and we spent the weekend drinking before I had to move on to Archway and my new digs.

My room was in a house about five minutes from the Tube station. It was in a modern terraced house owned by this wee Irish guy called Dennis. He was pretty old and retired and he rented out his two spare rooms to nurses. He was a good old boy and you never really saw him much. My room was at the top of the house with an enormous window on the slanted ceiling. It was small but clean and we had our own bathroom. Being back in London was nice, but I remembered about Connie and it stirred some feelings. What could you do? I just put them to the back of my mind. I had invited Annabelle over from Nairobi and she was arranging her visa and stuff whilst I worked as many shifts as I could.

Mostly, I ended up working at University College Hospital's A&E just off Tottenham Court Road. Virtually all my shifts had been booked there, and I really enjoyed it. I could work as many shifts as I wanted. All the staff were decent, and the work was varied and interesting. This being the centre of London, we did not get big road traffic accidents. Everyone knows traffic moves at a snail's pace in central London. We did get a lot of alcoholics and junkies in the department. Central London is where a lot of them were homeless and/or begged. We seemed to get an inordinate number of Scottish junkies and alkies. The team leader would always assign them to me saying 'They're from your country, you look after them!' She was joking. Or was she? The A&E saw its fair share of weekend nutters. Most of the time I didn't mind these. At least you could have a laugh. I would also get booked to do transfers to other hospitals because of bed shortages in London. The worst one I ever did has always stuck with me. We had a poor guy who tried to hang himself in the A&E toilets whilst waiting to be assessed by a psychiatrist. Luckily, someone found him and saved him. They had got a bed in a psychiatric unit outside of the city and I would be his escort. He just looked dazed. We drove there in a car and when we got to the entrance of the place, I could not find anyone to hand him over to. The place appeared bereft of staff. I heard some noise coming from upstairs, so I took him up there. Still no nurses to hand over to. I spied what looked like an office door ajar and I popped my head in to have a look see. Nobody there but I heard something weird, and I looked behind the door and found a member of staff hiding there! Strange. Were they hiding from me? This turned out to be the nurse I was to hand over my poor patient to. As for my patient, I will never forget the look in his eyes or on his face as I said goodbye. He said, 'Please don't leave me here, I'm frightened.' My God, I felt terrible. As I type this now, I'm reminded how I felt all those years ago.

One day as I was crossing the junction walking towards Archway Station, I noticed a couple walking a little bit ahead of me. I got close as we all walked in towards the entry gates. The girl was wearing these nice trousers, and I was really admiring her backside area when I suddenly realised it was Connie. I didn't know what to do. I did not want to be introduced to her boyfriend and make small talk. I stopped walking and turned to look at an underground map on the wall. They went inside and down the escalator. I followed slowly behind. Just as I reached the platform, a train arrived and checking they were not in my carriage, I jumped on. A few stops later, I saw her walk by me as I sat listening to music. She looked good.

Feeling sorry for my old landlord Dennis I took to sitting with him for a few hours at night watching TV. He was good company. We watched a lot of the Olympics together.

By November Annabelle had come over from Nairobi and I met her off the plane at Heathrow. We spent a few days in London, then we boarded the train to Glasgow. Thankfully, my sister let us stay with her and I worked at Stobhill Hospital's A&E. Ultimately Annabelle and I did not work out, but I was happy to see that she met someone and eventually got married. My wife and I bumped into her one day in the West End a few years ago. She told Janya that I changed her life by bringing her to Glasgow and that she will always be thankful that we met. Nice. Nice to help change the trajectory of someone's life.

Stobhill

It's funny that I ended up spending a lot of my agency shifts working in what was my local hospital when I was a Springburn kid. Stobhill was about a ten-minute walk from Galloway Street, but now I was living with my sister on Park Road in the West End. It was a bit of a faff getting a bus there, but I managed. The

Accident and Emergency Department was not that big. Most major traumas would go to the Royal or the old Southern. Stobhill had its share of nutters though, and a few amusing things happened whilst I was there.

We had a young girl who came in with her mother and after they had been triaged and seen by doctor; they were sent to me in the treatment room. The girl had a head laceration which was to be cleaned and then 'glued'. She was a wee bit scared, but I did my best to assure her there would be no pain. Her mother was very attractive, so I was doing my best to look professional and impress her. After cleaning the cut, I readied the glue. With gloved fingers, I closed the margins of the wound together and applied the glue. This stuff is like super glue when it goes off. As I was chatting up the mum, I failed to notice that my thumb and forefinger had slipped a millimetre or two. When I said to the kid, 'finished'! I tried to lift my hand, but both my fingers were stuck fast to her head. I tried to surreptitiously manoeuvre my stuck fingers, but they would not budge. I finally had to admit with a smile saying 'oops'. I yanked hard and freed my hand. I noticed two holes in my gloves. There were two patches of rubber glove stuck on the wee lassie's head. Joking aside I said not to worry because in a couple of days when her hair is washed, the soapy water will dissolve the glue and the rubber will fall off! I acted as professional as I could, but I don't think the mum was very impressed.

Friday and Saturday nights would be busy with minor injuries because of the pubs letting out and people getting into drunken fights. The police were regulars in the department. This night they brought in a cuffed guy who had obviously been on the losing end of a fight. He was effin' and blinding at anyone and everyone. He was not huge and skinny as hell. The police cuffed him to the stretcher trolley whilst I went about trying to take his vital signs. He was saying something slurry when I noticed that he was forming a glob of saliva on his lips to spit at me. He was that drunk or high that his actions seemed to be in slow motion so when he had enough spit; he took a slow breath in, ready to aim is secretions at me. I saw it a mile away and turned as saliva landed on the shoulder of my uniform. The police went mental, and they charged him there and then with assault. Zero tolerance is required for that kind of nonsense. I did feel a wee bit sorry for him though.

On a night shift I answered the phone to a guy who was having a lot of pain, possibly a kidney stone, and maybe a urine infection. I told him he should come in and get checked out, which he did. After being seen by the doctor, I was taking some of his pre-admission information. We got to talking, and it turned out that he was from Balornock and went to All Saints the year after I left Glasgow. I asked him about the wee guy who had tried to steal my bike in Springburn Park, summer of 1977. Just to see if he knew him, and it turns out that he not only knew him, but he was one of his best friends. As everyone knows it was this bike stealing incident that precipitated my leaving Glasgow and living on the Isle of Skye, and so changing my life forever. He thought it strange, but I asked if he could say a big thank you from me to his pal Eddie, because had he and his pals not tried to knock my bike all those years ago, I would have stayed in Glasgow. Thank God for the bike knockers!

Finally, I was often asked to stay on and do 'double shifts'. It was a frosty winter evening when someone called in sick for the night duty and the Charge Nurse asked if I would be willing to stay on until 3 a.m. They would arrange a taxi to take me home to the West End afterwards. I agreed, and the shift passed pretty quickly. The booked private taxi arrived outside the main A&E doors and I said my goodnights to all and jumped in the back. There I was expecting to take off when the car did not move. The driver was silent for a while and looking at me in the darkness through his mirror. Strange, I thought when he eventually said, 'Moore'?

'Yes,' I replied.

'Raymond Moore?'

'Yes' again, I replied.

'Where eff did you go tae?' Was his next question. Confused, I said 'What?'

He turned round and said, 'you remember me'?

'John, John Bird, Birdy?' He added.

'Yes, I remember you and your brothers,' was my weak attempt at conversation.

He said that he remembered me being in school, then the next thing I disappeared. He knew my brother and my family were still in Galloway Street, but he never saw me again. By this time, we were on our way back to Park Road. I had to fill him in on what I had been doing since 1977. It turns out that he still lives in old Galloway Street in a close near his old family home. We arrived at my destination and I said it was nice to see you. Gave him a tip and said, 'Cheerio!'

I wonder who else never moved away from Galloway Street?

Singapore

My papers finally came through to work in Singapore. It took that long that I had almost changed my mind about going and was planning something else, but as I had waited, I thought I should at least give it a shot. I flew into Changi and I was met by a girl from the National Kidney Foundation's HR department, who took me to my apartment. What she didn't tell me was that not only would I be sharing an apartment, but I would also be sharing a room! She said nothing until we set foot in the apartment. It was a nice enough place, but I told her my days of sharing rooms were over. They should have told me this during the application process. This was not the new beginning I had hoped for.

I called my mate Simon, who had moved to a nice apartment near Novena and asked could I stay with him until they sorted out my accommodation. He and his wife Trixie graciously put up with me for a number of weeks. I have a lot of time and respect for the NKFS, which provides free and subsidised Renal

Replacement Therapy for the poor and low waged of Singapore. They have a big fancy office building which I visited to sign some papers, then I was sent off to my training dialysis centre for a few weeks and I was subsequently posted to the Bedok Centre. Most NKFS dialysis centres were at the bottom of apartment tower blocks, just like a shop front. The journey from Novena to Bedok was long, and then I had to walk about 15 minutes to the actual building in the heat and humidity of Singapore. Not great.

Soon enough the National Kidney Foundation gave me my own apartment, which was very close to the Bedok staff's accommodation. This is great I thought. When I moved in, I found it to be small but fine, but it had no AC. None. Just fans on the wall. This was at one time a one-bedroom apartment that had obviously housed three people, as there were three single beds in the bedroom. All the beds were very cheap looking wooden affairs and had the thinnest mattresses in the world. My first night, there was a massive thunderstorm and as I turned to sleep not only did the power go off, the effin' bed collapsed. I slept on the floor that night. My only night. In the morning I was taking a shower when I noticed red marks on my back. On closer inspection, it turned out that I had been bitten allover by bed bugs! I was back at Simon's that night.

The work was arduous, but I enjoyed the challenge. The patients were relatively nice. Typical dialysis patients, but the salary was terrible. A sizeable chunk of mine going on my weekly MRT train ticket. I could not afford to go out socialising, and I realised that it would not work out for me. There were some really nice staff at Bedok. The nicest were the Chinese staff who worked as dialysis technicians. They all had given themselves Western names. My favourite girl was Evita. She was nice. Smart and funny. Very Chinese, of course, and really very friendly. She had been a doctor in China but could not make a living, so she came to work as a low-paid technician. I'm not sure how much these girls got paid per month, but it was a lot less than me. After three months, I gave up and handed in my resignation. To be honest, my heart was not really in it and that chest feeling had returned and it was effin' strong!

2001

Having returned from Singapore I was back in Glasgow staying at my sister's West End apartment. After a quick break, I began working agency shifts again, working mostly in Glasgow's Royal Infirmary. Then came September 11th – what a horrible day. I remember exactly where I was when I was told about what had happened in New York. It was the nursing agency office in George Square. I met up with my sister and we went for a drink in the Lansdowne bar and to watch the latest news from the USA. We sat in stunned silence unable to believe our eyes and ears. To say that these horrific events were era-defining is a total understatement.

The year 2001 also stands out in my memory as it was the time I got the phone call which everyone dreads. I was told that my Dad had been admitted to hospital. What actually happened was that my agency called and asked me if my father's name was Gerald, and I said yes with a sense of foreboding. They told me they had received a call from the Royal Infirmary's medical admissions ward, where I had done a lot of shifts. They had admitted my Dad via the A&E after he collapsed in a pub with a suspected stroke. He could not talk but someone in the pub told the ambulance crew I was a nurse and one of the Staff Nurses recognized my name and although Big Gerry could not talk, he understood what was being said. They asked him to confirm that I was his son and then called the agency. It was a Saturday evening, and I immediately jumped in a taxi to the hospital. When I got there, he was alert, and I tried to comfort him. I joked that it was lucky he had the stroke in the pub and that he probably just did it to get out of paying for a round! He laughed. I had seen many patients be admitted with the same condition, but to see my Dad like that, it was gut wrenching. I don't even like to think about it now.

Angela was in California on holiday visiting my Dad's sister. I had planned not to call her until I knew exactly what was happening. Unfortunately, a friend of my Dad's inexplicably called his sister to tell Angela about his admission. My sister dotes on her Dad so she flew back home as fast as she could. My Aunt Anne and Uncle Maury flew to Glasgow not long after my sister. I was glad that Maury came. I really found him a source of strength and support. We would often go for a beer in the pub beside the Royal. We did this after visiting as it was a way to decompress and to talk about how things were going with Dad.

His condition went downhill, and it was touch and go for a while. I had already had a conversation with the doctor about him dying. Thankfully, the big man was not ready to check out yet. He went to the rehab unit in the Royal and then got moved to another rehab on the South Side. On discharge from the rehab unit my sister had arranged for him to move into a flat in Govanhill, his first bachelor pad. He did amazingly well. His speech returned, and he had only a slight weakness on one side. Unfortunately, he lost some of his vision, but he was out and in his new apartment. He was only 61 when it happened, so he was not old. Coincidentally, his father passed away at the same age. Looking back on the weeks before his stroke, I remember him telling me that he had been feeling unwell and a bit off. I lazily told him to see his GP, which he did not do. He probably had undiagnosed hypertension for years. I felt/feel guilty about not forcing him to seek treatment, but he was a typical Scottish guy. He hated going to see a doctor.

After a few good years, the big man's mobility got worse, and he spent more time in his flat. This was fine by me. That man was hardly ever in the house for many, many years, so I was happy to let him rest. Latterly, he moved close to my sister in the West End, and this makes seeing him a lot easier. Big Gerry turned 80 in 2020. His next illness is unbeatable, but as I type this, he is receiving palliative care at home. My brother and my sister visit daily and I'm in constant touch with them. He is still asking for a dram, though!

Mull

The British Nursing Association for whom I worked as an agency nurse called me at my sister's; they asked if I fancied a 6-week stint at Dunaros Hospital on the Isle of Mull. It was autumn, and I thought, why the hell not. From Queen Street Station I jumped on a train to Oban.

Although my Aunt Margaret had the Oban Times delivered regularly when I lived on Skye, this was the first time I had been there. I had ample time to wander around and get something to eat before the ferry took me across to the island.

Less than an hour later, I was on land at Craignure. I had to get to the village of Salen. The place was not what I would call busy, but on a call box I found a taxi number which I rang. He arrived shortly afterwards, and I gave him the address of the bed and breakfast I was to stay at. Soon I was introducing myself to the couple that owned it, and they showed me my room. It was basic but fine and clean. The next day I walked towards the hospital for my first late shift.

Dunaros was a GP-run hospital with around 12 beds. Attached to it was an old folks' home. I walked in and met Dave, the Charge Nurse. He gave me a quick tour and handed over the keys and said his goodbyes! I was left with two patients and one nursing assistant. It was not the patients that worried me; it was the fact that Dunaros was the only hospital on the island. Although the local population was small the island received thousands of tourists so you could expect anything to come through the door. There was a hotline to call for an emergency airlift or boat ride to the mainland hospital in Oban.

I loved it. Salen was beautiful. The staff in the old folks' home were all very friendly, and I got on well with everyone, including the GPs. On evenings off I would go to the bar at the Salen Hotel and have something to eat washed down with a few pints of Guinness. Occasionally I would take a bus trip to Tobermory, which is an exquisite wee town.

Whilst there I got a visit from my Tawam buddies Vince and Andrew. I had the weekend off, so the three of us booked into a hotel in Tobermory and went and did some touristy things. At night we ended up in a pub which was having a quiz. We joined as the 'Badi Boys'. We came in second or third. We got totally wrecked and stumbled home to bed. The next day we made our way back to Salen as the boys were moving on to Skye. I miss those guys.

It rained a helluva lot on that first visit. I enjoyed the assignment that much that I returned about three times. The last time was just before Christmas of 2001. That trip they billeted me in the Hotel. This was great and as I never ate breakfast the owner gave me my evening meal free, but I had to pay for my Guinness. I could have lived on Mull permanently if it was not for that feeling keeping itself known in my chest.

The worst thing about Dunaros is when you saw a car or an ambulance pull up. You did not know what would come in the door. It was exciting and nerve-wracking too. As long as it was adults, I felt OK, but if a car pulled up with a kid, my heart beat ever so much faster. This happened one sunny afternoon. I was sitting in the office and a car stopped outside. I saw a woman and a girl. Thankfully, both did not look seriously hurt. I went out to greet them. It turned out that the girl had a tick in her head! I showed them into the treatment room and calmly told the kid and mother not to worry. We would have it out in a jiffy. I excused myself to 'gather my tick removal kit'. I rushed to the office, fired up the PC and Googled how to remove a tick! Not only did I not know how to eject one, but this was also the first time I ever saw one stuck on a human! I watched a quick video of the method that I chose and then went back to the waiting patient. I was a wee bit nervous, but I followed the video to a T and with this kind of twisty technique using forceps, I removed the beast. Phew!

My last shift at Dunaros was a night shift. During these shifts, the staff from the old folks' home would help me if needed. It was just my luck that someone had fallen. Thankfully, they were unhurt, but as we lifted them to their bed, I felt something go in my back! The rest of the night I lay in agony on the lounge sofa. I got my work done with the help of some painkillers, but the thought of travelling all the way back to Glasgow with my back in spasm was not thrilling me. The reality was slightly better as I had loaded up on pain relief, but I had to be careful on the train. Every movement sent my back spasm to torture me.

A few days before Christmas my back was still sore. My sister had bought me this cracking duck feather filled winter jacket. It had some weight to it and as I tried it on in her living room, my back went into meltdown with a big, horribly painful spasm. It took me to the floor. There I was, lying in agony in a centrally heated flat with a big winter jacket on. I was effin' boiling. It was too painful to remove it. I had to lie there for a round 20 minutes sweating like a B. Eventually the pain eased, and my mum and sister helped take the jacket off my sweaty body!

∽

Rolls Royce

As January 2002 rolled in, I got a call from my agency and they asked if I would be interested in a 3-month locum position? They would pay salary at an E Grade as opposed to the normal D. Where, I asked? They said it was in the Occupational Health Department of the Rolls Royce factory just outside of Glasgow. I immediately said yes. Luckily over the last year I had had experience working in Occupational Health. They had booked me for a week to travel with an Occupational Health Nurse who drove a screening van. This van was a mobile health screening clinic. For that week we travelled round building sights in Glasgow and checked the vital signs, visual acuity and hearing of men working on site. It was easy. It was also interesting, and the money was good. I had also spent a week at a chicken processing factory outside of Glasgow. This plant processed birds that would end up in ready meals for various super-markets. It was a pretty grim place. I was like a first aid nurse.

They split the factory into a clean and dirty area. My clinic was in between. The worst injury I had to deal with was an eye injury due to a chemical spill. I irrigated the eye for around 30 minutes, then sent her to the nearest ER. I would go into the cafeteria for lunch and man that place was really depressing; nobody looked happy and there was a horrible smell permanently permeating the air.

On arrival at the Rolls Royce factory security gate, I was given temporary clearance and an ID badge. They directed me towards the Occupational Health Department. Inside I met this short blonde suit-wearing girl called Gillian. She was the Occupational Health Nurse. Very friendly. We got on really well from the get-go. That's the thing about being an agency nurse you have to be a people person and leave yourself open to new experiences. It makes your life far easier. Also, it helps if you agree with whatever the permanent staff member is saying.

Gillian gave me the small tour. There was an office, a treatment room, and a health screening room. That was it. She explained that her colleague had recently left and that the company were in the process of finding a replacement. My job would be to do the health checks and to man the treatment room. She would be the one dealing with all the paperwork of which there were copious amounts. Occupational Health Nurses do a lot of sickness absence management and at Rolls Royce there had been a lot of long-term sick employees. She explained that this factory was where they fabricated the fan blades for the jet engines that powered most passenger jets. Not only was there a lot of heavy machinery work but also a lot of chemicals. Sounded interesting.

Gillian was married and from Airdrie and lucky for me, she was not one of these ladies that like to talk about their kids all the time! We had a good laugh together. She taught me how to use the audiology booth and also the spirometer to check the employees' lung function. Eye tests of course and the usual monitoring of vitals. They would test all employees every year. As there was a lot of metal polishing of the blades, she taught how to test for Hand Arm Vibration Syndrome, which was completely new to me.

I covered her when she went on leave, and as I had no access to the computers, my function was primarily as a first aider. It was fine. Mostly quiet. Some mornings I would lie in the treatment room and have a wee nap. The most serious incident I faced was a guy who came in after being clawed and bitten by his cat! They had a good cafeteria there, which was subsidised, so I ate well.

We got a visit from the company's head nurse who had had a report about me. She offered me a permanent job and that Rolls Royce would sponsor me to do the Occupational Health Nurses' course. I really was very tempted, but I had told her that my working life would not be in Glasgow. I had contacted my international agency and told them to send my CV out to hospitals in the Middle East. I was heading back into the sun. But where? Gillian wrote me a really great reference letter, and I was sad to leave the place.

Dammam

Having finished my stint at Rolls Royce, I was taking some time off. Well, not really time off, I just didn't work every day. I got calls about jobs in Saudi Arabia and I had kind of decided that it was there I wanted to work as I thought I should attempt to save some money. I had a number of offers from hospitals in Riyadh, but they were all private. My preference was to work for a government hospital. Maybe even military.

I got a call from Breda at CCM (who were my agents) asking if I would be interested in applying for a job with the Saudi Arabian National Guard Hospital group known as National Guard Health Affairs. They were in the process of commissioning two new hospitals and would I like to work in Al Hasa? Probably in the Renal Unit. The other choice was Dammam. I checked the map, and I saw that Dammam was on the coast and near to Bahrain, so the choice was easy. Send me to Dammam please.

Big Gerry was on the mend, but I was worried about leaving him just in case. He said I should go and not to worry about him. Instead of telling me to 'Go West', he announced 'Go East son'. So that was that. I awaited my visa and flight, which would take a month or two.

At the end of August, I was bidding farewell yet again to all and boarding another plane. I flew British Airways to Paris Charles De Gaulle, where I would board a Saudia Airways flight to Riyadh. Saudia does not serve alcohol, so my plan was to find a bar in Paris and down a few quick drinks. I didn't have much time in-between flights, but I found a small bar near my gate. I ordered a pint of white wine! Yep, a whole pint. I sipped on it genteelly until I saw the gate opening, and then I wolfed down the rest. Safe to say I was stocious on that flight. I sat beside a Saudi guy and I told him that I had had wine because of my fear of flying and to excuse me if there were any alcohol smells coming from my personage. He laughed and said 'mafi mooshkala' brother' meaning no problems. I was all set.

My flight to Riyadh was totally uneventful. I wish I could say the same about the flight from Riyadh to Dammam. Something was definitely up, but I don't know what. The plane waited and waited on the runaway. Then it seemed we were taxiing to take off when we suddenly stopped. No word from the Captain or crew. After about 20 minutes a number of Saudis made their way to the cockpit and I could see them arguing with the pilots. The plane moved back towards the terminal and we were all offloaded. It was after midnight and I had been travelling for a long time. I was totally knackered. They ushered all the passengers for Dammam to another gate, and they loaded us onto an already full 747 flight. Luckily, it's a quick hop to Dammam. When I cleared customs, I was two hours late and I could not find anyone from 'meet and greet.' I had the phone number of the Hospital but every time I rang, I only got an answering machine. In Arabic! Strange, I thought. Why would a hospital have an answering machine? I waited, and I waited, but nobody came. One of the young Saudi guys in customs saw me and obviously took pity on me. He offered to drive me to the hospital. It was early morning when he dropped me off at the Staff housing building. It was also super effin' hot.

For a staff housing building, there did not seem to be many people around. I eventually found one guy in a ground-floor apartment sitting watching TV. He explained to me that the accommodation was not ready so I would stay at the nearby Carlton Moaibed Hotel. I asked him why the hospital had an answering machine and he told me that the place had yet to open! WTF? The agency told me that although both hospitals were new; they were up and running! Obviously not. By this time all I could think about was sleep. They drove me to the hotel, and I fell into my room. I had some sleeping tablets in my travel bag, so I took one and zonked out.

Dorson

In my dream I could hear the faint sound of a bell ringing. Was it a machine alarm? An IV pump malfunction? As I came back to consciousness, I remembered that I was in a hotel room in Saudi Arabia and my phone was ringing. Picking it up, I managed a 'Hello'. On the other end, this American voice introduced himself as Dorson and arranged to meet me in the evening. I agreed and went back to sleep.

After showering I went downstairs to meet Dorson. I found this older African American guy sitting with a smile. We shook hands and went to the restaurant for some food. He had only arrived a few days before me. His job was a Nursing Coordinator, similar to a night Nursing Officer. He explained that the hospital was not open, and he had no clue when it would be. He also did not know how long we would have to stay in the hotel. Handy to know!

It was not too long before our staff accommodation was ready. We packed up our stuff and were transported back over to the hospital compound. We were to be housed in the 'bachelor' building. This building contained small one and two-bedroom apartments. I was told that I would share an apartment with Marius, a male nurse from South Africa. He was not a small guy. I told the housing staff that there was no way in hell I would share one of these tiny flats with anyone. They could send me back to Glasgow. They gave me a one-bedroom flat. Opposite Dorson's wee two-bedroom place.

The flats were brand new, so they were spotless. Comprising a small living room/kitchen, bedroom and a shower room. For me, it was totally fine. I was just happy I was not sharing with my South African buddy. He was too. He stayed right next to me on the corridor.

Fortunately, Dorson was familiar with the Dammam/Khobar area so we would go out on night-time trips to stock up on supplies. Mainly we hung about Khobar and all the wee shops near Alissa Souq. Close by there were two Thai restaurants where we would become regulars. Not that the food was great, but at least the place was relatively clean. Walking around the hot streets at night could be a challenge, but it was a good way to get to know the area. If I had not been friendly with Dorson, there is no way I would have bothered going out on my own.

Our hospital had no furniture, so they decided that all of us who arrived at the same time would travel every day to our sister hospital in Al Hasa. That's where we would do our orientation. This was two-and-a-half hours' drive away. Every day for two effin' weeks! Once completed we were all assigned to our units. I ended up in Male Medical/Surgical. There was an Australian lady who was the manager and who had arrived earlier than us. She welcomed us to an empty ward. No beds, no patients, no seats. Nothing. The only place that was 'open' was the Outpatients Department. This is where we would all do our medical and blood tests, so at least the staff there had something to do. I found a South African nurse who was willing to swap with me as she preferred the ward. I gladly swapped, and even though I would lose 1000 Saudi Riyals (approx 200 GBP), because of the shift allowance, I'm so glad I became an Outpatient Nurse.

Outpatients

Slowly, slowly, the hospital opened. As they added more clinics, we saw more patients, but it was hardly strenuous work. I worked with mostly Filipino nurses and our manager was a lovely tall South African called Sue. We lucked out with her. She was very easy-going. After six months, most of the hospital was open. We were told that Crown Prince Abdullah would come to officially open the hospital. The National Guard had always been his baby. He would eventually become King Abdullah.

We are all excited about the visit. At least it was something different. That day there was loads of security. I think the hospital had two patients, one of whom they took down to the CT scanner. He did not need a scan, but he was to be a prop when the Crown Prince passed by. I was one of the mix of staff chosen to stand in line in the ER as Abdullah walked by. He came, and he shook my hand and said something in Arabic. I just smiled. The Saudi TV channel was filming, and I later saw myself on the box!

Not wanting to write too much about this but I should at least say that for the first four years of working in the Outpatients department I was involved in a very toxic relationship with another nurse in the hospital. To put it mildly, she was 'aff her nut'. I didn't realise this though, so I kept making excuses for her. For example, when we began to see each other, she was so suspicious that I was married. She thought it strange that a 38-year-old Westerner did not have a wife. I told her more than a few times she did not need to worry. She even phoned my Mum and asked her – which, at the time, I thought was funny. She remained doubtful. Here's the kicker, though. It turns out that she was the one that was married and had two kids. She kept that secret from me! I should have quit there and then, but I thought I should try to put more effort into making the relationship a success. It was typical of me to waste my time and effort on something that is doomed.

We planned to go to visit Scotland, and I thought she would calm down once she saw my situation at home. Wrong. This is no word of a lie. We had just taken off on a Gulf Air plane on our way to Scotland when she accused me of staring at someone. I protested my innocence. I said I didn't even fancy the girl. She said that it was the guy I was looking at! She got up and sat in an empty seat for the rest of the flight. The vacation was a disaster. I think she had a personality disorder. Undiagnosed. I could go on and on about all the mad things that happened and about the arguments we had everywhere. On the streets, in fancy Bahrain hotels. In my apartment. We effin' argued every-where. After four years, I had had enough.

I was going to Glasgow for a break on my own, but I felt so guilty I thought I would give it one more try, so we went together. I will never learn! The funniest thing about that trip was that she met my pal Les and when I was in the toilet, she told Les that I was gay! He said, 'I know,' and laughed. He then saw that she was being serious. When we travelled back to Saudi, we did not speak the entire way. When we got out of the taxi at the staff accommodation, I said to her 'It's over,' and went to my place alone. I did not speak to her again. It's a small hospital and occasionally we would pass each other, and I would say 'Hello,' but that was it. After four effin' years of her complete lunacy, I was finally free! And it felt good!

Now when I think about that period of my life, I don't think I wasted it. I realised that I had to go through it all because ultimately it was that relationship and not wanting to repeat what happened that led directly to me meeting Janya, my wife.

Work was going well, no more craziness. Sue had left, and I covered the unit as Acting Manager until our new Manager arrived. Thea was one of the Night Nursing Coordinators, and she wanted off nights. She was German but had been long married to a Saudi Doctor and had many kids. She was an excellent Manager and so easy to work with. She let me do what I wanted regarding assignments and such. We made a wonderful team. We would end up working with each other for years.

I want to relate a story that happened during our former Manager Sue's time. She was into a lot of stuff like fortune telling and tarot cards and life after death. Me too. I like all that kind of 'out there' stuff, and I'm particularly interested in near-death experiences. Anyway, she knew of someone who worked in our Jeddah Hospital who did like a reading for you over the phone. You transferred some money into her account and then you would make an appointment to call her. Sue kept asking me to do it, but I thought it all a bit suspect. She finally wore me down and I transferred the 100 riyals to woman's account. The time was arranged, and Sue told me to light a candle and try to clear your mind, relax and then call. All this I did.

I made the call, and this ordinary, pleasant sounding English woman answered it. She explained to me that she would record everything on a cassette and send it to me. She also said that the only three answers I should give her are yes, no, and I don't know. What happened next made me think she definitely had something that was not fake. She said some kind of prayer or something as she began. I was listening and rubbing my neck, which had been hurting me all week. The first thing she told me was that my neck was very sore! She was right! I took it more seriously. She told me that I had a gatekeeper named Robert, who was French. She said I had lived before in Paris and that I would live there again, in another life! She talked about things that happened to me on the Isle of Skye, and she basically said my Aunt Margaret was looking over me from beyond. An interesting thing that she told was that I would build a house and it would be close to water. My Thai house which I built years later sits on a reservoir. There were loads of wee bits and pieces which were true, but there was also a lot that I said no and don't know too. At the call's end, she told me to go in peace and love. Strange thing was that for days after the reading I felt light inside. Like something heavy had been removed or lifted from my brain! I didn't call her again, though.

New Job

The reason I have stayed so long at Imam Abdulrahman Bin Faisal Hospital is that I like it here. Simple. I have been lucky over the last 18 years to have worked in different jobs within this hospital and as I have been here since the place opened, I feel a close connection to it. I have lived nowhere as long as I have lived in Saudi, and there is a reason for that. I like my hospital, my workmates and the local area.

After four years as a Staff Nurse in the Outpatients, I got a call from Riyadh and I was asked if I would be interested in becoming a recruiter for physicians. I fancied a change, so I said yes. My job title was Regional Recruitment Coordinator. I got a cool wee office in our administration building and I was out of nursing for two whole years. The position was a Saudi only position and ultimately, I would return to nursing, but this was a pleasant change. I worked very closely with our Medical Director, Dr Ahmed Shuaibi. He could be a challenge sometimes, but I have known him right from the start of my career here and I know that underneath it all he has a very good heart. He has always supported me and continues to do so today.

At this point I have to mention my pal Dr Zuheir Hamid. Not for any reason other than I told him if I ever wrote a book, I would mention him. He was one of the first Paediatric Consultants that I hired, and we have been friends ever since. Both of us sharing a love of all things technical. That's all you're getting, Zuheir!

I'm not saying the job was perfect, but it was not particularly difficult. I would get a lot of hassle from my supposed boss in Riyadh, who was an Irish girl and who had for some reason taken a dislike to me. It was a boring job too. If I got really bored, I would hang out with my pal Ali, who was the office manager for our Operations Director and my boss Dr Ibrahim Jaaman. Ali and I would gab for hours. Usually about sex. Dr Jaaman was a nice gentle soul. He supported me a lot, and I think he enjoyed having me around. He had studied in Manchester and had visited Scotland a few times and really enjoyed it. He left our hospital recently, and we sorely miss him. Ali left too. He is now living in Michigan. I still see him nearly every Ramadan when he comes home.

Love Online

By 2007 I felt ready to tip my twinkle toes into the shallow relationship waters once more. Being in Saudi Arabia limits your chance of meeting members of the opposite sex that are not fellow nurses. I decided that it was time to cast my girlfriend search net a little further afield.

Most other single (Western) non-nurses in this country generally are of a certain age and (like me), usually have some amount of emotional baggage in tow. So, I set my sights on the world of online love looking. Now I know what you're thinking, pervert! Just looking for casual hook-ups. No, a change was coming. I spent most of my adult life chasing something casual or something impossible. Now I was looking for something permanent.

Where to start? To be honest with you, looking for a Thai girl was the last thing on my mind. Like many people, I had a negative view of Thailand and had no desire to visit the place. I based this view on very little evidence and I soon realised that the dark side of Thailand is no blacker than any other country that I have lived in, including Saudi Arabia! As I did some research, I soon discovered that Thailand was not only a beautiful country, but its people were warm and friendly and very conservative. I eventually settled on a website run by a Western guy and his Thai wife. It was called Thai Love Links and unlike most websites was for people genuinely seeking proper relationships with a view to marriage.

As a guy, you paid a membership fee and posted your photo and a short bio. I soon discovered that there were far more female members than males and that my profile had generated a not an inconsiderable amount of interest. When you logged in you could then look through various profiles and, should you find anyone that piqued your interest, you could invite them to view your profile. This was all OK but what I did not like was that as soon as you logged online all members could see this and then they would try to start a 'chat'. I literally had loads of women wanting to contact me. By now you all know how incredibly lazy I can be. It really was too much work to chat with people, so I opted to surf anonymously! This gave you the chance to see the pics and read the ladies' profiles without always being disturbed by a chat buddy. If there were any members that you wanted to contact, there was a 'wink' button to press which they would see, and if they reciprocated with a 'wink' you could send them a message and start chatting!

Many of the girls had posted studio Sunday best type photos which for some reason did not interest me much. I preferred to see pics taken in a more 'natural' setting, for example with friends or family!

Out of the many profiles I viewed, I only 'winked' at three girls and the photo that I liked the most was posted by Janya. Her cousin Pen took it when they both were carrying on in her house. I thought it was funny and unlike most other members' profile pics.

Before I go any further, I have to tell you that at that time Janya was only 18! I know that you're thinking pervert again, but for some reason I ignored my head and followed my heart. After exchanging some messages with her and telling her honestly about my life/relationship history, we agreed to talk on the phone.

The first time I spoke to her was when I was on holiday in Glasgow, and it soon became apparent that she was a very funny and caring girl. I told her that I was worried about the (26 year) age difference, but this did not bother her at all.

She was interested in me because she believed that I was not a 'butterfly guy' (her words). Now I know people think of 'gold digger' and I totally understand this (I would think the same myself), but she knew I was a nurse and far from rich. Then people would think that she was only interested in getting a UK visa and again this I completely understand but I didn't let anyone's concerns put me off. What's the worst that could happen?

On my return to Saudi, we began to video chat and as the days turned to weeks, the weeks turned to months, I knew that I wanted to visit her in Bangkok. I needed to see if we really could make something of this online relationship.

I flew to Bangkok and met with her and her family, and it was one of the best experiences of my life. We laughed a lot, and she showed me around the city. The holiday whizzed by. Before I left, I had to have a serious conversation with her mother (who is only two years older than me). She asked me what my intentions were and if I was serious about her daughter. I told her I was very serious, and that I hoped our relationship would blossom (although I did not use the word blossom).

Back in Saudi, our video chats continued every day, and I was determined to return to Thailand to spend more time with my newfound love! Before long I was back in Bangkok and I truly developed a deep love of the big, crazy city! We hired a minivan, and her family and I went on a tour of the Thai countryside.

We ended up in Surin where her Dad is from and where her aunt lived and then we spent a week or so living there and touring around. We also visited her mother's place in Buriram, and planned to stay the night and meet her mother's family. Her Mum had land there and an old house.

When we arrived, it looked like nobody had lived in that run-down ruin for years. We practically had to kick the door in to get access. Luxurious it was not. Needless to say, there was no AC. We had a fan, though. I didn't mind, it was all an adventure. We finally bedded down in this dusty old house and very early in the morning her Mum awoke us. There was a party planned, and I was to be ceremoniously introduced to her kinfolk who lived nearby. I was not sure what was going on but followed Janya's lead.

We got ourselves presentable and went outside the front door. The first thing I noticed was a pig's head on a plate surrounded by vegetables. I thought to myself, 'oh no, I'm gonna have to eat that?' It was all I could think of. The pig's eyes were following me everywhere. We sat down and then a long line of local folk and family came and each one tied a piece of white string round my wrist. It was all very sweet and touching, but that effin' pig was still in the background. It turned out that the head was not for us, but a religious offering! Yaas! Thank you, lord I said inwardly. The rest of the day went great.

As my holiday was nearing its end, I asked Janya to marry me. She agreed, and we got engaged. I know people thought it was all too quick, and that we did not know each other. All that I understand, but I had decided, and I was determined to make it work. I'm not saying it was easy. It was hard for her sometimes, and there were tears. Mostly because of me being unreasonable! We worked on everything though, and I really did my utmost to make it a success.

Over twelve years and three kids later. I'm so glad I took a chance on love online. Without my wife, my life would have very little meaning. She truly saved me from the abyss that is loneliness and her love light shines bright in my heart. With Isis, Isaac and Noah we have three beautiful kids and I thank God for all four loves that make up my world today.

The moral of this story? I don't know. Don't wait for love to find you. Get out there find it yourself! Love is there to be found. It's waiting for the lonely and the worldwide web could be your love-finding tool. Don't be shy. Give it a try.

Home

Released in 2003, this Simply Red album slowly found its way to my ears. I was not a massive fan of Mick Hucknall, but I loved his voice. By the time I was getting to know Janya, this was playing more on my personal music device. 'Home' makes me always think about my wife, and I don't know why. 'Sunrise' is an ear anti-depressant. The relaxed vibe of the entire album just sat well with me. It was as if my ears were settling down along with my life. The cover version of 'You Make Me Feel Brand New' is exactly how Janya made me feel. She might have been a quarter of a century younger than me, but her heart made me want to love her and take care of her and start a brand-new life with her. When I met my wife, I did feel like I was home.

Bangkok Bound

By the summer of 2008, I had been told that there was a Saudi girl coming to take the position I had been working in for the last two years. I was expecting it, so I had no problems at all. It helped that she was nice, and it was my pleasure to teach Abeer all that I had learned about medical recruitment. I did have the option to return to the Nursing Department but as I was planning to marry Janya I thought that maybe it's time to leave Dammam.

It was around September 2008 that I said my fond farewells and boarded a flight to Bangkok. My very loose plan was to stay for around three months, get married and organise a UK visa for Janya. We had been renting this nice wee studio apartment, and it was there that I settled in for an extended holiday.

We visited Surin and whilst there we had an opportunity to buy a house near to Janya's aunts. It was a typically Thai country style. A wooden constructed house with a corrugated roof and it was literally just round the corner. As I had got my bonus and end of a service award from Saudi, we had enough money to buy it quick. It seemed that it was a done deal when suddenly the owner sold it to someone else! It was annoying, and I was a bit angry, but ultimately it worked out better for us in the end.

I bought half of her aunt's plot of land just on the waterfront so that we could build a house someday. We planned to build a small chalet-like building first, just for us to use on vacations. Later we would build something bigger. When the small house was finished it was basically like a studio apartment with a small kitchen area and a toilet and shower room. It was fine for our needs. Most of the time my mother-in-law stayed there with Janya's younger sister, Phu.

Back in Bangkok we needed to find out what was required to get a UK visa for Janya. I had absolutely no clue, so one afternoon we jumped in a green and yellow cab. Our destination was the British Embassy on Sathon Road.

Once inside, we collected all the relevant immigration paperwork of which there was a lot. This was going to take more than a few days, I thought. These effin' forms looked complicated. We stood outside the embassy contemplating our next move. Opposite the Embassy is an office building that contains numerous visa application 'shops' and they all have someone stationed outside the Embassy to drum up some business. As we sat at a bus stop, we were approached by one lady who began speaking to Janya and who then told me that her shop would do all the paperwork and get us on the way to Janya having a stamped UK visa in her shiny new Thai passport. Easy. And very cheap! Off we went across the road and followed this wee Thai lady up the stairs to her office.

Once inside, we got down to visa business. The woman asked if we were planning on getting married soon. We told her we wanted to but had not yet made a plan. She informed us that the visa application process for a wife was much easier and faster, she and Janya talked at length. I was then told that the woman suggested we get married ASAP. I said it's fine by me. The wee Thai woman said, 'Well why not do it today?'

I was not even dressed for the occasion, but after a wee while I thought 'Why put off the inevitable?' The lady informed us of the procedure and the cost. We said yes. She said they have a car waiting outside. That was quick. In a half to full daze I said, let's do it! Off we sped to the nearest registry office!

We arrived at an empty waiting room, and the wee Thai woman went looking for an official. The registrar was located, and he agreed to do the ceremony there and then! Luckily, we had all the needed legal documentation except one thing. Because of her age (18) she needed her father's signature for the marriage to take place. Janya's dad is a taxi driver and was working the busy Bangkok roads when we called. Serendipity was on our side as he was very close to the registrar's and could be there in less than 20 minutes.

We sat in the waiting room and watched as another couple approached the registrar with many documents in tow. He would wed them first and await the arrival of my father-in-law to be. He arrived and signed over the responsibility of his daughter to the old Scottish guy (me)!

Now came the surreal part. The guy who would marry us was ever so slightly eccentric and either had an ill-fitting toupee on or just had naturally weird hair. He sat between us and held both our hands and talked Thai! As he spoke, his grip grew tighter. His hands shook our hand as the Thai words flowed from his mouth. He then repeated in English what turned out to be the Thai wedding vows. Again, as he spoke, his grip grew tighter. His hands shook when he demanded that I love and take care of my wife till death. I agreed. I would. Till death.

He spoke gently in Thai, words that produced tears from my gentle fiancé's eyes. I didn't know what was being said. Janya told me it was some beautiful Thai words of marriage. They made her emotional and happy.

English again as the three of us and our hands shook and agreed to love, honour and obey till the end of the world (I'm paraphrasing). After approximately 10 minutes of shaking and talking, he pronounced us man and wife! Janya continued to cry as we thanked him and made our way out to her dad's waiting taxi. No bouquet or white dress, just the two of us in the back seat holding hands and wondering what the heck just happened. In a daze. We were married, and we were happy.

Our first visa application after getting married did not go too well. I was not even allowed into the waiting room of the Embassy. I had to wait outside in the hot afternoon sun. Janya was all alone there, and the interviewer was not particularly kind to her. They refused the visa. They wanted to see more proof that we had known each other for more than a year. Now we had to gather photographic and documented evidence of our relationship. Remember, this was before Facebook and most of the time we used to video chat, so finding such proof would not be easy! My phone at the time was a pre-Android Symbian OS Sony phone. This I had right from the beginning of our relationship, and it was this wee phone that saved us. Every day I would send Janya messages, so I had maybe two thousand on my phone! But how to get them off there? I found software that extracted all the SMSs and we got them printed out on A4 paper. There were effin' loads! Some of them a wee bit on the naughty side. At first, I went through them with a black redacting marker. Putting lines through anything explicit in an adult orientated sense. There was quite a lot. I soon gave up because there were screeds of paper. Let them read it all, I thought. At least all the messages are dated. With all these and a bunch of photos from my first visit to Thailand, we reapplied for the visit visa.

By this time, it was into December and I had exhausted my Thai visa extensions. For these I had to jump on a bus trip to Cambodia. Leave Thailand for ten minutes and then re-enter the country with a new 30-day visa. They fined visa over-stayers at the airport. This was all moot, as during my three months in Thailand there was massive civil unrest and political insta-bility. If you watched the news, you would have thought Bangkok was burning, but when we went outside, it was all fine. Ultimately, the Army took over governing of the country. At the airport there had been big protests to stop people flying, so all of us 'Farangs' were given a pass when it came to overstaying our visa.

Back Home

Just before Christmas 2008 I was back in Glasgow staying at Angela's. I was happy to see my family, but I was not happy because Janya was still in Thailand and we had heard nothing about her visa application. I was also freezing!

I needed to find a job so in the New Year I had an interview with NHS 24 and was successful in getting a position with them in their call centre not too far from the Southern General Hospital. We had also received news that Janya's visa was approved. She arrived at the end of February and I started my training with NHS 24. It was difficult for Janya. This was her first time away from home, and it was a freezing March. I was not that happy there too. The job was fine but the thought of going in day after day, doing night shifts and weekends was not very attractive. Truth be told, I missed my Saudi friends and the hospital. Janya and I talked about it and I got in touch with my old boss in the HR. Rashed informed me that there was a Nursing Coordinator's job going and given my past relationship with the place I would probably get it.

The story I tell people about wanting to come back to Saudi was that I did an agency shift in a respiratory ward at Glasgow's Royal. As I entered the unit, I was handed the ward keys by the only other Staff Nurse on duty and told to get on with the medication round. There were 32 patients, two nurses and a nursing assistant. This meant I had to look after 16 patients. It was then and there I decided to return to Dammam. It's a true story, but it didn't happen at the time I was thinking about coming back. It happened after I had gotten the job of Nursing Coordinator and I was waiting for my visa and ticket to come through. I left NHS 24 and over the summer of 2009 I was back working as an agency nurse.

Also, I put my flat in Edinburgh on the market. It had been lying empty for six months, and I was too lazy to find new tenants. I put in a new bathroom and kitchen and then gave it over to the estate agents. I got a very decent amount for it, though if I had played hardball, I could have held out for its full value. I didn't. I figured that for the ten years that I owned the place, I only paid the mortgage for less than a year. The rest of the time it was rented out cheaply to friends and they covered the monthly payments. I was glad when it was finally sold.

My travel arrangements and visa came in August, and I was to fly back to Dammam at the end of the month. The plan would be that Janya would go back to Thailand, stay in our wee holiday house and start making plans to build our forever home with the profits I made from the sale of my wee Edinburgh flat. Janya left Glasgow before me. Come the month's end, I was back on a Saudia flight bound for Dammam.

∽

Dammam Again

All in all, I stayed away from Saudi Arabia for less than a year. I was glad to be back at Imam Abdulrahman Bin Faisal Hospital. My Facebook friend Christine, who I met in Tabuk, remembers me saying that after my stint there I probably would never return to Saudi. Never say never indeed!

On my return, they moved me into a bigger two-bedroomed apartment. People were happy to see me, although they thought that I looked ill because I had lost quite a bit of weight whilst away. It felt good to be back. We had two new bosses in the Nursing Services, and my direct line manager Dawn Pleasant Parker from Texas was the Director of Nursing Services. She arrived around the same time as I did. I lucked out having her as a boss because since we met, she has always been incredibly supportive of my career moves over the last 11 years.

After a two-week orientation, I was to 'shadow' two of the Nurse Coordinators for two weeks until I was ready to be let loose on my own. Lynne was from Australia and originally an Operating

Room Nurse. Most of my first night duties I worked with her. She was great fun but could be very strict with the nurses on the units. I spent my first day duties working with my big pal Winston from London. We are still close today.

It did not take long for me to realise that working shifts was not good for my body. Especially working at night. The shift started at seven o'clock all the way through till around seven thirty the following morning. As a Nursing Coordinator you are the senior nurse on duty so basically you are in charge of the hospital at night and during the weekends. My big problem was that I did not sleep well during the day, so I always felt like crap on nights. It didn't help that at the time my flat had these really shitty single beds that had very poor mattresses. It was almost impossible to get any kind of good sleep. Thank God for Dawn as she eventually got the Housing Services to provide me with a decent double bed. She still tells the story of me and my bed woes to anyone who will listen! She also like to remind everyone about me being on the top ten users of the hospital internet. Yep, the IT department kept a monthly top ten of which I was regularly number one. They monitored your internet usage and if you went over your allowance; they reported it to your manager. It felt good to be number one at something! My problem was at night I would stream music and the radio, and this really ate into my monthly allowance! All this shifting though was getting to me. Lack of sleep. Working weekends. Getting up early. I needed a plan to get myself far away from these heinous shifts.

❧

Back in Outpatients

After less than a year as a Nurse Coordinator, in 2010 I had the opportunity to go back to the Outpatients Department as Assistant Nurse Manager. I jumped at the chance. This was seen as a demotion, but I did not mind. The salary was less, but it was worth it not to be working nights and weekends. I was back working with Thea and the team that I had left in 2006. The major difference from when I left was that now the department had many Saudi staff nurses. Luckily, they all accepted me, and it was an opportunity for me to share some of my experiences with them and help them to grow professionally. For me, this was the most important part of my job. I know many people think that I'm just a joker and don't take things too seriously, but when it comes down to being a mentor and a wee bit of a role model, I take that very seriously.

In Thailand, Janya was busy. Not only did she design the house, but she also had to be the project manager once she found a contractor and had all the plans drawn up. We had the lump sum from the sale of my flat and at the end of every month I would send most of my salary so that all the jobs could get finished. Anyone who has financed a self-build knows the stress and headaches involved. It doesn't matter if it is in Scotland or Thailand the stress is the same. I had the easiest job that year. Just sending the money. What was great though, was watching everything take shape right from the beginning. Janya sent photos every day. From preparing the ground in front of our wee house right until the roof was on and the major construction work was over. I would not get to see it till 2011 when I went for a holiday. We still could not stay in it because we needed furniture and AC. I remember arriving there from Bangkok and the first thing I thought was that we made it too big! If we had built a smaller place everything including furniture would be finished. Still, I was proud to have such a big, beautiful home in such a picturesque setting. We are still working on it to this day.

༄

Janya Saudi Bound

Although I'm employed on a single contract, I was lucky enough to have the support of my bosses that allowed me to bring Janya over to Dammam. The principal work on the house was complete, and we just wanted to be together. It had been nearly two years since we tied the knot. Luckily, she took to life here in Saudi and settled in pretty quickly. It was good to go home at 4pm to someone cooking your food and looking after you.

We had not been practising birth control since we got married and as I'm an old geezer I wanted to have at least one child before I was too old and demented. Not being in the same country makes trying to get pregnant quite difficult. Once she arrived in Saudi, I thought that it would happen very quickly, but I was wrong. How many pregnancy tests I bought I'm not sure, but I spent a fortune. Each month we hoped for good news, but 'no' was always the answer. I thought because of my age perhaps it was me that was the issue. I spoke to our doctor here, and she recommended doing a sperm test. They would check to see if my men were swimming strongly. I found it difficult to get into the donation mood and eventually gave up and didn't do the test. I read online that you could buy your own home test kits, and so I ordered a sperm test from eBay. No word of a lie, but the day that it arrived was the day that we confirmed by a blood test that Janya was pregnant. Both of us were over the moon and super-duper excited. I wanted to tell my family right away. We thought maybe we should give it some time, but I really could not keep the news to myself. Once they found out they all were so happy and pleased for us. This would be my folks' first grandchild.

We posted so many photos on Facebook about the pregnancy, I'm sure people were bored. For me I was walking on sunshine every day. Janya was fine and the pregnancy was going to plan. What I could not wait for was when eventually we could get the scan that would tell us about the baby's sex. I hoped and prayed for a girl. My dream was always to have a girl, and the suspense was killing me. Janya was on holiday in Thailand when they did that scan, and she teased me about it all day. I was here at work and just wanted to know either way. It was a girl! Yippee!

Isis

December 20th, 2011 was one of the happiest moments of my life. Waiting eagerly over the last few months, the admission day finally arrived for Janya. The birth plan was that she would have the pregnancy induced the next day. Excited and a wee bit scared, I made my way to the Labour and Delivery Unit of our hospital. This is where I would be for the next six hours. Prior to induction, Janya had refused pain relief either with morphine or an epidural. As the big contractions began, she changed her mind, and the doctor quickly inserted a needle into her back. For me, it was just a case of holding her hand and making sure I didn't faint. We had a wonderful South African midwife to guide us called Phumzile. What a difference she made. After over nine months this blob of baby was born and once I saw that squashed wee face, I knew my life was changed forever. I was elated and frightened. The responsibility of another life was now in my hands. They took her to do all the checks and then after a wee clean-up they handed our baby girl back to her mother. That night I visited both of them. Isis was in the nursery, fast asleep. Her mother was trying to get some shuteye. I walked home on air. I felt so good. So happy. It was worth the long wait.

Why name her Isis? This was before these cruel terrorists got their TV nickname. I had heard the name in a French movie years ago and I loved it. Isis is an ancient Egyptian Goddess. The mother of Horus. There are many beautiful meanings for the name. I told Janya that she could give her a name. A Thai name if she wanted. The only thing I insisted was that her middle name be Catherine after my Mum. When she could not think of a suitable name, we used my first choice. We love Isis. Today. Tomorrow. Forever.

The next day my pal Marwan came over to the hospital and gave the three of us a short lift home. That first night was tough. Isis cried a helluva lot. As new parents, we wondered if there was anything wrong. She was still lightly yellow, and we could not get her to settle. After a sleepless night, we asked

Thea for some advice. Thea is a German Super Mum and had loads of experiences with her kids, grandkids and everyone else's kids. What we did different for the next night was to wrap her tightly in a swaddling blanket. I had watched many YouTube videos on how to do it and was pretty decent at it. The second night was much better, and we both got more sleep. Janya was the one who did all the hard work.

My plan was that every night when I came home from work, I would look after the baby and try to give Janya some rest. She still had to cook our food, so I considered my job easy. For any new father, I would heartily recommend taking time with your baby. To get the feeling of genuine closeness to your child, you have to clean their bum, change their diaper and bathe them as often as possible. Every move we made, and every breath Isis took, we either filmed it or photographed it. All for my family to see on Facebook. Thank God for technology, that's all I can say.

At the weekend, I loved to lie on the bed with my baby and listen to music from my iPod. At night I loved it when watching a movie, she would sleep on my chest. We did have a baby cot for her, but it was very rarely used and until very recently my darling girl slept with us. My folks, my boss, my sister would always complain about her sleeping in our bed but it's a Thai thing and to be honest it made us all feel close. Over the next six months Isis became like a mini-Michelin man. With all that wholesome breast milk, she was so beautifully cute and round.

The summer of 2012 we took her to see her Scottish grand-parents and her auntie and uncle in Glasgow. We really had such a good time that vacation. That is apart from walking up the stairs with a stroller and bags of shopping to my sister's top floor Park Road flat. We had agreed to let my Mum arrange a Christening for Isis and have it this in a wee church just off Dumbarton Road. I'm not religious and Janya didn't mind, and it made my Mum happy, so why not? Afterwards there was a wee do in a nearby pub. I made Angela and my brother Gary godparents. We even got my old dad, Big Gerry, there from his Govanhill flat. I really enjoyed it. Even the church bit was fun. Isis looked chubby and gorgeous in her christening dress. We had a fair few people come including my good pals from

Annan, Maria and Andy, they brought their cute daughter, my goddaughter Georgia with them. My brother's girlfriend at the time Audrey was there as were a lot of my sister's friends. My two aunts, Margaret and Annie, were also in attendance with my cousin Veronica and her kid Jolene. The pub grub was good, and we ended up staying there till early evening enjoying the beer. Cracking day all round.

We would return to Glasgow that Christmas and Isis would have her first Scottish Christmas Day. She was too young to enjoy, but we all enjoyed it for her. Over the next eight years we would travel between Glasgow, Saudi and Thailand. We wanted to make sure that all the grandparents got to see as much of their grandkids as possible. This is challenging to say the least!

Soon my Isis will turn nine and I can say, hand on heart, that it has been an honour and a pleasure to be her father and watch her grow. She is funny, annoying, aloof, crazy, caring and beautiful. I love every last bit of that girl and I know deep down that whatever she wants to do with her life, she will never – *can* never – disappoint me. My goal is to make sure that for as long as she is in my care, her life is a happy as I can make it. Every single day with her has been a gift. Every single day I thank God for letting me be her dad.

Yeezus

I'm not a fan of Kanye West. I think he is off his chump, but I cannot deny that when I heard 'Black Skinhead' it did something for me. Strong and politically powerful, yet bare and honest. I bought the effin' album thinking 'Why not?' Produced by Rick Rubin and really stripped down to the basics, I say that this is one of the best hip hop albums of the last decade. 'I Am a God', is effin' brilliant. He might believe he is a god, and that undoubtedly puts people off his music. There is just something about this track that really gets me moving. 'New Slaves', wow what a song. 'Blood on the Leaves' I really felt. It's an album that I might not listen to regularly, but when I do I listen to it loud.

Work Change

Life was going along fine for us three in Dammam. Family life was grand and work life was pretty stress free. The problem was that the feeling in my chest was nagging at me again. For the most part I ignored it, but it was getting stronger so rather than leave the hospital I looked around for a new challenge. Our wee hospital does not have that many career-advancing opportunities, but I have always been lucky. One of the Nurse Educators who was Bahraini had recently taken over managing the CSSD. This is the department responsible for sterilising all the surgical instruments used in the Operating Rooms and around the hospital. I knew that at some point she was planning to leave, so I educated myself regarding Sterile Processing. Luckily there are many free educational activities online that I studied and studied. I also offered to cover the Manager when she was on vacation so this would give me an opportunity to introduce myself to the staff. Most people in the hospital know me. I'm the only Scottish guy here. Later on, the lady left and returned to Bahrain. Someone else was covering the department, and they advertised for a new Manager. I continued my studying and enrolled on some professional certification courses.

They had no luck hiring anyone from outside, so I made my move. I offered to take on the position as Acting Manager whilst I studied for my International Sterile Processing Certification. My boss Dawn agreed. I moved to the department in 2013 and after studying and qualifying I remain Manager to this day. The upside of leaving the Outpatients was that they advertised my position for Saudi candidates only. I encouraged a few of the nurses that I had mentored to apply, which they did, and I was part of the interview panel. Beforehand I told them that I planned to be very tough with them and I was. My friend and colleague Huda was successful, and I was happy to see her develop her managerial skills. It would not be too long before our long-serving colleague and friend Thea retired, and her position was up for grabs. Again, I encouraged some of my Saudi nurse co-workers to apply. I again told them that I would be very tough with the questions during the interview. The three top candidates were Huda, Maryam and Basma. Today Huda is the Manager, Maryam is the Assistant Nurse Manager and Basma is the Clinical Education Nurse of the Outpatients. I'm very proud of that wee team. It has not been easy but with the support of our boss and me, these young Saudi Nurses have done a brilliant job. I still go there every day to coach and annoy.

As another challenge, my boss made me Acting Nurse Manager of the Operating Room until we could find a suitable candidate. There I worked with Deirdre the Irish Assistant Nurse Manager and it ended up being almost two years that I covered the unit. I got to know all the staff very well and did my best to help every one of them during the working day. I'm still in close contact with the Saudi Managers today, which is something I feel proud of.

Isaac

We never practised birth control again after Isis was born, and we hoped that we could get pregnant quite quickly so that there would not be a big age gap between kids. I secretly hoped for another girl, but month after month of trying moved into year after year. Perhaps it was only meant for us to have one child and I was OK with that. I'm no spring chicken, so one child was enough.

Janya wanted to move to a bigger apartment now that there were the three of us and I was lazy to do so initially because I could not be bothered moving all of our stuff but eventually, I put in a request to move to what is known as the 'family' building, directly above my boss's apartment. Within a month of us moving there Janya was pregnant! After six years of us trying! We both were happy, as happy could be.

Luckily, the pregnancy was uneventful. Well, apart from Janya having gestational diabetes which meant she had to watch what she ate. When the scan was done that would give the baby's sex Janya was in Thailand again. She called me immediately and asked what did I prefer? A boy or girl? I said I really did not mind but if she pressed me hard enough then a girl. It's a boy! We were having a boy! I was surprisingly ecstatic.

We had another lovely South African midwife take us through the birth and after all the shouting, screaming and pain our son was born. It was beautiful. Isis and I visited him, and it thrilled her to now have a wee brother. Bringing him home we were a bit more prepared but unlike Isis this wee guy had a lot of colic, so he cried a lot. Many a night I would be walking around the apartment with him in my arms, rocking him till he slept. Sometimes I put him in his stroller and wandered around the house for up to an hour to get him to sleep. He was a tiring wee bundle of joy. It was Janya's turn to name him, and she didn't want a Thai name. She chose Isaac. The meaning of it is 'he laughs'. Right from the get-go, that boy smiled and laughed. His name suited him to a tee. He still liked to cry a lot too. Soon my boy will be three years old and it's hard to put into words what that wee guy has given me. I never thought having a boy would be so sweet and special, but Isaac is that and more. He looks so much like me (as does Isis) and he is a naughty, loveable, cuddly boy. In his first year he looked so much like my Granda Moore it was amazing. I cannot imagine my life without him, and I only hope to see him grow up happy. Whatever he decides he wants to do in this life, I don't mind. I just want him to laugh. I love that wee man.

Noah

Less than two years after Isaac in October 2019, we had our 'surprise' third baby Noah. What a shock! What a pleasant surprise to find out that Janya was so quickly pregnant. It was difficult for her with a young baby to care for and being heavily pregnant. She managed, though. She is strong. With the help of an Irish midwife, this time we had our wee Noah. The funny thing about his birth was that he came pretty quickly. Janya was in so much pain her eyes were rolling in her head. She said to me that she was going to die and just to let her go, I tried not to laugh and then our wee man popped out.

Why Noah? You know the Steve Carell movie 'Evan Almighty'? About a modern-day Noah? That's what gave us the idea. We liked it, and it suited him down to the ground. That wee guy is almost a year old now, and he is so unbelievably cute it's unreal.

The Lighthouse Family- Greatest Hits

I chose to mention this album last. Not because it is my most favourite record or band of all time. I chose it because I think the singer's voice has a medicinal quality. When I hear him singing, even sad songs, I feel good inside. 'Lifted' was one of their first hits, and it really has the power to lift your mood. 'Ocean Drive' makes me feel as if I'm walking down near the ocean sands. 'Goodbye Heartache' is a hopeful promise to all of us old romantics that heartache ultimately becomes love and happiness. 'Postcards from Heaven' is a dreamy day song to get you through the afternoon and 'Question of Faith' again fills me with the joy that is hope. My advice to hospitals and clinics is to pipe The Lighthouse Family through their waiting room PA, I bet it will soothe the frustrated soul and any complaints about long waiting times will disappear. Go on, try it. I dare you. Last, for my darling wife Janya 'Lost in Space' the lyrics ring true for me. It is her love that has saved me. It is our children that have found me, and without her love I really would be lost in space.

Corona

As 2020 rolled across the world we did not realise that this year would see the first pandemic flu of our lifetime. Discovered in late 2019 in Wuhan China, it quickly spread everywhere. Like a science fiction movie, countries shut down. COVID-19 is highly infectious, and it was not too long before it was knocking on the door of Saudi Arabia.

By the beginning of March Isis had finished her school term and the plan was that they would all go to Thailand for the next four months and I would follow in June. The four of them flew out from Bahrain to Bangkok about a week before the whole Middle East went into lockdown because of COVID-19. Our hospital began to only accept emergencies, and they put the entire region where a lot of our staff live under quarantine. In May, I was unfortunate enough to test positive for the virus. I was lucky that I had only mild symptoms, and I recovered quickly. After my two weeks of quarantine, I was back at work with no ill after-effects.

As I'm typing this, we are now into the end of October 2020. Countries are now reporting a '2nd wave' of infections. Saudi Arabia has eased restrictions, but nothing is back to normal. My family remained in Thailand because there have been no flights, and then Janya and I made the decision that they would stay there permanently. Fortunately, Thailand has seen a lot fewer cases than most other countries, and our area of Surin has not had many active cases. Isis and Isaac have started school, and because the lockdown has been less severe, they can still get out and about and have some semblance of a normal life. Luckily, we have our lovely big house and our Chevy pickup. The only thing that is missing is me. I see my family every day via video call and although I miss them desperately, I'm happy to see them enjoying themselves in the countryside of Thailand. Saudi Arabia under normal circumstances is difficult for kids because it's so hot in the summer. Under lockdown was an absolute nightmare as all kids are virtual prisoners inside their own houses. My Saudi colleagues were really suffering with their families. Schools have slowly started to open up, mostly with virtual classes, and the future remains uncertain as the virus does not seem to be going away anytime soon.

Lonely I might be, but alone I'm not. The most important thing to me is that my family is safe from harm, that they have a normal life, and that it won't be too long until I will join them for a vacation.

Janya is about to open her own small business after having completed several beauty courses. We hope she can open in November. If we are lucky, then after a few more years here in Saudi I will retire to Thailand! That's the plan, anyway.

My life story has yet to find an ending and there is undoubtedly another few chapters if not an entire book waiting to be lived and written. Stay tuned.

RN

I wanted to end this book with a positive message. Difficult to do amid a pandemic. My reason for documenting my life so far is so that my kids will be able to read about it later in their life.

If I have shuffled off this mortal coil, I take some comfort in the fact that they can check out my writings on their electronic device of choice. Maybe they will have a paperback copy who knows. It's the thought of them reading about their old dad that gives me a kick and the motivation to type.

I hope that you dear reader have enjoyed my life and that if you have made it this far; you have done so with a smile on your beautiful face. Thank you for sticking with me. Let me just end with a question that I'm asked and sometimes I ask myself?

What made you choose to become a nurse? This is a question that has been asked of me many times over the years. My answer is always 'I thought it would be a good way to meet ladies!' Of course, I'm joking. The truth is I don't have one answer as to why I became a nurse. There are many and varied reasons, all good and some bad! I sowed the seeds of my career between Portree and Linicro and it was Portree High School that enabled me to get enough qualifications to enter my chosen School of Nursing, which was North Lothian in Edinburgh.

Academia did not come easy for me, as I'm very easily distracted. The teachers at my Alma Mater ensured that the opportunities were available for me, and it was my personal responsibility to grasp them with sweaty palms and make the best of them!

I was the only person in our family to stay on at school and get some certificates, but my brother has always been smarter than me and my sister has held down the same job since she started as a Saturday girl in the 1970s and is the pride of Johnnie Walker, Glasgow and Diageo its owners! I'm proud of both of them.

Nursing allows you to see the best and sometimes the worst of humanity. It also affords you a glimpse at the personal struggles and health triumphs of complete strangers and gives you the opportunity to assist them in their time of need. Nursing can be emotionally demanding, and each individual nurse has their own coping mechanism to get them through the tough days. I chose humour as my sword and shield to enter the emotional battlefield that is caring for people fighting ill health.

It's been my sense of humour that has kept me going, even when occasionally I was on the precipice and about to go over the edge into mental chaos. Most nurses reading this will, I'm sure, agree that a sense of humour is important and the more morbid the better!

It may appear that we are sometimes aloof and unengaged, but again this is an emotional bulletproof vest to protect us so that we can continue to care. I have seen some sights that will be with me till my last day on earth, but I choose not to dwell on the horror that can be faced in hospitals I choose to be positive in the face of health adversity and promise to do my best to help those in need.

I might not remember their names, but I remember the faces of thousands of patients that I have nursed throughout the years. I was not always the perfect professional. I'm only human after all.

Sometimes I'm asked to recount a tale of a special moment in my career and there have been many, but I will tell you the one that meant the most.

Years ago, when I was a green student, I was looking after this old gentleman. A kind, grandfatherly sort who in typical Scottish fashion dealt stoically with his terminal diagnosis. On a back shift, before I would leave, he would ask me to roll up a pillow and squeeze it tight at his back as he prepared to sleep on his side. The reason for this? He said it reminded him of his deceased wife, sleeping back-to-back in their bed. That simple act gave him so much comfort, and I'm proud to have been able to accompany him on his last life journey.

So why did I choose to become a nurse you ask?

I didn't, nursing chose me.

Postscript
The Big Man

Over the last year, my old man, Big Gerry had been receiving palliative care at home. Sadly he passed away the day before his 81st birthday. This book had already been completed so I just wanted to take a wee minute and pay tribute to him.

Big Gerry was a big man with a big heart. He was a brilliant Dad to me, my sister Angela and my brother Gary. He was a well-known character in Glasgow, particularly in the country music scene. He loved his music and he loved to play his bass guitar and sing. Over the years he must have played thousands of gigs in and around Scotland. He loved to have a drink too!

Working abroad I didn't get to see him as often I would have liked but we managed the occasional video call and I spoke to him on a group video call with his grandkids a few days before he passed. He may be gone but he will never be forgotten. His memory forever etched on our hearts. He lives on in the eyes of my three children.

My Dad was a huge Hank Williams fan and I hope he is kicking it in the afterlife with Hank in some honky tonk in the sky. All that remains to be said is that we love you Dad. Now and always.

Saudi Arabia 23/8/21.

Lightning Source UK Ltd.
Milton Keynes UK
UKHW050955121022
410294UK00020B/666